Language Networks : The New Word Grammar

To Gay
with thanks for thirty six years of love
and encouragement

Language Networks

The New Word Grammar

RICHARD HUDSON

OXFORD
UNIVERSITY PRESS

OXFORD
UNIVERSITY PRESS

Great Clarendon Street, Oxford OX2 6DP

Oxford University Press is a department of the University of Oxford.
It furthers the University's objective of excellence in research, scholarship,
and education by publishing worldwide in

Oxford New York

Auckland Cape Town Dar es Salaam Hong Kong Karachi
Kuala Lumpur Madrid Melbourne Mexico City Nairobi
New Delhi Shanghai Taipei Toronto

With offices in

Argentina Austria Brazil Chile Czech Republic France Greece
Guatemala Hungary Italy Japan Poland Portugal Singapore
South Korea Switzerland Thailand Turkey Ukraine Vietnam

Oxford is a registered trade mark of Oxford University Press
in the UK and in certain other countries

Published in the United States
by Oxford University Press Inc., New York

© Richard Hudson 2007

British Library Cataloguing in Publication Data

Data available

Library of Congress Cataloguing in Publication Data

Data available

Typeset by SPI Publisher Services, Pondicherry, India
Printed in Great Britain
on acid-free paper by
Biddles Ltd., King's Lynn, Norfolk

ISBN 019-926730-8   978-019-926730-9 (hbk)
ISBN 019-929838-6   978-019-929838-9 (pbk)

Contents

1 *Preface*   vii

1 Introduction   1
  1.1 Conceptual Networks   1
  1.2 Classification and the Isa Relation   10
  1.3 Quantity, Optionality, and 'Variables'   18
  1.4 Multiple Default Inheritance   21
  1.5 Logic   31
  1.6 Spreading Activation   36
  1.7 Processing   41
  1.8 Learning   52
  1.9 Evaluating the Theory   59

2 Morphology   63
  2.1 Outline   63
  2.2 Lexemes, Inflections, and Features   68
  2.3 Words, Forms, Phonology, and Realization   72
  2.4 Variants and Syncretism   81
  2.5 Derivation and Inflection   87
  2.6 Compounding   93
  2.7 Morphological Structure   96
  2.8 Fused Words   100
  2.9 Clitics   104
  2.10 A Summary of Morphological Categories   115

3 Syntax   117
  3.1 Dependency Structure, not Phrase Structure   117
  3.2 Word Order, Landmarks, Precedence Agreement   130
  3.3 Selection and Constructions   151
  3.4 Agreement and Features   157
  3.5 Dependency Types and Constructions   160
  3.6 Mixed Categories   167
  3.7 Unrealized Words and Ellipsis   172
  3.8 A Summary of Syntactic Categories   181

4 Gerunds 183
  4.1 Introduction 183
  4.2 The Challenge of English Gerunds 184
  4.3 Previous Analyses 188
  4.4 Noun Classes and Noun Phrases 190
  4.5 Gerunds as Nouns 197
  4.6 Gerunds as Verbs 199
  4.7 The Debris of History: Possessives and *No/Any* 202
  4.8 The Route from Old English 206
  4.9 Conclusion 210

5 Meaning: Semantics and Sociolinguistics 211
  5.1 Meaning 211
  5.2 Language, Ontology, Signals and Symbols 214
  5.3 Evolution and Meaning 219
  5.4 Referents, Definiteness, Binding, Negation, and Tense 224
  5.5 Plurals, Quantifiers, and Sets 228
  5.6 Semantic Relations and Recycling 232
  5.7 Power and Solidarity 236
  5.8 Languages, Stereotypes, and Code-Mixing 239
  5.9 Acts of Identity and Inherent Variability 246

References 249
Index 265

Preface

This book is a collection of ideas about language—about how language is structured at every level, about the overall architecture of the whole system, and about how it fits into a larger framework of ideas about human cognition. The broad cognitive context is just as important as the detail about language structure precisely because my argument is that all the detail derives from this context. Language is not *sui generis*, a unique system which can, and should, be studied without reference to any other system; this may have been a healthy methodological antidote to the psychology of the early twentieth century, but the intellectual world has changed. Our intellectual neighbours have grown up into the healthy sciences of cognitive psychology and psycholinguistics, but intellectual isolationism is still strong on both sides. However well informed we may be about the neighbours' comings and goings, neither side really allows these developments to influence theoretical work on their side. (Just to give a small example, phonological theories ignore the popular psychological theory that working memory includes a 'phonological loop' (e.g. Baddeley and Logie 1999), which in turn evolved without any significant input from phonological theory.)

The structuralist tradition still dominates linguistics through the view that we can discover the structure of language just by applying the traditional methods of linguistics. This was especially true in the traditional Chomskyan approach, which presented the isolation of language not merely as a methodological assumption but as a matter of fact: language really is unique, so, as a matter of fact, there are no similarities to other cognitive abilities. But even Chomsky now questions this view (Fitch, Hauser, and Chomsky 2006; Hauser, Chomsky, and Fitch 2002), and the past decade has seen a great increase in the theoretical trend called 'cognitive linguistics' which explicitly rejects it, so maybe we are now moving towards what I believe will be a much more healthy period for linguistics (and maybe for psychology too). In this new order, linguists will allow psychological theories and findings to influence their theories of how language is organized.

To my mind, the most important example of this will involve the notion of **spreading activation**, a very basic notion in cognitive psychology which plays absolutely no part in most theories of language structure. It is true that this spreading of activation is a process, so it belongs clearly in a theory of performance rather than competence; but where it takes place is a structure, and that structure is what we all mean by competence—the permanent knowledge of language. Moreover, psychologists also agree that spreading activation interacts with longer-term activation levels that are sensitive to frequency and recency, so that frequent and recent items are relatively easy to access. Most linguists know these facts from psychology, but very few allow them to influence their thinking about language structure. This resistance may be based in part on the old idea that 'the lexicon' is different from 'the core' of language; so even if spreading activation is obvious in the lexicon, it may not be relevant to the core. This defence is undermined by the evidence for 'structural priming' which shows that even syntactic patterns activate each other (Branigan, Pickering, Liversedge, Stewart and Urbach 1995; Bock and Griffin 2000); but in any case the distinction between lexicon and core is itself very unclear and controversial even among linguists. Whatever the reason, it is a great pity that linguists have ignored spreading activation in this way, because it provides a crucial constraint on any theory of language structure: it must model language as a **network**. This conclusion is inescapable if the supporting model of language processing includes spreading activation and if activation can only spread in a network; but it has been ignored by most linguists, with a very few exceptions (notably Lamb 1966, 1998).

Another important idea which is well established in cognitive science (especially in Artificial Intelligence) is **default inheritance**, the logic of ordinary reasoning which allows us to assume that something has its expected ('default') properties unless we have evidence to the contrary (e.g. Luger and Stubblefield 1993: 387–9). This idea is simply common sense and underlies every traditional grammar which contains not only general rules but also their exceptions; but its implications deserve far more attention than they normally get from theoretical linguists. After all, if the mechanism of default inheritance is available in ordinary reasoning, then (by default) we expect it to be available in all kinds of reasoning including language. And if it is available in language, it is at least a promising candidate for handling all sorts of contrasts that linguists have tended to handle in terms of very different mechanisms, from the 'elsewhere' condition of phonology (where 'elsewhere' defines the default) to transformations which change the default structure into a special one (Hudson 2003c). In this case the idea has certainly had some impact on general theories of language structure, but outside cognitive linguistics this impact is mostly found in theories of the lexicon (e.g. Pollard and Sag 1994: 36). But what if the lexicon is just the most specific part of the general 'lexico-grammar' (Halliday 2002)? In that case default inheritance can also apply to general schematic constructions (as in Sag 1997).

Theoretical linguists could use the same defence against default inheritance as I suggested for spreading activation, namely that this is a matter of language use (performance), not competence. But once again the defence has the same fundamental weakness: the procedure of default inheritance has to apply to a structure in which there are 'inheritance hierarchies' (hierarchies of more and less general concepts, where less general concepts inherit from the more general ones above them). This being so, any theory of competence has to ensure that the structure of language includes the necessary hierarchies for inheriting, and to make them available not only in 'the lexicon' but also in 'the core'. Every theory includes some way of classifying elements in terms of both general and specific categories (often called 'features'), but not many theories provide the kind of consistent hierarchical classification that is needed to make default inheritance work smoothly.

Both spreading activation and default inheritance are widely accepted and used outside linguistics, but (rather surprisingly, to my mind) they are rarely combined in the same theory. This is especially surprising since default inheritance is a rather obvious solution to a widely recognized problem in network theories. One of the issues in the connectionist tradition of network modelling is precisely how to use a network to express generalizations and rules, and some researchers have identified this as a fundamental weakness of all networks (Browne and Sun 2001). The problem is not generalization as such; this can often be arranged as an automatic product of connectionist systems. Rather, it has two main sources. One is that most network theories have no mechanism for expressing properties that have variable reference—properties such as 'X has wings' (different birds have different wings) or (harder still) 'X suckles X's young'. The other weakness is the lack of any way of accommodating exceptions to general properties—in other words, of applying default inheritance. All that is needed, therefore, is a system that combines the virtues of network architecture with spreading activation and default inheritance.

Unfortunately, this is easier said than done, and my colleagues and I have spent a good part of the last decade trying to work out the details. Default inheritance may be elementary common sense, but the details are definitely where the devil is. Default inheritance is notorious among logicians for being messy and difficult, especially if the aim is an algorithm that is so clear that even a computer can understand it and mimic common sense reasoning. After all, if any generalization may be overridden, then no inference is safe until the entire database of knowledge has been checked for potential exceptions—a recipe for disaster, especially in the real world of humans where speed is more important than absolute reliability. What is needed for survival in the real world is an efficient logic which gives the right answer first time—and better still, one which only provides relevant information. After all, given that both time and mental energy are limited, there's not much point in inheriting dozens of irrelevant facts along with the one or two relevant ones. This is a serious challenge for any theory of human reasoning. However this book offers a simple solution based in part on spreading activation and in part on the distinction between types and tokens. In a nutshell (which is expanded in section 1.7), default inheritance only applies to tokens, and only inherits active facts.

To return to the main point: if spreading activation and default inheritance apply to language, then any theory of language structure must accommodate them; and yet very few do. But the problem does not stop with these two phenomena. Elementary psychological theory also has a great deal to say about other parts of cognition, such as categorization and the structure of memory, which are highly relevant to linguistic theory. The logic is very simple: if language is a type of cognition, and we know that general cognition has property X, then we must assume that language also has property X unless we have good reasons for denying it. Of course there may in fact be good reasons to deny it, but the evidence had better be strong. In this book I argue to the contrary, that language is indeed just like other kinds of cognition.

Moreover, reversing the logic gives a useful heuristic: if language has property X, then it is worth looking for property X outside language too. After all, we probably know more about the structure of language than about the structure of any other human faculty, so it makes good sense to treat language as a 'window on the human mind'. Some properties of language are, of course, unique to language; for example, it is only in language that we find words or topicalization. But many of these unique characteristics are either true by definition (words are surely part of language by definition) or can be explained in terms of the functions for which we use language (topicalization is useful for communicating); and a surprising number of the remaining elements of language can in fact be matched quite easily outside language. (Even in syntax, it is easy to find non-linguistic analogues of word order, dependency, and agreement.)

This book explores these very general ideas about language and cognition and tries to follow through their consequences for the theory of language structure. I am a linguist, not a psychologist, so language structure is my focus; while language use (and learning) and other areas of cognition are neighbouring territory—interesting and relevant, but ultimately not what I want to talk about. However, even within language structure we find the same tendency towards intellectual fragmentation, with each of the traditional levels of analysis (phonology, syntax, and so on) attracting its own structural theories which might be based on completely different principles from neighbouring levels. The problems of this tendency are obvious, not least that sooner or later the levels will have to meet up. Here too, I have tried to develop a general theory which integrates all the levels into a seamless whole.

As far as language structure is concerned, most of my ideas—especially the good ones—come from other people. My contribution has been to select them and fit them together. For example, at the start of my career as an academic linguist I chose Halliday's ideas about sentence structure and Chomsky's on competence and on generative grammar. Since then, ideas have come from people as diverse as (in alphabetical order) Anderson, Bresnan, Bybee, Deacon, Fillmore, Huddleston, Jackendoff, Labov, Lakoff, Lamb, Langacker, Levin, Levinson, McCawley, Pollard, Sadock, Sag, Slobin, Tomasello, and Winograd. To some, this list will look like an intellectual mess, a recipe for chaos; but to me, it is a reservoir of brilliant insights which, I believe, belong in any theory of language.

One of my long-standing interests has been the interface between linguistics and education (Brookes and Hudson 1982; Hudson 1981a, 1992; 2002; 2004b; Hudson and Walmsley 2005; Hudson 2001b). In my attempts to build bridges between linguistics and schools in the UK, I have tried hard to promote a general-purpose, theory-lite version of linguistics without bias towards any theoretical preferences (and perhaps especially not towards my own). And conversely, I have never tried to defend Word Grammar in terms of its benefits for education; if it's true, this will emerge from the evidence, and if not, it's no use for teachers. This book will say nothing about school teaching, but I do believe that some of the issues I discuss here are crucial to education. In particular, education needs to know whether language is an innate faculty which simply needs to be 'triggered' or whether it needs to be learned from experience; and whether it is a list of vocabulary and rules, or a network (Hudson 2007b). I hope the book will make a small contribution to building the bridge that some of us have been working on for some time; but the bridge deserves a separate book all to itself.

One problem I have not worried much about is the name of the theory. Is this really the same theory as the ones I described in 1984 and 1990, both called 'Word Grammar'? I do not know, just as I do not know whether I speak the 'same language' as the one Chaucer spoke. But I am sure it is not the same as the first theory I learned and worked on, 'Systemic Grammar' (Hudson 1971)—Halliday surely has the right to that name since he invented it. Nor can I call it 'Daughter Dependency Grammar', which is what I called the first theory I developed on my own (Hudson 1976a); after all, I no longer believe in grammatical 'daughters'. But since I started to use the name 'Word Grammar' in the early 1980s the package of ideas has changed at least as much as it did in the previous decade, so it is probably time for a slightly new name. Hence the startlingly original name in the title of this book: 'the new Word Grammar'. Like the contents, the label is half old and half new.

These changes would probably not have happened without the lively debates that occasionally erupt on the Word Grammar email list, so I want to thank the other participants in these (and other) discussions, and especially the following: And Rosta, Chet Creider, Eva Eppler, Geoff Williams, Haitao Liu, Jasper Holmes, Joe Hilferty, Mark P. Line, Matthias Trautner Kromann, Nik Gisborne, Sean Wallis, and So Hiranuma. The ESRC funded two research projects which helped me to develop some of these ideas (especially those about processing). Mark, Haitao, and Eva also gave me extensive and penetrating comments on all or parts of an earlier draft of the book, all of which have been acted on. I should like to thank John Davey for his encouragement and patience during all those years when the book was 'just six months away'. If only!

1

Introduction

1.1 Conceptual Networks

Word Grammar (henceforward: WG) is a theory of language which touches on almost all aspects of synchronic linguistics and unifies them all through a single very general claim (Hudson 1984: 1):

(1) **The Network Postulate:** Language is a conceptual network.

This claim is not unique to WG and could even be described as a common-place of modern linguistics. After all, we all see ourselves as successors to the early structuralists who saw language as 'a system of interdependent terms in which the value of each term results solely from the simultaneous presence of the others' (Saussure 1959). Any system of interconnected entities is a network under the normal everyday meaning of this word, so the structuralist legacy can be interpreted as the view of language as a network—a view that every modern linguist would surely accept, at least in contrast with the idea that a language is merely a collection of otherwise disconnected units. However, I suggest below that the network idea is actually quite controversial when taken seriously.

The modifier *conceptual* is not much more controversial. It is obvious that language is conceptual in the sense that it exists in the minds of individual people; this is what we mean by 'knowing a language'. Some linguists have emphasized that language has a social mode of existence in addition to this conceptual mode—as a 'social fact' (Saussure 1959), as a 'social phenomenon' (Sapir 1921) or as 'social semiotic' (Halliday 1978). This is equally obvious; after all, language is the foundation for society as we know it, and it is from others in our society that we learn our language. Indeed, I shall argue in section 5.7 that it is impossible to separate language from the social relations between speakers and those with whom they interact, so I have considerable sympathy with the view that language is a social fact.

However, I also believe that social facts are relevant only to the extent that they are conceptual—i.e. only to the extent that they are known by individual people. In contrast, an extreme version of the social view is that 'our primary object of interest [is] the speech community', and 'the individual does not exist as a linguistic object' (Labov 2001: 34). This must surely be wrong—linguists often study the language of one individual to produce very successful descriptions. The only problem they face is in not being able to generalize from that individual to a whole 'community', but the notion of speech community is in any case highly contentious (Hudson 1996: 24–9). Moreover, the only way to study the language of a community is by first studying individual members, so the individual must be the primary object of study. If there are social patterns as well, they can be studied, but this research must build on the study of individuals. In short, I agree that our primary object of study should be 'I-language ... where "I" is understood to suggest "internal", "individual" and "intensional".' (Chomsky 1995*b*: 6)

The conclusions so far, then, are more or less uncontroversial:

- Language is a system of interconnected elements.
- Language is conceptual in the sense that it is 'in the mind', even if there is also a sense in which it is 'in society'.

But however bland it may seem at first sight, the idea of language as a conceptual network actually leads to new questions and highly controversial conclusions. The words *network* and *conceptual* are both contentious. We start with the notion of language as a network. In WG, the point of this claim is that language is **nothing but** a network—there are no rules, principles, or parameters to complement the network. Everything in language can be described formally in terms of nodes and their relations. This is also accepted as one of the main tenets of cognitive linguistics (Langacker 2000; Goldberg 1995; Lamb 1998), so WG fits very comfortably in this new tradition which has developed in parallel with WG. In WG, the whole of language has a uniform structure, and consists of abstract patterns which all share the same basic formal characteristics (though some are much more general than others). The same is true of the other theories in the cognitive linguistics tradition (Cognitive Grammar, Construction Grammar, and Stratificational Grammar), and also of Systemic Functional Grammar, the theory from which WG ultimately derives (Hudson 1971; Halliday 1985).

For example, in WG the generalization which combines any finite verb with its subject is analysed and described in the same way as the one which combines the verb *hit* with its object, though the former is much more general than the latter. This claim is very different from the view that rules belong in the grammar—the 'computational system'—while idiosyncratic facts belong in the lexicon, which is merely 'a set of lexical elements' (Chomsky 1995*b*: 130). This radical split between rules and the lexicon is central to a lot of work in modern linguistics—for another example, consider Pinker's claim that in morphology, regularities are handled by rules, while irregular and semi-regular exceptions are handled by a lexical network (Pinker 1998). But it seems to have more to do with the traditional division of linguistic facts between grammar books and dictionaries than with any reality that can be observed in language. It creates an artificial boundary between 'general' and 'specific' where there is actually a continuous gradation, and generates more analytical problems than solutions. We shall consider one such example below.

The claim that language is a network therefore conflicts with the claim that information is divided between the grammar and the lexicon. In a network analysis, the same network includes the most general facts ('the grammar') and the least general ('the lexicon'), but there is no division between the two. Indeed, we shall see in section 1.7 that the network includes even more specific facts than the lexicon, namely unique uttered (or written) tokens of words (or other items of ongoing experience). I shall use the terms 'token' and 'type' with their established meanings, so types are stored and tokens are not; this contrast will play an important part in the theory. The idea that the network includes one-off tokens as well as permanently stored types is even more controversial, but it will turn out to be really helpful in explaining both how we process experience and how we learn from it. To summarize, therefore: there is no clear boundary between the network of 'the lexicon' and the rules of 'the grammar', nor between stored knowledge of types and temporary tokens.

This means simply, turning to the 'conceptual' part of the claim, that language is in the mind. It says nothing about how language gets there, and on this question too the WG answer is controversial: very little of language is innate, so almost all is learned from experience. This is the standard answer in cognitive linguistics, where language is assumed to be 'usage-based' (Barlow and Kemmer 2000), and it also attracts strong support in computational linguistics (Bod 1998); but it is diametrically opposed to the 'nativist' idea that most of language ('universal grammar') is innate. The debate is in part about learning mechanisms and other psychological questions which may be outside the scope of linguistics; but it also has major implications for purely linguistic theory.

For example, if the basic structures of language are already in place at birth, or develop automatically soon after, all the learner has to do is to set parameters and fill in a lot of lexical items according to a standard template. The result will be free of redundancy because the general patterns exist before the details are registered and need not be stored twice. In some sense, language will be 'perfect'. The usage-based view is very different. If language is induced from experience, all the details are stored before the general patterns become apparent so there is no way to avoid redundancy. The resulting knowledge will be very rich, very redundant, and very 'messy'. This is not to deny the general patterns or their clarity, so for example a usage-based grammar will still include the very clear rule of English that requires finite verbs to have subjects. Such generalizations are an important part of language; but so are the myriad idiosyncratic and sometimes irregular details about particular words and constructions. For example, the English passive is normally realized as a passive participle, but exceptionally it may be realized as a present participle just in case it is the complement of a verb that means 'need' (i.e. NEED, REQUIRE, WANT):

(2)   This pot needs cleaning.

A theory of language structure must accommodate such messy details as well as the broad generalizations. In short, language is mostly learned (rather than innate), and the learning process combines massive storage of examples with induction of generalizations. Consequently, the end state contains a great deal of redundant detail as well as high-level generalizations.

Networks turn out to be convenient for modelling this spectrum of information which ranges from fine detail to broad generalization precisely because there is no clear dividing line between the two. For instance the pattern of *needs cleaning* in (2) is idiosyncratic, but it also goes well beyond any one lexical item so is it a rule or a lexical fact? In the absence of general principles, most of us would prefer not to choose at all. In contrast, a uniform network analysis accommodates general and particular facts in the same way, so it forces no choice.

I hope to have shown that the conceptual-network idea is not merely a matter of our choice of metaphors for thinking about language or what kinds of diagram we draw. It also has important consequences for the theory of language structure, such as the supposed split between the grammar and the lexicon. However its importance goes well beyond questions about the internal architecture of language, because it raises even more basic questions. We shall consider five:

Question 1.   Is language different from other kinds of cognition?
Question 2.   Is language separate from other kinds of cognition?
Question 3.   Is there a specialized short-term memory system for language processing?
Question 4.   If language is a network, what kind of network is it?
Question 5.   Is the network of language distributed or local?

The point of the discussion is not so much that we can already answer these questions satisfactorily, but rather that we can ask them and find relevant evidence.

Question 1.   Is language different from other kinds of cognition? How does the language network fit into general cognition? It is a commonplace of cognitive psychology that long-term memory is a network (Reisberg 1997: 257), though it is a matter of dispute whether this network is symbolic, with one node per concept, or distributed, with each node represented by a particular setting of connection weights across the entire network (ibid. 292). (I shall return briefly to this question later.) Similarly, computer models of general knowledge often analyse it as a 'semantic network' (Luger and Stubblefield 1993: 35). If language is a network, then we can compare its network with the networks that are found in other areas of knowledge in order to decide whether it is basically the same or different. But if language contains structures of a type that is only found in language, obviously this question does not even arise.

The question is not whether the language network can be distinguished from the network for our knowledge of people, places, and so on. It is different by definition: what we mean by 'the language network' is, put simply, our knowledge of words and their properties. (This is why the theory is called 'Word Grammar'.) Rather the question is whether the networks for words are different kinds of networks from those that we use for storing our knowledge of people, places, experiences, and so on. The null hypothesis is presumably that there are no differences, so what we need to look for are potential differences. Are there any features of language which are unique to language? For example, are there any general link-types which are only found in language? Does a language network have architectural characteristics which are special to language? Ultimately, of course, these are questions for those who know about other kinds of knowledge but in the meantime it is possible for a linguist to assemble informal evidence, and my tentative answer is that every apparent peculiarity of language turns out to have a close analogue outside language. However, the main point is not the answer, but the fact that the question can even be asked. One of the purposes of this book is to highlight the similarities between language and other kinds of knowledge, as I did in earlier work (Hudson 1984: 37–9; Hudson 1990: 53–83). My tentative conclusion, therefore, is that knowledge of language is very similar to other areas of knowledge in terms of its organization and even in some of its general analytical categories.

Question 2.   Is language separate from other kinds of cognition? In other words, is language a distinct 'module' of the mind? This question is closely related to the previous one, since the clearest evidence for a separate module would be distinctive organizing principles; but even if (as I have just argued) language has the same organizing principles as other kinds of cognition, it might still be stored separately, giving a version of **modularity**. For example, when Fodor argues that language perception is a distinct mental module, his main evidence is not its internal organization but rather what he calls 'information encapsulation' (Fodor 1983)—the property of not being influenced at all by information which is available elsewhere in the mind. It is very clear that some areas of experience are encapsulated in this way, and immune to general knowledge; a clear example from everyday experience is the effect on us of a stationary escalator (a staircase which normally moves): however clearly we can see that it is stationary, we still stumble awkwardly when we get on because we 'expect' it to be moving. On the other hand it is equally clear that our perception of language is heavily influenced by higher-level factors such as the phonological contrasts of our language (Harley 1995: 222), and that interpretation at higher levels is driven by contextual information as well as by bottom-up perceptual input (ibid. 225).

One conclusion is that 'it may be that we have to rethink the concept of module and allow for a kind of continuum, from peripheral perceptual systems, which are rigidly encapsulated (not diverted from registering what is out there), through a hierarchy of conceptual modules, with the property of encapsulation diminishing progressively at each level as the interconnections among domain-specific processors increase' (Carston 1997: 20). Another possible conclusion is that it is wrong to think in terms of modules, and that instead we should be looking for a network model of cognition in which some defaults are much harder to override than others—for example, in the case of immobile escalators maybe we cannot override the default motor-programme that we associate with escalators.

Another kind of supposed evidence for modularity comes from neuro-psychology, where it is often suggested that some areas of the brain are dedicated exclusively to language. If this were the case, then these areas would define the language module physically. However, the neurological evidence in fact seems to suggest the opposite:

The traditional theory equating the brain bases of language with Broca's and Wernicke's neocortical areas is wrong. Neural circuits linking activity in anatomically segregated populations of neurons in subcortical structures and the neocortex throughout the human brain regulate complex behaviors such as walking, talking, and comprehending the meaning of sentences. When we hear or read a word, neural structures involved in the perception or real-world associations of the word are activated as well as posterior cortical regions adjacent to Wernicke's area. Many areas of the neocortex and subcortical structures support the cortical-striatal-cortical circuits that confer complex syntactic ability, speech production, and a large vocabulary. However, many of these structures also form part of the neural circuits regulating other aspects of behaviour. (Lieberman 2002: 36)

Modularity creates far more theoretical problems than it solves. As Tomasello puts it: 'The major problem for modularity theories has always been: What are the modules and how might we go about identifying them?' (Tomasello 1999: 203) For example, should we think in terms of separate modules for the traditional 'levels' of phonology, morphology, syntax, and meaning, or in terms of one module for the lexicon (which contains information from all the levels) and another for the general rules of grammar? It is true that research has revealed strong tendencies for particular kinds of information to cluster together in the brain or to be injured together in pathology, but this is exactly as predicted in a non-modular, network-based account: nodes that are directly connected are more likely to be located near each other and to be affected by the same traumas than nodes that are distantly related. But these tendencies are a far cry from the absolute module-wide patterns that we should expect if modules are like boxes which are located and affected in their entirety. My conclusion, therefore, is that the language network does not occupy a distinct part of the human mind or brain, but is intimately embedded in the general cognitive network.

Question 3.   Is there a specialized short-term memory system for language processing? Another basic question about conceptual networks concerns the theory of memory. A traditional view, which has had some influence in linguistics, is that our minds contain two separate kinds of memory, long term and short term. Long-term memory is our linguistic competence, and has one kind of structure, be it rules and lists, a network, or whatever. Short-term memory, on the other hand, is a kind of workbench with a very different structure, onto which we copy material from long-term memory in order to combine it with incoming data such as a sentence that we are currently trying to understand. It is our short-term memory, for example, that we use to hold arbitrary lists of numbers and which has a limited capacity (the famous 7 ± 2 of Miller 1956). It is a short step from this idea to the idea that we have distinct short-term memories for different tasks, including a special one for processing language; so a great deal of psycholinguistic work has been devoted to exploring the structure of this supposed area of the mind in terms of syntactic parsers and phonological buffers with very specific characteristics. For example, the syntactic parser might be unable to cope with more than two constituents under the same syntactic relation (e.g. subject within subject) (Lewis 1996), and the phonological buffer might only be able to hold up to two seconds worth of speech (Baddeley and Logie 1999). A recent version of this general approach is that 'linguistic working memory' is a 'workbench' or 'blackboard' with three separate divisions for handling phonology, syntax, and semantics (Jackendoff 2002: 200).

On the other hand, more recent work on memory has suggested that 'working memory' (the preferred term for short-term memory) 'consists of a set of processes and mechanisms and is not a fixed "place" or "box" in the cognitive architecture. ... its contents consist primarily of currently activated LTM representations ...' (Miyake and Shah 1999: 450). This idea has been promoted by some leading psychologists (Cowan 1997, 1999; Ericsson and Kintsch 1995; Ericsson and Delaney 1999). In other words, maybe there really is only a single memory, the network of long-term memory, and working memory is just the 'working' part of this network. (As I mentioned earlier, this network actually includes not only permanent long-term nodes but also some temporary short-term nodes for tokens.) If this is so, then all our models of the mechanism for processing language need to be rethought to the extent that they depend on specific workbench structures. I shall return to this question in section 1.7, where I shall present the outlines of a WG theory of processing. Meanwhile the tentative conclusion is that there may not be a separate 'work-space' for processing language (or anything else).

Question 4.   If language is a network, what kind of network is it? Do all nodes have the same status? Are the links differentiated from one another in any way? If so, what kinds of links are there? We shall consider all these questions, and come to the conclusion that language is a network in which all concepts, including relations, are richly classified. This is probably the most distinctive claim of WG, but the question to which it is an answer simply does not arise in a more conventional approach to language. Even more interestingly, we can try to fit language networks into the typology of networks that has recently been discovered in graph theory (see Barabási 2003 for graph theory, and Chipere 2003: 28–31 for its relevance to language). For example, are links distributed randomly among the nodes, or are there 'hub' nodes which have far more links than others? In technical terms, is language a 'random' network or a 'scale-free' network? This is a quantitative question which can only be answered by counting the number of links per node; in a random network the distribution of links shows a bell-shaped curve in contrast with the power-law distribution found in scale-free networks. Recent work on existing databases has suggested that language is scale free (Ferrer i Cancho, Solé, and Köhler 2004; Ferrer i Cancho and Solé 2001; Solé 2005), but we need studies on more theoretically sophisticated databases before we can be sure of the conclusion.

Another quantitative question is whether nodes are linked more or less evenly across the entire network, or whether there are sub-networks where the links among the members are denser than those to non-members (so-called 'hierarchical modularity'). At present we have nothing approaching a full network grammar of a language so we cannot even start to answer these questions, but we can at least look forward to the day when we shall be able to. Meanwhile we may be able to learn from small-scale experimental computer network models of processes such as vocabulary attrition (Meara 2002).

Question 5. Is the network of language distributed or local? This is the question about connectionism which I touched on earlier. Is knowledge represented locally, with a separate node for each concept, or globally, with each concept distributed across all the nodes. In other words, is it a symbolic network or a connectionist network? On this question, my impression is that linguists answer with one voice (Bybee 1995, 1998; Corbett and Fraser 1993; Croft and Cruse 2004; Culicover 1999; Givón 1998; Goldberg 1995; Lamb 1998; Langacker 2000); see, for example, the trenchant criticisms in Lamb 1998: 2. We all agree that, if language is a network, the network is symbolic rather than distributed; in other words, one node represents the word *dog*, another node represents each sound, and so on. Indeed, it is hard to imagine doing linguistics (as we know it) without this assumption. A symbolic network allows us to explore the structure of the network and challenges us to think clearly about the details; in short, it is a good tool for research on linguistic structure. But a distributed network has none of these attractions; it may be able to learn simple correspondences such as between verb bases and their past tense forms (Rumelhart and McClelland 1986), but what is learned is just a table of numbers—no help at all in understanding the structure of this part of English grammar.

To summarize this section, WG is based on the Network Postulate that language is a conceptual network, a system of interconnected elements in the mind without any clear boundary between the network of 'the lexicon' and the rules of 'the grammar'. It is mostly learned (rather than innate), and the learning process combines massive storage of examples with the induction of generalizations, with the result that the end state contains a great deal of redundant detail as well as high-level generalizations. The network for knowledge of language may be very similar to other areas of knowledge in terms of its organization and may even share some of the same general analytical categories; and there may not be a separate 'work-space' for processing language (or anything else). In terms of its formal properties, the network is symbolic rather than distributed and all nodes and links are classified. All these claims will be developed in later sections.

1.2 Classification and the Isa Relation

What then can we say about the language network? What kind of network is it? We can now start to enter into questions of detail. We already know a great deal of detail because most of what any linguist knows about language can be translated quite easily into network concepts. Later chapters will give network analyses for significant areas of morphology, syntax, and semantics, and will include a lot of the well-known facts about language that have emerged over 2,000 years of study. What we know about the structure of language is far more detailed and highly structured than our research-based knowledge in any other area of human cognition, so we can treat language as a particularly clear window into human cognition.

One very clear conclusion is that links are of different 'types' according to the kind of relation that they represent: some links show class membership, others show part–whole relations, and so on. In other words, we are not dealing with mere associative networks in which all links have the same status and the same meaning. For example, the significance of a class–member relation is quite different from that of a part–whole relation, and a word's sense is different from its grammatical subject and from its morphological realization. Moreover, links are all directional, so that their significance varies according to which end of the link is under consideration: for example, in *John snores*, *John* is the subject of *snores* but not vice versa. To a linguist most such distinctions are obvious and completely uncontroversial, and what we miss in the distributed connectionist networks mentioned above.

What kinds of links are there? This is not a matter of logic or philosophy, but of linguistics and ultimately of psychology: what kinds of links does a working linguist need in order to analyse linguistic competence? The following generalizations are based on my own experience of descriptive analysis, and are fundamental to WG theory, but of course they are as tentative as any other theoretical generalization.

One relation stands out from all the others as particularly fundamental: the **Isa relation** used in classification, as in 'Dick isa Linguist' or 'Penguin isa Bird'. This relation and its name are familiar from the 'semantic networks' of early Artificial Intelligence (AI) (Reisberg 1997: 280), but of course it is also one of the ordinary meanings of the verb *be* (as in *Dick is a linguist*) and it underlies any thesaurus or ontology. It is hardly necessary to stress the importance of this relation. As the basis for all classification, it is also fundamental to all generalization. For example, anything we know about Bird generalizes to anything which isa Bird—in other words, to any particular bird or type of bird. This process of generalization is 'inheritance', which I discuss in section 1.4. Inheritance plays such a fundamental part in all conceptual networks that I shall call these networks 'inheritance networks'. In short, these networks allow generalizations thanks to the links which are labelled 'isa'.

I now have three brief comments on terminology and notation.

1 The usual name for this relation is 'isa', which works well in simple cases such as '*and* isa Conjunction', but raises grammatical problems when used in sentences where ordinary grammar demands a form other than *is*. I have tried a number of alternative solutions (such as 'is-a', 'are-a', 'be-a'), but the most popular one seems to be to use *isa* even where other forms such as *are*, *was*, or *be* would be expected; so with regret I shall write such things as 'Penguin and Sparrow isa Bird' and 'the subject must isa noun'.

2 My practice in naming concepts in the text is to give the name a capital letter, as in ordinary English. Thus Penguin is the name for the category 'penguin', and Noun means 'the category noun'. (I make an exception for words, where the usual italics signify the name; so *penguin* means 'the word *penguin*'.) When I use category names as common nouns, of course, I do not give them capital letters: 'a noun is a word'. I shall argue below that relations themselves are also concepts, so I shall follow the same practice in naming them; thus the Isa relation will be called 'Isa'. Diagrams are obviously different from the sentences of this text, so capital letters are unnecessary.

3 Isa has a standard notation in WG diagrams: a small triangle whose base is next to the supercategory and whose apex is connected to the subcategories. (The triangle is iconic: the base is larger than the apex, as the supercategory is larger than the subcategories.) The line may point in any direction, so all three diagrams in Figure 1.1 (over) are equivalent.

A WG network is built round a 'skeleton' of Isa relations because every node is involved in at least one such relationship. Most nodes, of course, isa some 'higher' node (taking 'higher' in its metaphorical sense rather than literally in terms of the diagrams; as we have just seen, a superordinate node may appear below its subordinates in a diagram). And similarly, most nodes are supercategories for other nodes. Of course Isa hierarchies must have a top node, but it is possible that every hierarchy leads to the same super-node, the node shown as a dot in Figure 1.3 (p. 13); this is merely speculation given the present state of research. However what does seem clear is that every other node is classified by at least one Isa link to a supercategory. This claim follows, in fact, from the WG theory of processing

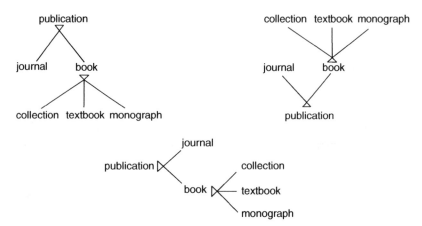

FIGURE 1.1.   Three equivalent Isa diagrams

and learning (see ss. 1.7 and 1.8), since the very existence of a node presupposes some classification. The only possible exceptions are nodes which are innate, but if there are innate nodes, most of them must surely play an important role in classification.

The Isa skeleton is much more complex than a mere hierarchy because one node may isa more than one other node. This multiple membership is part of everyday life; for example, Dog isa Pet as well as Mammal, and each of us isa many different supercategories. For example, I myself isa Man, Brit, Linguist, Cyclist, and Londoner. Multiple Isa relations are also commonplace in language; for example, the lexeme *attempt* isa Verb, English word, and Formal word, and the inflected word *attempts* isa this lexeme and Present singular. In general, these separate supercategories carry orthogonal (i.e. independent) properties, but they can conflict and when they do, the conflict cannot be resolved except by fiat; this, I suggest, is why we cannot say **I amn't* although we know perfectly well what it would be if we could say it (Hudson 2000*a*). Figure 1.2 shows WG diagrams for the examples just quoted.

So far, then, we have identified just one basic relation: Isa. This relation has its own notation (the triangle) in WG diagrams, and its own logic (default inheritance, to be discussed in (s. 1.4)). I shall introduce four other similarly basic relations in later sections: Argument and Value (later in this section), Quantity (s. 1.3), and Identity (s. 1.7). All the other links are treated in a different way from these primitive relations. In WG, these relations are themselves concepts, whereas the primitive relations are probably not; for example, they might be manifested neurologically by distinct neuron types rather than by distinct relations to other concepts. The

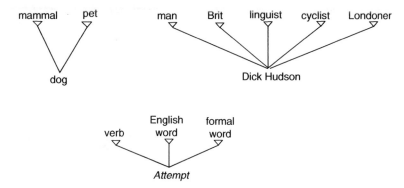

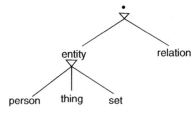

FIGURE 1.2. Isa hierarchies showing multiple membership

WG ontology (i.e. its classification of concepts) probably includes something like the hierarchy in Figure 1.3 in which Relation is contrasted with Entity at the top level (Hudson 1990: 76). (As expected, it is difficult to find natural-language names for some nodes at this level, so the top node has no name; but this does not matter because we shall see later that names are not important.)

In addition to the basic Isa relation, then, we also recognize a multiplicity of more specific relations ranging from very general (e.g. Part) to very specific (e.g. Beak). Figure 1.4 (over) shows two specific relations which link the typical bird to its beak and its tail. The number 1 is explained in the next section, but in a nutshell this diagram shows that a typical bird has a beak and a tail. It is surprisingly hard to find distinctive terminology for relations because nouns in English (and perhaps in all languages) tend to refer to entities rather than to relations, and to do this even if the entity is defined by its relation to some other entity. Take the word *father*, for example, a clear example of a relational noun: a father is a person, not a relation, although the particular person is picked out by their relation to someone else. Strictly speaking, therefore,

FIGURE 1.3. The top of the ontology

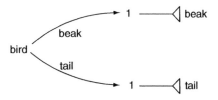

FIGURE 1.4.   A bird has one beak and one tail

Father isa Person, not Relation; and yet 'father' is the obvious name for the relation. Even more confusingly, non-relational nouns such as *hand* or *car* are often used relationally as in *my hand* or *Mary's car*; each one picks out a particular object on the basis of its relation to some other person or object. Once again the hand or car is an object and not a relation, but the relation needs a name and it is tempting to lend it the object's name. For example, this naming system would give the label 'car' to the link from Mary to her car. Similarly, the relation between a bird and its beak is called 'beak', which of course is different from the label 'Beak' on the node for the general category of beaks. This potential ambiguity of labels between relations and entities is harmless because networks use arcs for one and nodes for the other, but in any case I shall explain shortly that the terminology is simply a matter of convenience, so nothing theoretical hangs on it at all.

It is easy to see that relations themselves must also be concepts because we sometimes have ordinary non-technical names for them such as *friendship*, *distance*, and, of course, the word *relation* itself. If the sense of a word is a concept, then these relations must be concepts. Of course, a relation is fundamentally different from the other kind of concept, Entity, in that it must relate two entities, but there are also important similarities.

One of these is that, like entities, relations can be classified; so in everyday life we recognize a variety of relations between people—family relations, work relations, personal relations, and so on—as well as spatial, temporal, and causal relations. Similarly, grammarians have for a long time recognized a hierarchy of syntactic relations in which, for example, Complement subsumes Object and Predicative. The natural conclusion is that relations, just like entities, must also be organized in isa hierarchies. The importance of this conclusion cannot be exaggerated, because it solves the well-known analytical problem of relations: 'If each type of relation is represented by a specific type of associative link, then we risk losing the simplicity of the network idea and thereby render the whole proposal less attractive' (Reisberg 1997: 280).

The usual approach to this problem is to assume that the list of possible link-types is given in advance, and that the list is finite and hopefully quite

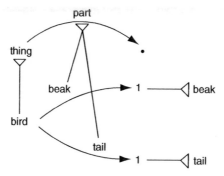

FIGURE 1.5.   Beak and Tail isa Part

short. But this hope is dashed as soon as we start considering even simple examples such as a bird's parts. The fact is that a bird's relation to its beak is quite different from its relation to its tail; each part has a distinct location within the bird, and even more importantly it has a distinct use. We cannot simply talk about parts, but must refer more specifically to the bird's beak and its tail in order to formalize even simple statements like (3) in which *a bird's beak* and *its head* invoke different relations.

(3)   A bird's beak is attached to its head.

But if this is so, there is little hope of finding a limited, or even finite, set of predetermined relations.

The solution is based on the fact that precisely the same problem arises with entity concepts: where does the list 'come from'? It is generally accepted that at least most of these concepts are not drawn from a predefined list, but are learned from experience. Given the diversity of human experience, we predict an open-ended variety of entity concepts which are held together conceptually by isa hierarchies (and other links). The solution to the problem of relations is to apply the same kind of treatment to the non-primitive relations that link entities, and the result is an open-ended hierarchy of relations. Similar suggestions have been made before for limited domains such as semantic cases (Charniak 1981) and grammatical functions (Bresnan 2001: 97; Hudson 1990: 189–218), but so far as I know the idea that all relations are classified is unique to current WG. It is clearly controversial, and if true it is important. In short, our fundamental Isa relation applies not only to nodes, but also to non-primitive links. Figure 1.5 shows how this claim applies to the earlier example of bird-parts by expanding Figure 1.4 to show that the relations Beak and Tail both isa Part.

Classified relations appear to put the networks with which we are dealing onto a higher formal plane than the networks that are usually discussed in the literature. We might call them 'second-order' networks because the links are themselves interrelated in a separate network of Isa relations. This is a major change in the logical and formal status of networks which makes the whole network idea less attractive. After all, if we can now show that cognition is a second-order network, maybe next year we shall find evidence for third-order networks and so on and on ad infinitum. Every extra order that we discover implies more computing power in the mind, and one thing that is certain is that computing power is limited, so theories about higher-order networks require careful consideration.

There is in fact an alternative theory of relations which assumes a less obvious answer to the question whether relations are network links or nodes. The obvious answer is that they are links; this is what I have assumed in the discussion so far, and indeed I shall pretend to assume it in the rest of this book. But the alternative treats relations as nodes, just like entities; for example, the relations Part, Tail, and Beak are not represented by arrows, as in Figure 1.5, but by nodes just like those for the entities Bird, Tail, and Beak.

One advantage of this analysis is to explain the similarities between relations and entities that I have already discussed, and in particular to explain how it is that relations can be classified and learned just like entities. Furthermore, this analysis is more consistent with the diagram of the top of the ontology (Fig. 1.3) in which Relation and Entity, as sisters, have the same status. Given this analysis, the Isa hierarchy of relations is of the same order as that for entities, so there is no need to worry about second-order networks.

Of course the price paid for these benefits is that we have no links (except Isa links). For example, if the relation Part is a node rather than a link, then it obviously cannot link entity nodes to each other. And yet we know that something links entities, and indeed that their distinctiveness depends entirely on the distinctiveness of their links. The solution is to introduce yet more links, but this time primitive links (like Isa). As primitives, they have properties that are 'built in' rather than inherited via an Isa hierarchy, and these properties are exactly the same for every link. Moreover, like Isa they are directed (so 'A isa B' is different from 'B isa A'), and they control the logic of inheritance. The obvious names for these new links are **Argument** and **Value**, so the two facts 'Part Argument Thing' and 'Part Value X' combine to express the fact that a thing's part is X which, in the previous system, would have been expressed by a single fact: 'Thing Part X'. In other words, the solution to the problem of relations is that there are, in fact, very few true relations: just a handful of primitives (Isa, Argument, and Value, plus two others to be introduced later). However there is also a large collection of relational nodes (e.g. Part and Beak) which function as 'pseudo-relations' thanks to their Argument and Value links to entity nodes, and can grow without limit thanks to the ordinary processes that are responsible for the learning of entities.

Decomposing every non-primitive relation into a node plus two primitive relations may provide a satisfying theory, but it multiplies the problems of diagramming. Even if we use obvious abbreviations for 'Argument' and 'Value' ('of' for Argument and '=' for Value), quite simple networks become unreadable. For example, it would be hard to expand Figure 1.6, which just shows how the entities Bird and Beak are related via the relational node Beak. The diagramming complications come from the Isa, Argument, and Value links to the relation nodes, so the rest of this book will ignore these links in most diagrams and pretend that each relation corresponds to a single arrow whose classification is shown just by the label attached to it.

The discussion in this section raises important questions about the mental resources that a mind needs in order to handle a cognitive network. In a simple associative network, the basic unit of thought consists of two nodes (A and B) connected by a simple relationship, R: 'A R B'. This constitutes a 'fact', so manipulating a fact in this network would involve just three cognitive

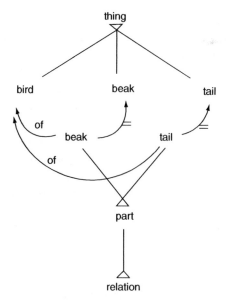

FIGURE 1.6.   Birds, beaks and tails with relations as nodes

units and holding this fact in working memory would take just three units of mental resources. In an inheritance network as defined here, the relation R itself has an Isa link to a super-relation R+, so this figure rises to at least five: two nodes (A and B), two relations (R and R+) and one Isa link (between R and R+). (The figure could be higher, given the possibility of multiple Isa links between any one of the nodes and supercategories.) The idea that cognition is an inheritance network may raise fundamental questions for comparative psychology; for example, are non-human animals capable of creating inheritance networks? If our uniqueness lies in our ability to conceptualize symbols (Deacon 1997), is this because only we are able to learn relation-types (such as the relation Meaning, which I discuss in more detail in 5.1)? Section 5.3 considers these questions in more detail.

Another important consequence of accepting inheritance networks is that a network consists of **nothing but** nodes and links; the labels that we put on either nodes or links are simply mnemonics for our own purposes, and have no theoretical status whatsoever (Lamb 1966, 1998: 59). For example, Bird is uniquely defined by its relations to nodes such as Beak and Wing, so the label 'Bird' is redundant; and likewise for every other label, provided the network is firmly 'anchored' to external units such as perceptual categories. Indeed, both Figure 1.4 and Figure 1.5 contained nodes that had no label (except a dot or a 1) which illustrate the point well. For example, the dot in Figure 1.5 is defined as the typical part by its Part relation to the super-general category Thing, so the label 'part' would have been redundant; and similarly the two nodes labelled '1' are uniquely defined by their relations as the typical wing and tail. From a theoretical point of view, then, we could in principle remove all the labels for relations and rely entirely on the isa hierarchies that relate them to one another, though the practical value of such diagrams would be close to nil.

To summarize this section, I have argued that language networks, and more generally human conceptual networks, consist of nodes and links. The links are all of three primitive types: Isa, Argument, and Value (with two more to be introduced later), and the nodes include relations as well as entities. (But, to simplify the diagrams and the discussion, I shall reduce a relational node plus its Argument and Value arrows to a single arrow.) Every node (except one) isa at least one other node, and every entity node is the argument or value of at least one relation node.

1.3 Quantity, Optionality, and 'Variables'

We have so far considered three primitive relations: Isa, Argument and Value. Another relation that early AI workers also considered very basic is what they called 'hasa', as in 'Book hasa Title' or 'Bird hasa Beak' (Reisberg 1997), but this is actually very different from Isa. Any 'hasa' statement is really just a way of counting relata (whatever is picked out by the relation). For example, if we say that a bird has a beak, we are asserting the existence of one beak per bird; if we deny it, we are asserting that the relevant number is zero; and if we say it has two wings, our claim is that there is one two-member set. In contrast, Isa is not dependent on any other relation and does not involve either an existential claim or a numerical one; it is simply about class membership. In other words, 'hasa', unlike Isa, combines two separate bits of information: a relation (e.g. 'beak', 'part'), and a quantity, which may be a number (1 or zero) or a range (>zero, ≤1, any number). In an earlier version of WG (Hudson 1990: 16), I did treat 'has' as a basic relation which always combined with a 'quantifier' such as 'a' (=1) or 'ano' (=a or no, i.e. either 1 or zero). However, current WG dispenses with the 'has' relation altogether. In diagrams, it sometimes (but not always) uses the quantity as a label for the node concerned; for example, Figure 1.4 shows that the number of beaks for a bird is 1. A simple dot shows that the number is unconstrained—i.e. either that the relatum is optional and may be multiple, or that the quantity is inherited from elsewhere.

But however convenient this notation may be when drawing networks, it is no more than a notational trick. If labels are basically mere mnemonics, as I claimed at the end of section 1.2, then it is wrong to pack so much information into labels. To be theoretically pure, these numerical labels should be replaced by separate relations, so we must consider this underlying reality.

Take the example of a bird's beak. The network must show not only that this node isa beak, but also that it is an obligatory part of the bird's anatomy—in other words, every bird typically has precisely one beak. The WG solution is to recognize numerical quantities as entities with the same properties as other entities. Thus '1' is an entity which is related, *inter alia*, to the value of the 'beak-of' relation (i.e. x in Fig. 1.7). The relation between a numerical quantity and another entity is '**quantity**', represented in diagrams

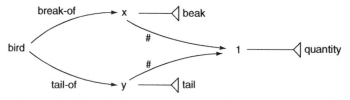

FIGURE 1.7. 'Quantity' as a separate relation

(when needed) by an arrow labelled '#', and implied by a number (zero or 1) standing in for the node itself. This is another primitive relation, like Isa, Argument, and Value.

The effect of treating quantity in this way is to separate it from other properties, which is clearly right. For example, the physical and functional properties of beaks are quite separate from the questions of which creatures have them and how many they have. Similarly, throughout language structure a revealing analysis must separate quantity from other properties such as word-class and position. For example, syntactic subjects have a large number of properties that typically converge, such as word-class, position, and semantic role, but (as we shall see in s. 3.7) these other properties are independent of whether or not the subject has a 'realization' (i.e. an audible or visible form); so we know that an imperative verb normally has an unrealized subject, but we also know what (and where) the subject would have been if it had been realized.

Quantities are important for processing because they determine what we expect to meet in experience. For example, if we see a cat we expect four legs and if we hear the verb *give* we expect a subject, a direct object, and possibly an indirect one—one subject, one direct object, and either one or no indirect object. Every token of experience, by definition, has a quantity of one, so when we process experience we have to match the expected quantity against this observed quantity. Even if the three-legged cat's overall properties match well those of a cat, the missing leg is registered as an exceptional feature; and of course ungrammatical combinations of words are commonplace in everyday speech. If by default every concept's quantity is 1, this can be overridden in the usual way by other quantities (including zero, ≤ 1 and zero $\geq$, meaning respectively 'impossible', 'optional up to 1', and 'any number'). However it is also possible that quantities reflect frequency, so that a commonplace experience is stored with quantity 1 but a rare one is stored with a lower figure, while an impossible one (such as unicorns or Father Christmas) has zero quantity. A system like this would allow us to distinguish commonplace experiences from unusual or even astonishing ones, but it also raises serious research questions that I cannot even try to answer here, such as how to make it sufficiently context dependent.

Nodes that have a quantity specified in this way are naturally those that have no specific referent such as a particular individual or a general concept—nodes with meanings such as 'the father of a typical person' or 'the subject of a typical verb' or even 'the subject of the verb *go*', bearing in mind that *go* has different subjects in different sentences. Since their reference varies with the situation we might call them 'variables' (as indeed I did in Hudson 2007a), but this would be misleading because they are different from the variables of predicate logic. For one thing, they are never completely empty of content because they always have an Isa link to some other concept, so they are more like Jackendoff's 'typed variables' (Jackendoff 2002: 42). This being so, there is only a difference of degree between them and 'constants' such as the concepts for John or the typical man: 'variables' are relatively poorly specified and constants are relatively richly specified, but in between we find a continuum of richness. Another difficulty in applying the constant/variable contrast to the concepts of WG is the principle introduced in section 1.1 that all the information in a network resides in the relations rather than in node labels. If we cannot use the labels to distinguish constants and variables, how can we distinguish them at all?

The conclusion must therefore be that WG has no variables as such; but one survey of inference in network models claims that, in a 'localist' network, variables are essential for generalization (Browne and Sun 2001). This claim may be true of other systems, but fails for WG because although the networks are localist (rather than distributed—that is, each concept is represented by a single node) and have no variables, they certainly do allow generalization. The discrepancy can be explained if we note that none of the networks in Browne and Sun's survey allows default inheritance, the mechanism for generalization in WG. For example, WG allows us to refer to a bird's beak, or a verb's subject, even though different birds have different beaks and different verbs have different subjects. As in a logic-based system, the beak or subject is represented by a node, but this is allowed to have variable referents because default inheritance creates a new token node for each inference. This will be explained more fully in section 1.4, and section 1.5 will show how WG expresses the distinctions of predicate logic such as quantification. Furthermore, since the notion of 'variable' is closely linked in classical logic with the notion of 'binding', I shall also explain in the discussion of binding (s. 1.7) how WG shows which nodes need to be bound.

1.4 Multiple Default Inheritance

Default inheritance is the logic of the Isa relation. By definition, if (say) Penguin isa Bird, then facts about Bird generalize to Penguin (and to all other subclasses of Bird). This is what Isa means, and no other relation type has this meaning. The technical term for this downward spreading of facts is 'inheritance', so Penguin is said to inherit facts from Bird. In other words, the facts listed in the network directly for Penguin are supplemented by those which are listed for any other concept that Penguin isa, which in turn are supplemented by their supercategories and so on. This is not only an efficient way of storing predictable information, but it is also an important way of supplementing our existing knowledge. For example, we may not know from personal experience whether or not penguins have hearts, but if we do not know we can easily inherit this information from a higher concept.

Apart from the technical term, this logic is merely a matter of common sense. Given that we are trying to model how humans actually store information, it is obvious that some kind of inheritance system must be available because everyday experience confirms that this is the logic we live by—we see something, we guess what supercategory it isa, and then we assume that it has all the unobservable properties of the supercategory. For example, if we guess that something isa Cat, we assume it likes to be stroked because this is one of the facts that are stored in our knowledge of Cat. There is very little doubt that inheritance of properties plays an important part not only in ordinary human reasoning, but also in our knowledge of language. For example, as soon as we learn a new word and assign it to a word-class, we can infer a great deal of unobservable information from that word-class.

What is less clear is the extent to which we (as learners rather than as analysts) actually exploit inheritance in order to minimize storage. Are inheritable facts ever stored, or do we always avoid storing them because they are redundant? For example, given that Peacock isa Bird, and that Bird has feathers, we certainly do not need to store the fact that Peacock has feathers; but do we in fact store it? The experimental evidence suggests that we do store it for Peacock, though maybe not for other birds with less memorable feathers (Reisberg 1997: 270). In any case, redundancy is not a major issue given the vast storage capacity of our long-term memories, so we may assume that some facts which could be inherited are in fact stored directly.

This raises a serious problem if we are trying to model human competence: how can we know for sure which facts are stored and which are inherited? For example, in a detailed analysis of inflectional morphology can we assume that regular inflections are always inherited? Evidence from experiments and from language change suggests that we cannot (Bybee 1999; Ellis and Schmidt 1998; Harley 1995: 161): at least some regular forms are in fact stored, and especially so if they are used frequently. Indeed, it is hard to see how it could be otherwise if generalizations are induced from observed 'usage'—i.e. from a collection of memorized instances—as I shall argue in section 1.8. Once a generalization has been made on the basis of stored instances, those instances may be redundant but there is no mechanism for deleting them from memory, so we must assume that at least these stored cases persist; and if these redundant memories can coexist with the generalization from which they could be inherited, why not other memories too? What this means for linguists is probably that we cannot claim to model actual knowledge; all we can model is an idealized knowledge with minimum redundancy. This will define the minimum of stored knowledge, while recognizing that actual speakers may add vast amounts of redundant links.

Returning to the general principle of inheritance, its psychological reality is surely uncontroversial. It is also relatively easy to combine with a network model of knowledge such as WG, provided that this network includes Isa relations. Inheritance can be represented schematically as the relation between the two networks shown at the top of Figure 1.8. In this figure,

- the dotted line shows '**transitive-isa**', i.e. a chain of one or more Isa relations, so if X isa Y and Y isa Z, then X transitive-isa both Y and Z (and so on up the Isa hierarchy).
- the double-headed arrow means a relation pointing in either direction.
- the broad horizontal arrows show that the network on the left can be expanded by inheritance into the one on the right.

It might be thought that inheritance would apply the source fact (A R B) to the inheriting node (A') in the simplest possible way, by providing an extra link from A' to B; in this approach, a person X would inherit Name from the default person in the form of a direct link from X to Name. However this would lead to serious logical problems because it would imply that Name (the typical name) belonged not only to Person but also to person X, so anyone else inheriting Name would also inherit this link to X. To avoid this logical problem, inheritance works by creating a new and distinct copy of the inherited fact: A' R' B'.

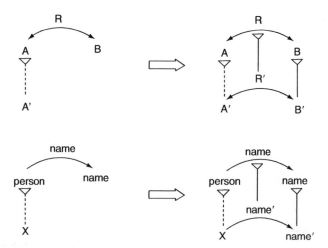

FIGURE 1.8.   Inheriting defaults in a network, e.g. a person has a name

The general idea of inheriting information from general to particular is uncontroversial in cognitive psychology (though it is noticeably absent from most network models of knowledge). Much more controversial is the idea that we only inherit information 'by default'—hence 'default inheritance'. Once again this can be seen merely as a matter of common sense. Our stored information defines the typical bird, penguin or whatever, but we can also cope with non-typical examples such as plucked birds (which have no feathers), albino penguins, and so on. We happily classify something as a cat even if one of its legs is missing, and in language we accept non-typical features such as irregular morphology and even spelling mistakes. The same is true of stored concepts; for example we recognize that Ostrich isa Bird even though it doesn't fly. In other words we allow its 'walking' to **override** the default 'flying' as the typical means of locomotion (and similarly for its size). In case common sense needs experimental support, this is available in abundance from work on 'prototype effects' (Reisberg 1997: 311–29). Categories have relatively 'good' (i.e. typical) or 'bad' members (e.g. robins are better birds than ostriches are), and they may have borderline members (e.g. what counts as a piece of furniture—how about TV sets and ashtrays?). These effects are exactly as expected if categorization allows exceptions: good members inherit all the default properties, worse members override some of them, and borderline members override so many that it is debatable whether they are members at all (Hudson 1990: 45, Jackendoff 2002: 185).

Default inheritance is clearly a fact of ordinary life, and it can be modelled in a network. The two pairs of networks in Figure 1.9 show how an existing

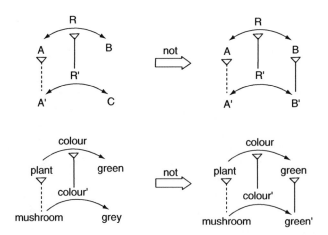

FIGURE 1.9.   Overriding a default—the colour of mushrooms

proposition blocks the inheritance of any competing proposition (i.e. one with the same relation and entity). For example, given that mushrooms are plants (rather than animals) but that their colour is grey, we do not try to inherit the default green.

Nevertheless, default inheritance is controversial in the research world of AI because it 'compromizes the nature of definitions themselves. ... If we define a penguin as a bird that does not fly, what is to prevent us from asserting that a block of wood is a bird that does not fly, does not have feathers, and does not lay eggs?' (Luger and Stubblefield 1993: 388). The answer is surely that no human mind would make this classification because it would be unlearnable, given the principles of processing and of learning that I shall outline in sections 1.7 and 1.8. The stored classification is based on the classification of some token of experience, which in turn is based on the 'best fit' principle of choosing the classification which provides the best global fit between the token's observed properties and the existing network. How could a block of wood qualify as a bird in this scenario?

Another standard objection to default inheritance is that it is very hard to implement in a working computer model (Shieber 1986). The problem is that this logic is assumed to be 'non-monotonic', but I shall show shortly that in WG this assumption is false. Inference is said to be monotonic if it is simply cumulative, so that later inferences never overturn earlier ones; in non-monotonic inference, on the other hand, any conclusion which is drawn may turn out later to be wrong. For example, default inheritance would be non-monotonic if the default was inherited and then later abandoned because of exceptions. Non-monotonicity makes every inference provisional because there is no way to know in advance which will be overridden, so no firm conclusions can be drawn until every inference has not only been drawn, but also checked for possible overriders. If these assumptions are true, it is easy to understand why those working in logic and AI are uncomfortable with non-monotonic inference.

In spite of these widespread anxieties about default inheritance, I believe they have been exaggerated and the problem has an easy solution: **default inheritance only applies to tokens.** In other words, tokens can inherit from stored types, but types cannot inherit from each other. To start with a non-linguistic example, suppose I have a stored concept Cat and I want to apply it to a particular token of experience X which I have classified as a cat; so all I know is that X isa Cat. I can apply default inheritance to X, so if I know that Cat (the typical cat) enjoys being stroked, I can assume that X does too. On the other hand, because inheritance only applies to tokens, I cannot apply it to Cat in order to find out whether Cat has skin; but if I want to know whether

X has skin, I can inherit this fact from any concept that X transitive-isa (e.g. Animal) because it is transitive-isa, rather than plain isa, that allows inheritance.

One of the advantages of restricting inheritance to tokens is that it explains why default inheritance does not clog the network with redundant properties. As mentioned earlier, there is in fact a great deal of redundant information, but it is fair to assume that most of this information results from direct experience rather than from inheritance. Putting this assumption in functional terms, there is very little point in enriching a stored node by inheritance, because inheritance itself already makes the added information so easily available; but it is absolutely essential to apply inheritance to a token node because that is the only way to enrich it beyond the properties which are directly observable.

It could of course be objected that we can in fact draw inferences about stored concepts; for example, we can infer that birds in general—i.e. Bird, the typical bird—have a heart because we know that they are animals and that animals have hearts. However, it is easy to accommodate this kind of inference by assuming that what we are actually doing is setting up a hypothetical token and inferring to that. This explains why we can use ordinary anaphoric pronouns to refer to such tokens as in the following exchange (which I owe to Mark P. Line):

(4)   A.   Can a bird fly?
      B.   Yes.
      A.   What if it's a penguin?

The normal rules of interpretation give the pronoun *it* the same referent as its antecedent, which in this case is *a bird* in the first line; but this is only possible if this referent is a token which is distinct from both Bird and Penguin (the senses of *bird* and *penguin*), because its superclass must be able to shift from Bird in the first line to Penguin in the third.

However, if inheritance only applies to tokens, another crucial characteristic follows: **inheritance works bottom-up**, i.e. starting with the lowest node in the Isa hierarchy, and then working up from there. This is again a very natural assumption in terms of network structure—what could be more natural than to enrich a token node from the nearest node first? It is also very easy to design a recursive algorithm for inheriting first from node A, then from A's supercategory B, then from B's supercategory C, and so on. But most important of all, this solves the problem of non-monotonic inheritance, because default inheritance will, in fact, be monotonic. No inherited property will ever be overridden, because more specific properties will always be inherited before more general ones and the first property always wins.

This is an important conclusion because it explains why inheritance is so fast and so trouble free. All the processor has to do is to visit a clearly defined series of nodes, and for each one inherit onto the token any relations for which it does not yet have a value. (We shall see in s. 1.7 that spreading activation may make inheritance even easier than this if inheritance only applies to relations which are already active.) In particular there is no question of searching the total database for potential overriding properties.

Even more controversial is the use of **multiple** default inheritance, which follows automatically in WG from multiple isa, i.e. the fact that one node may isa several other nodes. The classic discussion of the problems of multiple inheritance is Touretzky 1986, which illustrates them with the so-called 'Nixon diamond' in Figure 1.10. This refers to the historical fact that the American president Richard Nixon was both a Republican and a Quaker. These two reference groups typically hold opposing views on warfare (represented crudely in the diagram by the relation 'war?'), with the consequence that Nixon could inherit contradictory views.

This is generally presented as an argument against multiple inheritance on the assumption that a logic should not lead to contradictory conclusions; but in my opinion it actually shows the rightness of multiple inheritance. After all, the ultimate test of a logic is whether its conclusions are correct, and in this case the conclusion is in fact correct: Nixon's situation was contradictory. For consistency he should have renounced one of his reference groups, but in fact he resolved the conflict by fiat—by deciding in favour of the Republican value. A more accurate representation of the situation would therefore be as in Figure 1.11, where Nixon's preferred (and stipulated) value correctly overrides that for Quaker.

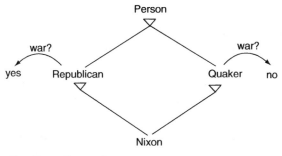

FIGURE 1.10.   The Nixon diamond

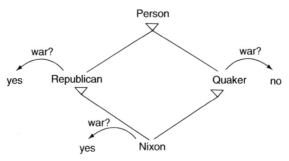

FIGURE 1.11.   The Nixon diamond resolved

However controversial it may be, multiple inheritance seems exactly right for language structure. It is extremely common for linguistic categories to intersect, the obvious example being inflectional morphology where an inflectional category such as Plural-noun intersects with some lexical item such as DOG to define a combined category 'DOG:plural'—the plural of DOG. Later chapters include a general discussion of mixed categories in syntax (3.6) as well as an extended discussion of multiple inheritance showing how gerunds inherit both from Noun and from Verb (ch. 4). I have also used multiple default inheritance to explain the rather odd gap where we expect *I amn't* (or *I aren't*) as in (5) Hudson 2000a:

> (5) *a* He's tired.
>   *b* He isn't tired.
>   *c* You're tired.
>   *d* You aren't tired.
>   *e* I'm tired.
>   *f* *I amn't tired.

In a nutshell, the missing form inherits from both Negative (like *aren't*) and First-person (like *am*), but since neither of these categories transitive-isa the other, the conflict cannot be resolved.

In the last few sections, I have presented a general theory of classification and inheritance that may strike the reader as simply a matter of common sense—as a formalization of existing practices, or perhaps as a notation for recording information about how concepts are classified and defined (in terms of links to other concepts). However, the theoretical package which contains inheritance networks and default inheritance makes a considerable difference to the analysis itself. Here are some very general consequences of adopting this theory:

- Subclassification may distinguish just one subclass. It is tempting to think of classification as the division of a larger class into at least two smaller ones, but this is wrong in an inheritance network. A subclass contrasts not with other subclasses, but with the superclass. For example, a person might recognize just one subclass of rose, e.g. dog-rose, without necessarily lumping all other roses together as non-dog-roses; rather, the rest would simply be ordinary (i.e. default) roses. In linguistics, this is how we recognize 'markedness'. The unmarked member of a pair is the superclass, while the marked member is the subclass—for example, singular nouns are simply default nouns, the unmarked member, with Plural-noun as the exceptional subclass.

- Features are independent of classification. Most linguistic theories assume that classification is done in terms of contrastive features (also widely known as 'attributes') such as gender, number, and tense. This approach is probably most fully developed in the theory that I learned first, Systemic Grammar (now called Systemic Functional Grammar), in which these features are organized in contrasting sets called 'systems' and systems are interrelated in a 'system network' (Halliday 1985; Hudson 1971). An earlier version of WG assumed that features were part of the classification system; for example, I suggested (Hudson 1990: 93) that English verbs were divided by the feature finiteness into finite and non-finite, with mood dividing finite into imperative and tensed. However, I now think features are merely a particular kind of relation; for example, the 'feature' Gender is a relation between a noun and one of the values Masculine, Feminine, or Neuter, just as Meaning is a relation between a word and its meaning. Where features are needed—in section 3.4 we shall consider some situations where they are important for syntax—they can be recognized, but they are predictable from classes, rather than providing the foundation for these classes. To take the example mentioned in the previous bullet point, we can recognize Number as a feature of nouns, which relates them to the abstract values Singular or Plural, while also distinguishing singular and plural nouns through the Isa hierarchy (where singular nouns are in fact just default nouns, with plural nouns as exceptions). In this analysis, the default value for Number is Singular, but exceptionally plural nouns have the value Plural (Hudson 1999).

- Subclasses and members are not distinct. Standard set theory makes a fundamental distinction between subsets, which are sets, and members, which are individuals. This distinction has no place in WG because categories are all more or less abstract and schematic 'types' rather than sets. (In fact, Set is one special type which we shall exploit in ss. 1.5 and 5.5.) The category Dog must be the same kind of thing, logically speaking, as the particular dog Fido, because otherwise Fido could not inherit the characteristics of Dog; and in particular, Dog is not a kind of set. (Dog is the typical dog which has a tail and barks, but sets do not have tails or bark; conversely, sets have members and numerical sizes, which dogs do not have.) In WG, types, sub-types and individuals have just the same status and are mixed up together in the network; for example, under Noun we might find both Proper (a subclass) and DOG (a member). Indeed, even individual tokens of experience, such as a particular cat or a particular instantiation of the word DOG, are part of the same inheritance hierarchy as the more general categories, and have just the same logical status (apart from being tokens rather than stored types). This merging of individuals and general types seems psychologically sound; for example, we can recognize exceptional and dated cases of an individual (e.g. John when unwell, or John when he was a small child) just as we can with general types (e.g. person when unwell or small children). Moreover, according to the WG theory of learning (s. 1.8), general types are induced from more specific types, which in turn are learned as tokens; if this theory is right, individuals and subclasses must have a very similar cognitive status and compatible formal properties.

All these principles follow from the general properties of inheritance networks, and they all affect the way we analyse knowledge in general, and language in particular.

In conclusion, then, the logic of WG is multiple default inheritance, defined by the following facts about a concept A which isa B:

- **Inheritance**: normally A inherits all the characteristics of B and any other nodes on the isa chain leading up from B (i.e. any node which A transitive-isa).
- **Default inheritance**: but it does not inherit values for relations which already have a value.
- **Multiple inheritance**: if A transitive-isa any other concept, it inherits from this in the same way as from B.

It is this inheritance system that lies behind all classification and all generalization, so it is a very important part of any conceptual network—hence my description of such networks as 'inheritance networks'. We shall return in section 1.7 to the details of how it may be implemented in a model of processing.

1.5 Logic

It may be helpful at this point to compare the expressive power of a WG network with that of the predicate calculus. This is an important comparison for readers who are already familiar with the predicate calculus and who may be wondering to what extent a mere network of nodes can achieve the same effects. I shall try to show that WG has a similar expressive power, though of course the two systems can never be exactly equivalent because they are based on contradictory assumptions. Classical logic allows no exceptions, but exceptions are part of everyday reasoning so WG does allow them (through default inheritance). Thus given the axioms 'If something is a bird, then it flies' and 'A penguin is a bird', in classical logic it follows unavoidably that a penguin flies; whereas in WG this conclusion may be blocked by the exceptional axiom: 'A penguin does not fly'. However I have already explained in section 1.4 that WG can achieve this effect while maintaining monotonicity so that although the general case is not always true, it will only be applied when it is true.

We start with **universal** quantification. In the predicate calculus, axioms are defined by propositions which consist of a predicate and its arguments expressed as variables which are bound by a quantifier; for example, the axiom that people die would be expressed by the predicate Die, the variable x, and the universal quantifier $\forall$:

(6) $\forall x, \text{Person}(x) \rightarrow \text{Die}(x)$

(For all x, if x is a person then x dies.) In WG this axiom is defined by the network in Figure 1.12: the typical person is the die-er in one instance of Die (i.e. dying). The effect of the universal quantifier is achieved by assigning the property to the general category Person; default inheritance applies it universally (subject to possible overriding). In contrast with predicate logic, WG makes no distinction between predicates and variables for the reasons I explained in section 1.3. As far as the underlying network is concerned, Die

FIGURE 1.12.   Everybody dies in WG

and 1 are both just nodes, distinguished by their relations to other nodes but not by their labels.

Both systems allow predicates to have more than one argument, but they do this in different ways. In the predicate calculus a predicate may have any number of arguments (including none at all); and it distinguishes these arguments only by their order. For example, the proposition that people give their children presents on their birthdays might be expressed with a four-argument predicate: Give (w, x, y, z), combined with quantifiers and propositions that classify w as a person, x as w's child, and so on:

(7) $\forall(w)$, Person(w), $\forall(x)$, Child(x, w), $\forall(y)$, Birthday(y, x), $\exists$ (z), Present(z),
       Give(w, x, y, z)

(For every person w, for every child x of w, for every birthday y of x, there is a present z which w gives to x on birthday y.) In WG, in contrast, every relation is necessarily binary—a link between two nodes in the network—so four-argument relations cannot be expressed directly. Nor is it possible in WG to rely on the order of arguments to distinguish them, because there is no left–right order in a network. Instead, each proposition is represented by a single node for its predicate, and the arguments are linked to it by binary relations whose classification distinguishes their roles. The proposition about birthday presents is therefore expressed by the network in Figure 1.13. This network claims that on every birthday of every child of every person there is an act of giving whose giver is the person, whose receiver is the child and whose time is the birthday; in this act of giving, the gift is some present.

It is difficult to evaluate these different ways of handling propositions and arguments, which each arise out of an established tradition in semantics—the logical tradition for the predicate calculus, and the traditions of AI and lexical

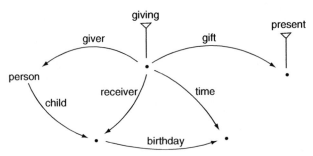

FIGURE 1.13.   Everybody gives birthday presents in WG

semantics for the WG approach. However the main attraction of the WG approach is that it allows generalizations which are not possible at least in the classical version of first-order predicate calculus. On the one hand, we can generalize across predicates by relating them in isa hierarchies—man isa person, lend isa give, and so on. In contrast, this classification would require 'Give (Lend)' in the predicate calculus, but predicates are not allowed to apply in this way to other predicates. On the other hand, we can also generalize across argument-roles because these are stipulated categories which can be related in isa hierarchies; for example, we might generalize about givers or children (or, in linguistics, about agents or subjects).

Returning to quantification, I have already explained how WG expresses universal quantification but we can now consider **existential** quantification. Figure 1.13 contains two examples, both shown by unlabelled nodes. Consider the node which isa Present. This means 'some present', not 'every present', because not every present is given to a child on its birthday. (More precisely, this node means 'some present which is given to some child by that child's parent on that child's birthday'; but the main point is that it is distinct from the Present node which means 'every present'.) Similarly, the node which isa Giving means 'some act of giving', not 'every act of giving', because not every act of giving involves a child's birthday present. However, it is important to stress that the notation achieves this effect because of the way in which default inheritance works, not because of the difference between labelled nodes and unlabelled dots; as I stressed earlier labels in themselves have no theoretical status. If something is classified as a present, it inherits all the properties of Present, but not of specific sub-cases of Present—that is, properties are inherited down the Isa hierarchy, but never up it. Consequently, the properties of the sub-case of Present which is shown in Figure 1.13 cannot be inherited from Present, so they are not 'universally quantified'. The same principle explains why inheritance works as shown in Figure 1.8 in section 1.4: if A' inherits from A a relation to B, this relation must not relate it to B itself, because it would then be available for inheritance to any sub-case of B. Instead, A' inherits a relation to B', a sub-case of B.

In short, any node X always means 'every X', regardless of whether it has a distinctive label (e.g. Person, Present) or a mere dot or number, and regardless of whether it has a generic or an individual reference. What this means is that any other node X* which isa X must inherit X's properties. But if X isa Y, then it is merely 'some Y', so its properties are not inherited by other instances of Y. Even more briefly, nodes are universally quantified, but their sub-cases are existentially quantified.

The **logical operators** ($\land$, $\lor$, $\neg$, $\rightarrow$) of classic predicate logic can also be expressed in a network, though again the means of expression are very

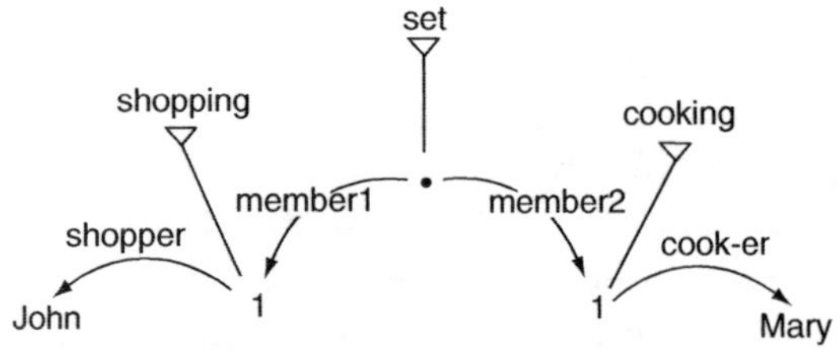

set

shopping   cooking

member1 • member2

shopper   cook-er

John   1   1   Mary

FIGURE 1.14.   John shops and Mary cooks

different. We start with the 'and' and 'or' operators (∧, ∨), which are expressed in terms of sets. As I mentioned briefly in 1.4, WG treats a set as a particular kind of individual which has properties such as size and members. This approach works well in semantics; for example, the referent of a plural noun is a set whose typical member isa the lexeme's sense; so *dogs* refers to a set whose typical member isa dog (Hudson 1990: 139–45), and a word like *families* or *sets* refers to a set of sets. Sets are also important for the grammar and semantics of coordination, where the meaning is a set (ibid. 410–11); for example, the meaning of (8) is a two-member set whose members are the events of John shopping and Mary cooking.

(8)   John shops and Mary cooks.

The semantic structure is shown in Figure 1.14.

One advantage of this approach compared with the logical operator ∧ is its ability to handle combinations of things other than propositions. Thus we can recognize exactly the same structure in terms of sets in the meaning of conjoined nouns as in *John and Mary bought a house*. The semantic structure for the collective interpretation of this sentence (where they bought it jointly) is shown in Figure 1.15. The crucial part of this diagram is that the buyer is the set consisting of John and Mary.

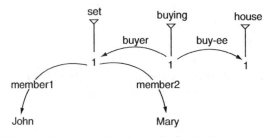

FIGURE 1.15.   John and Mary bought a house (collective)

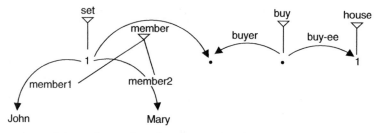

FIGURE 1.16.   John and Mary bought a house (distributed)

The sentence's other interpretation is the distributed one in which they each bought a house. This is a little more complex, but builds on the same set structure. As can be seen in Figure 1.16, the buyer is the typical member of the set of John and Mary, so by inheritance it generalizes to every member. Another difference is that the number of events is no longer restricted to one; in a more complete analysis (as explained in s. 5.5), the number of events would be tied to the number of members of the set.

How then can we distinguish 'and' from 'or' in the analysis of sets? In 1990, I offered a rather unsatisfactory analysis involving two elements '&' and '/' whose status was undefined, but I can now do better. As we might expect, the 'and' meaning is the simpler of the two, and in fact requires no further structure. The last three figures all force a universal interpretation in which both events exist (Fig. 1.14) and both John and Mary are involved in the house buying, either collectively (Fig. 1.15) or singly (Fig. 1.16). The effect of changing *and* to *or* is much the same as that of changing universal to existential quantification because we change from 'every member' to 'some member'. As with existential quantification, we can achieve the desired effect by referring to an arbitrary sub-case (here, an arbitrary member) rather than

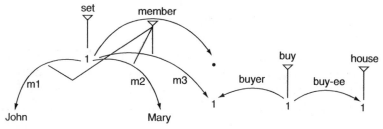

FIGURE 1.17.   John or Mary bought a house

the entire set. The semantic structure for this sentence is shown in Figure 1.17, where the third member (labelled 'm3') is the arbitrary member which is to be bound to one of the others (i.e. to John or Mary). The meaning of the sentence could thus be paraphrased as 'some member of the set consisting of John and Mary bought a house'. As can be seen, this approach has the attraction of keeping the syntax and semantics closely in step, so that phrasal or word coordination can both be represented as sets of individuals. This strikes me as much better than the predicate calculus, where disjunction is always a relation between entire propositions so that coordinated words have to be interpreted as though they were coordinated clauses.

The third operator is $\neg$, meaning 'not'. Negation is very easy because we already have exactly the right apparatus: the relation 'quantity' which I introduced in section 1.3. Negation is shown in semantic structure by the value zero. For example, *It is not raining* has exactly the same semantic structure as *It is raining*, except that the quantity of the event is zero rather than 1. Similarly, *no student* has just the same semantics as *a student* except that its quantity is zero; and likewise for its plural, *no students*, though of course in this case it is a set rather than an individual that has zero quantity.

The last logical operator $\rightarrow$ has roughly the same meaning as *if*, but it has a more precise meaning which can be defined truth-functionally: '$P \rightarrow Q$' is false if P is true and Q is false; otherwise it is true (or irrelevant). In logical form, '$P \rightarrow Q$' means the same as '$(P \wedge Q) \vee \neg P$'. Since we already know that WG can express the other three operators ($\wedge$, $\vee$, $\neg$), we can be sure too that it can also express this particular combination of them.

In conclusion, a WG network has all the strengths of first-order predicate logic without (so far as I know) any of its weaknesses.

1.6 Spreading Activation

One of the many attractions of the network view of language structure is that it provides a strong bridge to current work in psycholinguistics and cognitive psychology, where network models are also popular. Linguists and psycholinguists are studying the same object—language—so their theories must eventually converge on one which is supported by both linguistic and psycholinguistic evidence. The psycholinguistic evidence for networks is overwhelming. The crucial difference between a network and a collection of rules is that only the former defines the notion of 'topological distance', i.e. the distance between nodes, which in turn supports the notion of

spreading activation, whereby activation spreads blindly from one node to its 'neighbours' (a notion that makes no sense outside a network).

The psycholinguistic evidence for spreading activation comes from two sources:

1 Speech errors in which a target word is replaced by a different one which is almost always one of its neighbours in the permanent network, as well as often being one of its neighbours in the network of the current utterance. For example, when Dr Spooner told a student that he had 'tasted the whole worm', the word *tasted* showed the influence not only of its permanent neighbour *wasted* but also of its utterance neighbour *term*.

2 Priming experiments, in which a preceding word 'primes' a later word by making it more accessible so that an experimental subject can retrieve it more quickly. Not surprisingly, it turns out that words prime their network neighbours. For example, experimental subjects take slightly less time to decide that *doctor* is an English word if it follows *nurse* than if it follows an unrelated word such as *lorry*. Both semantic and formal (phonological or spelling) similarities are relevant to priming, though semantic priming lasts much longer than formal priming (Harley 1995: 146, 149).

Every experiment which shows that one word primes another is evidence that these words are near to one another in the network. For example, the words *nurse* and *doctor* might be separated by as few as four links, as in Figure 1.18. Once again, all that counts is the number of links, and not their classification or direction.

There is very little doubt about the reality of spreading activation. Moreover, it is important to stress that errors and priming are found at every linguistic level, including those which are often thought of as the domains of 'rules' rather than network activity. Starting with errors, the interfering items may be neighbours of the target at the following levels, and at some levels they may also be near to each other in the utterance ('utterance neighbours'):

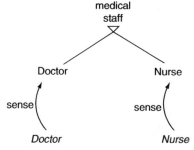

FIGURE 1.18.   Links needed to explain the priming of *doctor* by *nurse*

- Phonology:

(9)   There were lots of little orgasms (for: organisms) floating in the water. (Aitchison 1994: 20)

(10) utterance neighbours: the mirst (for: first) of May. (Harley 1995: 352)

- Morphology:

(11) the chung (for: young, children) of today. (Harley 1995: 352)

(12) utterance neighbours: slicely thinned (for: thinly sliced). (Levelt, Roelofs, and Meyer 1999)

- Syntax:

(13) I'm making the kettle on. (for: making some tea + putting the kettle on). (Harley 1995: 355)

- Meaning:

(14) Get me a fork (for: spoon). (Harley 1995: 352)

- The environment of the utterance:

(15) (Addressee is sitting at a computer.) You haven't got a computer (screwdriver) have you? (Harley 1990)

Examples such as the last one are particularly interesting because they reveal the intimate connection between the language network and the rest of cognition. The computer in this example has nothing whatever to do with language as such; it is simply part of the physical context which the speaker is processing non-linguistically. And yet it interferes with the choice of words in just the same way as it might have done if the discussion had been about computers, which shows that activation spreads as easily from 'general cognition' to 'language' as it spreads within the language network. The example is not isolated; Harley lists hundreds of attested examples.

The evidence from priming experiments leads to the same conclusion. Once again, we find that spreading activation can affect elements at all levels, including some general 'syntactic' patterns which might be associated with 'rules' rather than networks.

- Phonology:

verse primes *nurse* (Brooks and Macwhinney 2000; James and Burke 2000)

- Morphology:

hedges primes *hedge* in a way that can be distinguished from phonological priming. (Bauer 2003: 287)

- Syntax:

Vlad brought a book to Boris primes other sentences containing Verb + Direct Object + Prepositional Phrase. (Harley 1995: 356; Bock and Griffin 2000; Chang, Dell, Bock, and Griffin 2000)

- Semantics:

bread primes *butter* (Harley 1995: 17)
The most significant category in this list is the syntactic priming. It is relatively easy to accept that lexical items are interrelated in a network, but syntactic patterns are widely believed to be stored in a different way, as separate rules or schemas. The existence of priming effects suggests strongly that they too are stored as items in a network. I shall explain in Chapter 3 how syntactic patterns can be stored in a network as properties of general word-types.

How exactly does spreading activation work? How does such a crude, unguided process help us to achieve our cognitive goals, rather than leave us drifting aimlessly round our mental networks? It is very unclear exactly how it works in mathematical terms, but the WG hypothesis is that a single formula controls activation throughout the network. (As I admit in s. 1.9, this hypothesis can only be tested, of course, in a computer model.) What is clear, however, is that processing is goaldirected; for example, when we hear a word we (normally) look for its meaning and are frustrated if we cannot find it. In some activation-based models the directionality is 'hard-wired'; thus a model of production will lay down a series of steps through which the processor must pass in order to achieve the predefined goal (Levelt, Roelofs, and Meyer 1999; Jackendoff 2002: 198). This is not how WG handles directionality. Instead, it assumes that goals are defined by current interests and goals, which in turn are expressed as spreading activation.

For example, when I hear a word, it is the context which decides whether I am most interested in its meaning, its syntax, its etymology, or even its pronunciation. (The latter situations are familiar to any practising linguist or phonetician.) No single hard-wired model of speech perception will accommodate all these interests, but they are easy to explain if we assume that each interest involves a different kind of property (such as meaning, etymology, and so on). These are defined in WG in terms of relations (as explained in 1.2)—classified links from one node to another. Each relation link is in effect a concept, so it may receive activation and pass it on to other related links. In this way, spreading activation applies not only to nodes, but also to the links between nodes. Consequently, when Meaning is active, a word may have an active link to

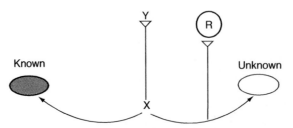

FIGURE 1.19.   How activation from an active function defines the processing target

its meaning but not to its etymology; and more generally, activation spreading through the relation hierarchy activates links differentially.

How, then, does this activation of links help to direct processing? Imagine a situation where I have heard a word in the course of ordinary conversation. When I hear the word, my mind is already oriented towards meanings by virtue of the activation in the (general) Meaning link that is left over from the previous words. There is no need for hard-wired 'extrinsic ordering' of processes leading from sound to meaning because the word's sound and meaning already provide focuses of activity from which activation spreads. These active nodes define the goal of the processing: to find the best 'path' from the (known) form to the (unknown) meaning by selectively activating intervening nodes which receive activation from both directions and damping down the activation on all other nodes. In other words, the node which stands for the unknown meaning defines the target by 'pulling' the activation towards it. This process is illustrated schematically in Figure 1.19, where R is the relation which is currently active (e.g. Meaning). Its activation selects one target node, which is poorly defined ('empty') but active and in turn spreads activation to neighbouring nodes. Nodes which receive activation from this source as well as from the highly active 'known' node stay active while other nodes lose activation quickly, and these active intervening nodes provide properties which enrich the empty node. Exactly how this happens is the topic of the next section.

Although further details must wait until the next section, there is one processing issue which we can address immediately: the nature and limitations of **working memory**. Activation involves physical resources (energy and time) which are limited. This limitation has tended to be discussed in terms of the number of items of information which we can hold in short-term memory (Miller 1956) but nowadays a popular view (mentioned earlier) is that 'working memory' is simply the active part of permanent, long-term, memory:

What is working memory? ... Working memory is those mechanisms or processes that are involved in the control, regulation and active maintenance of task-relevant information in the service of complex cognition, including novel as well as familiar, skilled tasks. It consists of a set of processes and mechanisms and is **not a fixed 'place' or 'box' in the cognitive architecture.** It is not a completely unitary system in the sense that it involves multiple representational codes and/or different subsystems. Its capacity limits reflect multiple factors and may even be an emergent property of the multiple processes and mechanisms involved. Working memory is closely linked to LTM, and **its contents consist primarily of currently activated LTM representations,** but can also extend to LTM memory representations that are closely linked to activated retrieval cues and, hence, can be quickly reactivated. (Miyake and Shah 1999: 450, emphasis added)

A reasonable hypothesis is that the 'capacity' of working memory is simply the amount of available activation. If this quantity is limited, then only a limited number of nodes and links can be highly active at a given moment so (for example) it will not be possible to keep more than a few unrelated items of information active—hence the famous limit of about seven to the number of arbitrary digits we can hold in memory.

What I hope to have established in this section is that spreading activation is massively supported by psychological experiment as well as by observation of spontaneous speech errors, and that it in turn gives overwhelming support for the Network Postulate in section 1.1, the claim that the whole of language is best modelled as a network. I have also shown that activation need not be directed along a predefined path provided that it spreads not only from the current 'known' node but also from an 'empty' target node. This section thus provides a bridge between the earlier discussion of how we store information and the following sections which deal with how we use this information in processing and how we learn it. We shall see that spreading activation plays a crucial role in processing.

1.7 Processing

The central claim of WG is that language, that is, knowledge of language, is a network. In itself, this claim says nothing about processing, but one of its attractions has always been (since the early days of Stratificational Grammar—Lamb 1971) that a model of processing is relatively easy to add, and in principle 'the theories of competence and performance should line up' (Jackendoff 2002: 30). Spreading activation is not unique to WG, of course, and has been a common element in computer models of speech and language processing. In psycholinguistics, spreading activation models have been constructed or proposed in:

- letter and word recognition (McClelland and Rumelhart 1988),
- word sense disambiguation (Quillian 1968; Anderson 1983; Hirst 1988),
- morphology (Marslen-Wilson 1984; Bybee 1995; Roelofs 1997),
- parsing and syntactic disambiguation (McClelland and Rumelhart 1988; Macdonald, Pearlmutter and Seidenberg 1994; McRae, Spivey-Knowlton, and Tanenhaus 1998; Roland 2001; Sturt, Pickering, Scheepers, and Crocker 2001; Vosse and Kempen 2000, Rushton 2004), and
- information retrieval (Crestani 1997).

However, 'activation of words alone is not sufficient to account for understanding of sentences' (Jackendoff 2002: 58) so the WG theory of processing rests on a distinctive combination of other assumptions:

- As explained in section 1.1, the network is **symbolic** rather than distributed, so each node or link corresponds to an identifiable concept.
- Processing is highly **interactive** rather than modular. The single very general-purpose mechanism (outlined in this section) is responsible for all processing of symbolic structures, whether inside language or outside, whether in production or perception, and across all 'levels' of language. There are several other interactive models for sentence-comprehension (e.g. McClelland and Rumelhart 1988; Macdonald, Pearlmutter, and Seidenberg 1994; McRae, Spivey-Knowlton, and Tanenhaus 1998; Roland 2001; Sturt, Pickering, Scheepers, and Crocker 2001; Vosse and Kempen 2000), but many of these models divide processing into a series of stages which apply in a fixed order (Levelt, Roelofs, and Meyer 1999). One of the attractions of highly interactive models is the possibility of using contextual information (which in these models is part of the same network as the grammar) to guide language processing, for example by resolving ambiguities. Again, there are other models of general and linguistic knowledge that explain how these interact, notably ACT-R and SOAR (Anderson and Lebiere 1998; Laird, Newell, and Rosenbloom 1987), but both these large-scale systems combine a network architecture with procedures that trigger specific actions, which makes them very different from the purely declarative networks of WG.
- Following the principles outlined in the previous section, processing takes place in 'long-term working memory' (Ericsson and Kintsch 1995), rather than in a separate part of the mind called 'short-term memory'. The processor adds new temporary 'token' nodes to the permanent network, rather than simply tracing paths through the existing network. These token nodes, for transient items of experience, form a constantly changing fringe on the edge of the permanent network. When

first created, they are highly active, but their activity dissipates rapidly and most of them soon vanish from the network (or at least become unusable).

– There is a **typology of links** rather than an undifferentiated set of 'associations', and the processor treats different types of link in different ways. Isa links allow **multiple default inheritance**, while the argument and value links of section 1.2 allow relation nodes to classify other links and to pass spreading activation, via the Isa hierarchy, directly from relation to relation, rather than only via entity nodes.

– There is also a **typology of entities** which distinguishes stored **types** from **tokens**. As with links, the typology affects the way in which the processor treats nodes. In particular, the procedure of binding only applies to tokens.

The following account of WG processing will develop these claims. The leading idea in all the psycholinguistic research cited earlier is that the network is not just a static collection of nodes and links, but a highly active organism in which the nodes and links may be 'active' in some metaphorical sense which ultimately translates into chemical and physical activity in neurons. A good comparison would be a circuit-board in a computer, which allows electrical charges to pass from node to node; but it is actually much more dynamic than that because the 'wiring' is constantly changing in a way that will become clear below.

Consider a very simple non-linguistic example: what I do when I see a fly in the air. The main task is simply to recognize it as a fly, so my network has to establish a connection between it and my general concept Fly. In terms of network activity, this requires the following operations:

1 First create a node for the perceived object; call this node E (for 'Experience'). E is linked to its observed properties (size, colour, movements, noise, and so on), which are stored as links to the relevant permanent concepts, so E is in the centre of a sub-network. Since we can not react to any experience until we have classified it, the top priority is to find a 'type', a permanently stored concept, of which E is an example; we can call this node T. At this stage, all I know (or at least hope) is that I shall be able to classify E, so I provisionally introduce a node for T and add an Isa link from E to T.

2 Then let activation spread from the observed properties and converge on the node Fly, as the only node which combines them all. Bind T provisionally to this node, thus classifying E as a fly.

3 Then apply default inheritance to inherit as much inheritable information as possible from Fly to E. (This inheritance may prioritize

information which is already active and therefore relevant to the immediate context; for example, if I try to swat the fly, its movements are more relevant than its colour.)

This example has nothing to do with language and yet it contains all the ingredients of language processing:

- **Node** creation **and definition**—creating two new nodes for the current word token: E, for the experience itself, and T, for its 'type' (which may already be classified as a word, so T isa Word). The procedure is basically the same whether E is the word currently being perceived or the target of speech planning; but in one case it is the form that is already known whereas in the other it is the meaning. These new nodes are the current focus of attention, so they receive a great deal of activation which will continue until E is classified and otherwise 'dealt with'. E is, of course, linked to all its observed properties.
- **Spreading activation** which leads to **binding**, binding T to the stored node S which matches these attributes best. Spreading activation guarantees that S satisfies the **Best Fit Principle**, i.e. it ensures that S is a better model for E than any other stored concept is.
- **Default inheritance**—selectively inheriting other attributes from S to E.

We shall now consider these processes in more detail.

1. *Node Creation and Definition*

A word token is distinct from the corresponding type, so WG gives them distinct names (Hudson 1984: 24). For example, in the sentence *I speak English*, the word token *speak* might be called 'word 2' (or 'w2') but it isa the word type *Speak:present*. Most linguistic theories do not make this distinction explicit in their notation because they use ordinary orthography for labelling both the token and its type, but this is highly misleading because the two things have quite different properties—e.g. the token has a specific speaker/writer and time or place, but the type does not. Indeed, their properties can even conflict, as when the token is in some sense defective—for example, mispronounced or mis-spelt. The conceptual distinction between the two is very clear and hardly a matter of dispute. Consequently, the first step in processing a word token is to assign a new conceptual node to it.

One of the most controversial claims in WG is that utterance tokens are 'part of the grammar'. (This is what I meant when I said that processing is done in 'long-term working memory', rather than in a separate 'short-term memory'.) Consequently, the conceptual node which represents a word token (or a token of any other unit) is linked to nodes in the permanent network. Ultimately it will isa some word type such as *Speak:present*, but even at the first stage the token must be connected to the network in order for the activation invested in the node for w2 to spread through its attributes to the permanent network. As mentioned earlier, tokens of experience can be thought of as a constantly changing 'fringe' attached to the permanent network, with the possibility that some of them may stabilize and become permanent. (This is the basis for learning as I shall explain in s. 1.8.)

The same principles apply whether we are producing or perceiving (speaking or listening, writing or reading). In perception the token stands for an observed word, and the aim is to enrich it so as to discover its unobservable characteristics such as its meaning. In production, the token is the target word and this time the enrichment will provide its pronunciation or spelling. Either way round, the token needs its own node, and this node will be enriched by integration into the network. As I explained earlier, the most active relation produces the most enrichment, so when listening, we devote most resources to meanings, and when speaking, to pronunciations. For example, when we perceive the word *speak* it is pronunciation or spelling that is observable, as well as a sentential environment consisting of the words already processed and a contextual environment consisting of a speaker, an addressee, and so on; and the target is a meaning node which is waiting to be enriched under the guidance of activation from all these sources.

On the other hand, in production our starting state is some kind of meaning, plus the sentential environment so far and everything we know about the situation, the audience and so on. If we choose and say *I speak* it is because we are aiming at some word whose sense is Talking and which is compatible with *I* as its subject—in other words, our target is a finite verb. I am ignoring important questions about timing—no doubt *speak* has already been selected by the time the word *I* is uttered, but the point is simply that the words chosen have to be put together into a grammatical sentence structure. The meaning may not fully determine the choice of word—for example, the verb *talk* would have done equally well in other contexts. Just as in perception, therefore, production starts with a rich but incomplete definition of a word token, and the aim is to enrich it by consulting the grammar.

Another similarity between perception and production is that in both cases the token word is important to the user, so it receives considerable activation which spreads through the little network that defines it; and thanks to spreading activation, the nodes in this network (e.g. the constituent phoneme tokens) share their activation with nodes in the permanent network. As we shall see in the next step, this is what allows the target word type to be selected.

2. *Spreading Activation and Binding*

Suppose a listener or speaker has identified some word token w2 and built a mental network for it as just described. In the processor's mind, w2 is linked to permanent concepts for its constituent sounds (in hearing) or for its meaning (in speaking), but the classification of w2 consists so far of nothing but the provisional token T, standing for some 'type'. The next step is to enrich T by binding it to at least one permanent word-type. This binding process is the basis for classifying new tokens of experience, but the same process in fact plays an even larger role in processing because it goes well beyond mere classification and applies to all **bound tokens**—tokens which need to be bound to some other entity. For example, if I hear an example of *dog*, I can inherit for it a referent node and a syntactic parent node, which must be a determiner. Each of these nodes needs to be bound to some other node for enrichment, so I need a dog for the referent and a determiner for the parent. In other words, it is binding that is responsible for reference-assignment in pragmatics and also for finding grammatical relations ('parsing') in syntax. According to WG, all these processes—classification, reference-assignment, and parsing, and perhaps other processes as well—are handled by a single mechanism. In the following paragraphs, I shall present binding in relation to classification, but it should be borne in mind that the mechanism has a much wider application.

Binding applies, then, to impoverished tokens, and the aim of processing is to 'enrich' these tokens by binding them to one or more other node. (The notion of enrichment is taken from Relevance Theory—Sperber and Wilson 1995.) We can illustrate this by supposing that I hear the sounds [spiːk]. By step 1, I have represented this experience by the node E, with suitable links to the nodes for the constituent sounds. I also know that E must isa some word-type, which is also represented by a node. The state of play is shown schematically in Figure 1.20, where the unknown category is shown provisionally

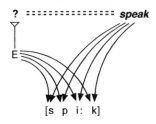

FIGURE 1.20.   Binding an example of [spiːk] to the stored word *speak*

as a question mark—a notation which I replace in the next paragraphs. All being well, I will decide that I have just heard someone say the word *speak*.

How does the processor know which nodes to bind? Binding applies only to token nodes, so the processor can ignore all stored nodes; but it only applies to a subset even of the tokens. For example, contrast the referents of definite and indefinite noun phrases such as *the dog* and *a dog*. The choice of *the* is a signal that the referent should be bound to some pre-existing 'dog' node. In contrast, *a dog* refers to a newly created node which needs no binding. This distinction can be made in the network by a property which is inherited by definite referents but not by indefinites. The property concerned involves **Identity**, but it is directional because it links a 'known' (which inherits it) to an 'unknown' (which will be found by the Binding procedure). For example, take this little story-opening:

(16)   A man had a dog. The dog barked all night.

Both *a dog* and *the dog* have referents, but the referent of *the dog* inherits the property of being identical to some other node. This much is inherited by the word tokens concerned, but Binding will then establish an identity link from the referent of *the dog* to that of *a dog*. The network after Binding will include the links in Figure 1.21, using the obvious notation for identity (an extended '=' with a head to show directionality). Identity joins Isa, Argument, Value, and Quantity on the list of primitive and unclassified relations; as far as I know it completes the list.

Given the relation Identity, therefore, the binding system 'knows' that a token needs to be bound if it inherits an Identity to link to one other node. This will be true for all classification, for all syntactic valents (i.e. expected dependents and parents) and for definite referents. The next question is how the processor chooses among the many thousands of available nodes. We

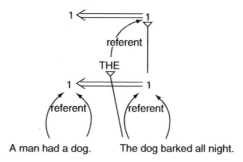

FIGURE 1.21.   The anaphora from *the dog* to *a dog*

can start by noting that the search is usually limited to some general category of things; for example, in the case of word-recognition, the target must be a word because this is what the processor is expecting in the current context. Of course there are occasions where we hear a sound which we think is a word but which turns out to have been something else, such as a mere cough, but in general, classification is a matter of refining an initial guess rather than starting completely from scratch. The task, therefore, is to select the best **eligible** candidate, where nodes qualify as eligible if they have a transitive-isa link to the relevant supercategory (such as 'word').

This choice is in turn guided by the **Best-Fit Principle**, which is familiar in AI (Winograd 1976; Luger and Stubblefield 1993:117) and fundamental to WG (Hudson 1984: 20). The main feature of this strategy is to prefer the match which makes the best **global** fit, even if some of the individual attributes are 'wrong'. The mechanism behind the Best-Fit Principle struck me at one time as entirely mysterious (Hudson 1990: 46) but I now believe it too can be explained in terms of spreading activation. The principle is very simple: the winner is **the most active eligible node**. For example, when we read the letters *speak* we take the known properties of our token w2, and look for a stored type which best fits everything we know about w2 at the point of processing the utterance *I speak* … In this case, the Best-Fit Principle works smoothly and without conflict, but it would have given the same decision even if the input had been the deviant *I speaks* because globally *speaks* matches *Speak:present* better than it matches any other stored word, and only deviates in one minor respect. The Best-Fit Principle seems psychologically plausible because it recognizes that we can classify deviant tokens while still noticing the deviations; and it is worth reiterating that this is only possible if w2 is a distinct node from its stored model, so that its properties can be different.

In production, Best Fit itself may be responsible for **speech errors**, which illuminate the activation which underlies speech production. These show that the most active node may not in fact be the 'correct' target. This can arise when a word is closely enough related to the target word to share some of its activation but also receives activation from some other source. For example, consider the attested example (17), in which the target word was (presumably) *corporal* but the word actually selected was *capital* (Aitchison 1994: 19):

(17)   Corporal punishment is a last resort. It is difficult to use *capital* punishment
       in any institution. A beating is very valuable: it shows people you have come
       to the end of your tether.

Why did this mistake happen? We can only guess, of course, and whatever explanation we offer has to deal with the fact that the word *corporal* was correctly used in the previous sentence. A plausible explanation is that the phrase *capital punishment* is more frequent than *corporal punishment*; this is confirmed by a search on Google, and is probably true of everyday experience. However, both phrases are stored in memory and both are similar not only in meaning but also in pronunciation, as shown in Figure 1.22 (which, ideally, would also show relative activity levels based on frequency). Consequently, activity on one phrase automatically spreads to the other, so they are always in direct competition. In the first sentence the choice was made correctly for reasons that we can only guess at, but after this choice both nodes remain highly active and the higher frequency of *capital punishment* proved decisive.

Examples such as this support the idea that Best Fit favours the most active candidate. One of the most interesting consequences of this principle is that it always favours the most specific candidate, because this is the one which collects activation from the most sources simply because it is the most highly specified candidate. For example, any word-token could be classified simply as a word, but this would ignore the activation coming from its pronunciation and other information which distinguishes it from other words, so its link to some specific lexeme will always be stronger. By the same token, multiple class membership will always be preferred to single class membership because each class contributes more activation, so if a word can be classified in terms of inflectional categories as well as a lexeme, it will be. The specific intersection classes (e.g. *speak:present*) need not be available as stored nodes; the processor can combine the activation from the lexeme and the inflection 'online', though the details of how this happens are still unclear; so it will find both the lexeme and the inflectional category. We can therefore draw two general conclusions about classification: the search for a supercategory will

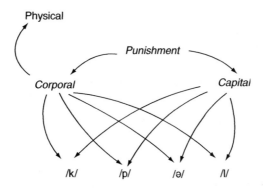

FIGURE 1.22.   links needed to explain the use of *capital* instead of *corporal*

favour lower (more specific) nodes over higher nodes, and it will favour larger numbers of nodes over smaller numbers.

To go back to our example of *I speak English*, the output of the previous process was a network in which w2 was linked via all its observed properties to the corresponding properties stored in the permanent network. Activation spreads out from w2 and affects all these stored nodes; for example, it goes from w2 to the phonemes /s/, /p/, and so on. Thence it spreads to all the word-forms which contain these phonemes, but the activation is spread so thinly that it dissipates very fast; so the winner is the form which receives activation from all the phonemes—the form *speak*—and all the others deactivate almost immediately. As I pointed out above, activation spreads via other routes as well, but in a simple case like this it all converges on the same answer, so by Best Fit, *speak* (or more precisely, *Speak:present*, since the pronoun *I* selects a finite verb) is the winner.

3. *Default Inheritance*

Both the previous steps are merely a preparation for this one, which provides the functional motivation for them all. Merely classifying a piece of experience is not in itself a useful activity; the benefit comes from all the enriching information that derives from this classification and cannot be known otherwise. This is the result of default inheritance. In the case of speech perception this provides information about unobservables such as meaning and syntax; in speech production it provides non-semantic information such as morphology, pronunciation, and (again) syntax.

Default inheritance is a process that takes time. In a classic experiment, (Quillian and Collins 1969) subjects were given English sentences such as 'A cat has fur', 'A cat has a heart', and 'A cat has wings', and their task was to decide whether each sentence was true or false. The dependent variable was the time taken to make this decision, and Collins and Quillian found that sentences like 'A cat has a heart' took longer to judge than did sentences like 'A cat has fur'. The obvious explanation for this difference is that the property of having a heart is stored at a higher level in the Isa hierarchy, maybe at the level of Animal, whereas fur is a memorable (and remembered) property of cats; so we retrieve fur simply by finding it ready-made among the characteristics of cats, but we have to infer hearts by inheritance. This experiment showed that inheritance takes time, but of course it does not prove that all inheritable properties are in fact inherited rather than retrieved directly. On the contrary, it is experiments like these that provide the evidence that I noted earlier which showed that properties which could be inherited may in fact be stored redundantly (Reisberg 1997: 269). For example, to judge by reaction times, we seem to store the property of having feathers not only with the super-category Bird, but also with particular species whose feathers are memorable, such as robins or peacocks. The main point of these experiments is that if properties are inherited, then this process takes a measurable amount of time.

There is also evidence that we take time to deal with exceptions which override defaults. This time the evidence comes from language, where regular and irregular morphology offer an ideal testing ground. Here we can be sure that an irregular past-tense form such as *took* is stored whereas a relatively rare regular one such as *extrapolated* is not. Given the results of Collins and Quillians' experiment, we might perhaps expect *took* to be easier to produce than *extrapolated*, because the latter involves inheritance rather than direct retrieval. However, the experimental results are actually the reverse of this expectation: irregular forms like *took* are slower than regulars like *extrapolated*. Moreover, the brain area activated for *took* is larger than (and almost includes) that for *extrapolated* (Jaeger, Lockwood, Kemmerer, Van Valin, Murphy, and Khalek 1996). In short, the advantage of being stored directly is outweighed by the disadvantage of being irregular because irregularity involves reconciling a competition between two forms: the stored irregular and the inherited regular form.

This finding is important for a theory of processing, because it excludes what at first sight might be an attractive theory of default inheritance. According to this theory, when we are searching for a past-tense form, we start at the bottom, with the most specific information we can find (e.g. the entry for the particular verb in question), and move up the Isa hierarchy until we find a form; and then we stop searching, so that we never in fact access the regular form. The extra time taken by irregulars shows that this must be wrong: we must retrieve both forms and choose between them by applying the logic of default inheritance outlined in section 1.4. In short, default inheritance has at least two separate components, each of which takes a measurable amount of time: climbing the Isa hierarchy in search of relevant properties, and choosing between any competing properties that may result from this search.

All the examples given so far have involved single words, but the same principles will in fact allow us to explain syntactic processing. Naturally this explanation presupposes the WG theory of syntax which is the topic of later chapters, but the most relevant fact about this theory is that words relate directly to one another via dependency links. To take a very simple example, the syntactic structure of (18) is as shown in Figure 1.23.

(18) I actually live in London.

Each word-type has a dependency structure which is inherited by its tokens; for example, *live* needs a subject and a complement, *in* needs a complement

FIGURE 1.23.   Syntactic dependency structure of *I actually live in London*

and a parent, *actually* needs a word (such as a verb) to depend on. As I explained in section 1.4, inheritance automatically creates a new token for each inherited property, so each inherited dependency links the observed word-token to an unknown one which is waiting to be bound. For example, the token *live* inherits not only the subject relation, but also the fact that the word concerned needs to be bound to some other word-token. What parsing does is to apply Best Fit to all these tokens which need binding to some other word in the sentence. Once all these identifications are done, the syntactic structure is complete.

In this section I have reviewed the outlines of a very general procedure for applying any kind of network to any kind of 'experience'. The procedure applies equally to non-linguistic or linguistic behaviour, and to the under-standing of other people's behaviour or to the planning of our own. The steps that have to be taken are as follows, using E as the name for the piece of experience in focus:

- **Node creation** and **node identification**, to produce a representation of E which includes all the information currently available—the perceived information about the incoming experience, or the partial description of the planned experience.
- **Spreading activation** activates some part of the network and **Best Fit Binding** selects the most active node (A) in the network.
- **Default inheritance** enriches the description of E (or any other token) once E isa some node F by creating a new copy of every property of F, and especially of properties which are highly active.

1.8 Learning

Learning raises two kinds of question:

1 How do children learn the general properties of words, and in particular that words combine a sound with a meaning (and, eventually, that they have morphological structure, belong to word-classes and have a syntactic valency)?
2 How do they learn the specifics of individual words?

The first question is clearly more fundamental, and harder, than the second, and to some it seems too hard to explain in terms of learning. It also raises even more fundamental questions about why other primates cannot understand how words work. However, I do believe that learning is possible even for such abstract properties and in section 5.2 I shall offer a brief explanation of how infants may be cognitively prepared, unlike other primates, to learn one of the essential word properties, that words have a meaning. In this section I shall focus on the easier question of how children (or for that matter adults) learn new words and their properties, and in the process I shall try to put together a coherent theory of learning to accommodate this particular kind of learning.

The main thrust of the last section was that conceptual networks, including the language network, are dynamic. New links and new nodes are continually being established, and activation levels throughout the network are affected by spreading activation. There is a great deal of evidence that these effects of experience are not ephemeral but, at least in some cases, very long-lasting indeed. The most obvious examples of this are the 'recency effect' and the 'frequency effect', which show that words are more accessible if they have been used recently or frequently (Reisberg 1997: 51). If we explain these effects in terms of spreading activation, it seems that activating a node has a more or less long-term affect on it, making it more easily activated on future occasions. This is the variable called 'entrenchment' in Cognitive Grammar (Langacker 2000), and once again one advantage of a network model of language is the possibility of at least debating this important variable, and possibly even finding a suitable theoretical basis for it. Unfortunately this is an area of WG which has not yet been developed except in relation to sociolinguistic data (s. 5.9, Hudson 2007c).

This dynamic interaction between the network and experience is the basis for **learning**—i.e. for permanent extensions to the network. I am impressed by the evidence for massively 'usage-based' learning, in which the learner stores large numbers of very specific experiences—specific utterances of words or word-groups—and then uses this database as a source of inductive generalizations which constitute the grammar/lexicon (Bybee 1998; Langacker 2000; Ellis 2002; Tomasello 2003; Bod 1998). Inductive generalization is particularly evident in morphology, where it is generally agreed that children first store all observed forms, whether regular or irregular, and do not recognize general rules until they have stored a significant collection of regular forms. (As noted earlier, one consequence of this inductive approach is that at least some regular patterns must be stored, because generalization presupposes stored examples; see Jackendoff 1997: 122.) I should like to show now how this kind of learning may be a by-product of the processes described in the previous section.

Suppose a child hears a new word in a sentence such as this:

(19)   Let's get rid of those nasty germs.

The new word is *germs*. Segmentation is easy if the child already knows all the other words in the sentence, so let's assume that its sounds have been identified as a word-segment. At this point the child has created a new node w7 to represent this word, and knows already that w7 isa Word, which allows all the general characteristics of words (e.g. having a speaker and a referent) to be inherited; the child can even supply specific values for some of the inherited variables: the word's pronunciation, its speaker, and its time. Spreading activation from the earlier words (especially the preceding determiner *those* and the adjective *nasty*) has already strongly activated the Common-noun node and the Plural-noun node; so Best Fit adds new Isa links from w7 to Common-noun and Plural-noun. So far, then, w7 isa Common noun, Plural noun, and Word.

Once again default inheritance applies, giving *germs* the morphological and semantic structures of a typical plural noun. The morphological structure consists of a base and the suffix *s*; the details of this structure will be explained in Chapter 2. This allows the child to identify the morpheme *germ* as the base of w7. The Plural-noun node also provides a schematic semantic structure, showing that the word refers to a set each of whose members isa the word's sense, so the child 'knows' that *germs* refers to a set of things each of which is called a germ. That is the end state after processing, unless the child can make a guess (right or wrong) about what kind of thing a germ might be.

What happens to w7 after this? One possibility is that it weakens (in some sense) to the point where it no longer counts as a part of the network. This is presumably the fate of the vast majority of word-tokens, at least to the extent that they become inaccessible to any kind of retrieval system. A great deal of psychological research has shown that to the extent that we can remember sentences we remember them in terms of their content, not their exact wording (Harley 1995: 313). Another possibility, however, is that, because of its novelty, w7 is sufficiently salient to receive a great deal of activation, and that this activation is sufficient to keep it accessible until the next time the child encounters the same word—in short, a token node turns into a type node simply by persisting in memory.

It could be objected that this is logically impossible because types and tokens have completely different statuses; after all, in most theories, types belong to competence whereas tokens belong to performance. But I have already explained that this is not so in WG: although token nodes and type nodes can be distinguished, they both have the same formal status in the network. Admittedly, types and tokens have different psychological statuses since one comes from memory while the other comes from perception or planning; but even this contrast is blurred by those word-tokens that we can recall from memory, of which we all have a large stock. We can all recall individual datable tokens of particular words—tokens which stand out in memory for some reason such as being our first encounter with them. In WG these tokens are permanently stored as examples of their respective types, from which most of them are distinguished only by the fact that they have specific values for the deictic categories of time, place, speaker, addressee, and so on. For example, our imaginary child may remember the word *germs* for some time, together with some of the details of who used it and when; and the same may even be true of the new type *germ* which *germs* isa.

It could also be argued that a node that carries specific deictic details which tie it to a specific situation cannot be a type because types are by definition general; so even if we remember a token, it is still just a token, not a type. It only becomes a type by losing its specificity, and only then can it be used as the supercategory for another token. However, this argument ignores the effects of Best Fit and Default Inheritance. Even if the child's memory of the first token of *germs* is tied to a particular time and speaker, another token of the same word will strongly activate this memory and this activation will be enough for Best Fit to choose it as the new word's supercategory. The deictic contradictions between them do not prevent this identification because Default Inheritance allows defaults to be overridden. In any case, it seems likely that most deictic details will fade into oblivion through the normal processes of memory loss, so most tokens will automatically become more abstract the longer they are stored.

My proposal, then, is that our first encounter with a word produces a new node for that token, which is attached to everything we know about it—who said it, when they said it, and who they said it to, as well as its observable form (whether pronunciation or spelling) and (probably) a word-class and (possibly) a meaning. Since it is a new word, we don't assign it to an existing lexeme, so we register it as new and therefore interesting and important. Its novelty has the effect of distinguishing it from tokens of familiar words, and prolonging its life so that it may act as a supercategory for the next token of the same word. If the next token enriches the description of the word (e.g. by providing a richer or different meaning), it too will survive, so gradually the stored information about this word becomes more and more rich and informative. Best Fit guarantees that the richest node will always be selected so this is the one which will prosper, while its poorer relatives fade away and become less and less accessible. In other words, the richest concept becomes the 'official' representation for the item concerned.

Here then are the elements of my account of how we learn a new word W:

- We hear a token of W and create a node for it, called E.
- We store all the known characteristics of E, including:
  - its observable form (spoken or written),
  - its deictic characteristics (time, place, speaker, addressee, etc.),
  - its high-level classification as a word,
  - any general characteristics that can be inherited from Word, including a new node for its meaning.
- We apply Best Fit to find as informative a supercategory for E as possible, given the currently active nodes; these reflect the morphology, the grammatical context, and the conceptual context, so they may produce more high-level classifications in terms of syntactic and semantic categories (e.g. Plural-noun for *germs* and Set, Nasty, and Invisible for its meaning).
- We add these inferred characteristics to the store of known characteristics of E and its meaning, giving:
  - its word-class(es)
  - its rough meaning.
- All the preceding steps are parts of normal processing, but unlike most word-tokens E does not fade from memory; because of its novelty it remains accessible to future processing. In other words, this token node E turns into a type node simply by staying active and 'alive'.
- The next token of W isa E by the usual classification procedure. If its characteristics add to those of E, it survives and replaces E as the provisional representation of W. This process repeats until the internalized representation of W stops changing because there is nothing more to learn.

This theory has the attraction of explaining how we can learn a new word (or any other kind of concept) after meeting it just once, while also allowing subsequent experiences to enrich and correct the first attempt.

Individual lexical items are the 'basic-level categories' of language (Rosch 1976)—the most informative categories, which combine the largest number of non-inherited characteristics, and provide the best fit between form and function. Outside language they are fundamental to learning; for example, we presumably learn Chair and Table before we learn the higher-level category Furniture and lower-level distinctions between types of chairs and tables.

Similarly in language: we learn individual lexical items before word-classes, so the above account of how this happens is fundamental to a theory of language learning. However this theory also needs an explanation for how grammar goes beyond the individual lexeme in two directions: in terms of size and in terms of generality. The first produces syntax, and the second produces rules and generalizations.

Syntax is already implicit in the account of how we learn lexemes if, as in WG, syntax consists of nothing but pair-wise links among words. (This is the main theme of the later chapters on syntax; see ch. 3 for a summary.) The accompanying words are highly salient characteristics of a word token, so if a child hears the utterance *Dogs bark*, it can store the fact that they occurred next to each other in this order along with all the other information stored about each word separately. Stored word-sequences are the basis for learning dependencies because most of the time adjacent words are in fact linked by a dependency; in English, for example, estimates of the number of words that depend on an immediately adjacent word range from 63 percent (Pake 1998) to 78 percent (Eppler 2004: 156–8) for conversation and one estimate for written English is 74 percent (Collins 1996). In other words, most words have a syntactically relevant link to the preceding word (either as dependent or as parent). Moreover, words that are not adjacent are much less likely to have a significant relation, so a child benefits greatly from having a limited span of only two words since this helps to filter out irrelevant links (Elman 1993).

This strong tendency for adjacency to favour syntactic links means that a strategy based on nothing but adjacency will provide a very useful database of word pairs for future learning; but of course actual language learners learn meanings alongside words, so they can in fact distinguish the semantically relevant links from the irrelevant ones. For example, *buy cherry yogurt* contains two adjacent pairs, one of which does show a semantically relevant link (*cherry yogurt*) while the other does not (*buy cherry*). Presumably adjacent pairs are more likely to be stored for future reference if they are also related semantically on the principle that rich links attract more activation. As the dependency system becomes more sophisticated the learner can rise more and more above mere adjacency, but adjacency is a very good starting point.

The other direction for growth is towards increasing **generality**. According to the 'usage-based' approach described in section 1.1, learning is based on experience and generalizations are built by induction from stored examples of experience. Inductive generalizations produce the stuff of grammar— word-classes, constructions, dependency types, word-order rules, and so on. The benefits of higher-level categories are very clear, and especially so in learning; for example, in our earlier example the child could infer that *germs* was a plural noun because it already knew the categories Plural noun and Noun, and this in turn allowed the form *germs* to be segmented into a base and a suffix. However, it is less clear exactly how induction works in a network as described so far, and it may well involve psychological processes that go beyond those that I have assumed so far. The following remarks are pure speculation even as a model of mind, let alone of its underlying neurology.

Somehow the learner's mind 'spots' a similarity among a range of nodes (which we can call A, B, C) and creates a new node D such that:

(a) A, B, and C all isa D
(b) D has the characteristics which A, B, and C share.

One possible explanation is that we have a special 'induction mechanism' which randomly activates nodes during slack periods (e.g. during sleep) in search of correlations—bundles of two or more characteristics that tend to occur on the same nodes. Suppose the characteristics that A, B, and C share are their links to two other nodes, X and Y. In that case, activity on both X and Y will make A, B, and C more active than any other nodes, which indicates a correlation between their links to X and Y. Following Hebb's principle that 'nodes that fire together wire together' (Hebb 1949), the induction mechanism creates an explicit link among A, B, and C ('wires them together') by building an Isa link from each one to a new supercategory D. Once this supercategory exists, it will inevitably attract all other nodes that have similar links to X and Y and presumably its properties can also become richer in the same way as I suggested above for new lexeme-type nodes.

Whatever the mechanism, it is clear that inductive generalization is a lifelong process. For example, a detailed study of irregular past tenses such as *kept* and *told* showed that speakers are more likely to recognize them as a distinct subclass of verbs as they become older (Guy and Boyd 1990). The speakers (in Philadelphia, USA) sometimes 'drop' the final t/d from these words by a process called t/d deletion which applies more frequently in mono-morphemic words such as *apt* than in regular bi-morphemes like *walked*. Young children never use the suffix t/d in irregular verbs like *kept* and *told*, but at some point in later life everyone uses it at the same rate as in mono-morphemes, which shows that they have not yet recognized the possibility of a morpheme boundary. However some adults later reduce their 'dropping' rate in these irregular verbs to that of bi-morphemes, from which we may conclude that they have recognized that these words form a distinct group which contains a semi-regular suffix alongside an irregular base—a clear example of late learning based on induction.

If new concept nodes can be created by induction, the same must be true of relation-types. The discussion in section 1.2 (around Fig. 1.6) led to the conclusion that non-primitive relations are also concepts (even if my simplified diagrams do not show them as nodes), so these must be generalizable by the same inductive processes as entity concepts. Once again the induction mechanism looks for correlations which are revealed by random activation, but this time it is on relations rather than entities that the activation converges. Imagine two relations R1 and R2 whose tendency to link the same pairs of nodes is revealed by random activation; the result is the creation of a super-node which is 'defined' in terms of R1 and R2. This is the kind of process that explains abstract relations, including those of syntax. Take the Subject relation, for example. This is famous for bringing together a bundle of disparate characteristics from word order to semantics (Keenan 1976), each of which is a simpler relation such as Before (word order) or Agent (meaning). The induction mechanism just sketched explains how the correlations among these simpler relations can lead to the creation of a super-relation which has the simpler ones as its inheritable characteristics. Each of the relations concerned helps to define the others and to make them available, by inheritance, during processing.

To summarize this discussion, I have made the following rather tentative suggestions about how basic-level lexical items are extended in terms of both length and generality. Two-word syntactic constructions (dependencies) can be induced from stored pairs of adjacent words, most of which are in fact linked by syntactic dependency and some semantic relations; these dependencies can be stored as facts about the words concerned, and recurrent patterns will reinforce each other. More general categories are built, by induction, out of the basic-level lexemes. It is possible that inductive generalizations are spotted by a random activation-generator which discovers correlated link-patterns, and which then records the correlation by creating shared supercategory nodes. The same process applies to the relations among lexemes, so that increasingly general and abstract syntactic (and other) relations can be induced. In short, 'rules' are learned and stored as facts about general categories which are (therefore) inherited by their members.

1.9 Evaluating the Theory

The theory that I present in this book is primarily intended to specify the nature of language structure, but a background assumption is that this cannot be done in isolation. This theory must meet up sooner or later with theories of how the structure is used and learned, and of how other kinds of knowledge are structured, used, and learned. It would be very easy to build a theory which failed at the last post because it failed to mesh with established psychology, so my view is that the integration should happen sooner rather than later: better to build some elementary psychology into the theory from the start than simply to hope for the best and leave it till later. In short, a theory of language structure can and should aim at the 'psychological reality' that has been on the agenda for some decades now (Chomsky 1965; Lamb 1971; Bresnan 1978). Moreover, just the same arguments apply to the relations among analyses at different levels of language: sooner or later they must meet up, so the sooner the better. The aim of this theory, therefore, is to integrate the structures at one level with those at the other levels as well as with more general conceptual structures.

This rather ambitious aim makes evaluation problematic. The standard criteria for any linguistic theory still apply, so the theory must allow accurate and revealing solutions to well-known descriptive problems. This bread-and-butter work has taken up all my working life, and I include in this book a number of examples to show that at least some problems are solvable within the WG framework. The main showpiece is an extended discussion of gerunds in English (ch. 4), but the book also outlines descriptions of other complex phenomena, of which the following are just a sample:

- Latin verb morphology (s. 2.2)
- Slovene noun morphology (s. 2.4)
- Beja clitics (s. 2.9)
- Serbo-Croatian clitics (s. 2.9)
- German Partial VP Fronting (s. 3.2)
- Zapotec prepositional pied-piping (s. 3.2)
- Icelandic case agreement (s. 3.7).

Each of these discussions supports some part of the general theory, but this also rests on a great many other descriptive analyses which I mention in passing. These briefer discussions go well beyond the core areas of morphology and syntax into semantics and sociolinguistics. The obvious gap remains phonology—both segmental and prosodic.

Any linguist can evaluate these analyses in relation to the facts and to other analyses of the same data expressed in terms of other theories. However, the most important fact about them is that whether they involve morphology, syntax, semantics, or sociolinguistics, they all assume the same theory. A theory of language structure which integrates separate sub-theories for morphology, syntax, and so on is more comprehensive and therefore more explanatory than a library of unintegrated theories for different levels; so given a straight choice between the single theory and the library of theories, the single theory must always win.

The problems of evaluation multiply when we look beyond language. At this point, of course, the best judges are psychologists. When I make claims about spreading activation and its effects in priming and speech errors, I think I am simply repeating what can be found in virtually any textbook of psychology (e.g. Reisberg 1997). The idea that spreading activation implies a network is both obvious and widely accepted among psychologists, though I recognize that some psychologists are uneasy about the idea of using nothing but networks to model knowledge:

There is surely widespread agreement that memory does draw on associative processes and spreading activation. There is likewise no doubt that network theorizing can encompass an enormous range of memory data. But there is considerable uncertainty about whether network theorizing, either in a traditional version or in PDP [Parallel Distributed Processing], can explain all of mental functioning. This is still 'work-in-progress' on an immensely complex and subtle topic—merely the task of describing All of Knowledge. Moreover, we can take considerable comfort from the fact that, unsolved mysteries or no, we have at least a part of the puzzle under control. (Reisberg 1997: 303)

However, I believe that a linguist may have an important contribution to make in this debate about psychological theory because the structure of language is so much better understood than any other area of knowledge. What I am offering is a theory of networks which accommodates all the complexity that linguists know about; and in particular, which includes a theory of how relations are classified (which is one of the main weaknesses in associative theories). So far as I know, psychologists have never considered a network of this type, so all the evaluation remains to be done.

Another characteristic of WG networks is the procedure for enriching token nodes through default inheritance. This idea belongs to Artificial Intelligence rather than to psychology, though it also explains the prototype effects that psychologists find in categorization (s. 1.4). However, default logic is very controversial in those parts of the AI world (and of logic) which prefer 'clean' solutions; after all, a logic which allows earlier conclusions to be overridden later is a potential disaster not only in terms of logic but also in terms of computer programming (Touretzky 1986). After a survey of the problems, one textbook concludes:

Unfortunately, most commercially available inheritance software does not provide a clean enough implementation of inheritance to avoid these problems. This is because many of these problems have not yet been solved or the solutions that are available are either too new or too inefficient to affect the design of current programs. (Luger and Stubblefield 1993: 389)

However I believe that the approach to default inheritance that I describe in section 1.4 avoids most of the problems described in this literature by restricting inheritance to tokens. As with the design of networks, I believe this is an innovation so it remains to be evaluated.

Since the research tool of AI is computer modelling rather than experimentation, it may be that the only way to evaluate this area of WG is to build computer models and to match their performance against observed human performance, warts and all. A computer model would fail if it performed differently from the typical human being, regardless of whether its behaviour was worse or better; for example, it should make some errors (so long as these were like the errors that humans make), and it should take longer to retrieve a rare word than a common one. This approach to theory evaluation is already quite familiar in psycholinguistics (e.g. Levelt, Roelofs and Meyer 1999), and it would certainly be a good way to evaluate WG. If WG is right, it should be possible to apply a single 'inference engine' equally successfully to networks for any area of language or for other kinds of knowledge such as kinship systems and social behaviour. Once again, this research has not yet been done, though a start has been made on a general-purpose network simulator (called Babbage) which can be adapted to different network models, including WG. (Interested readers should consult the Babbage website at **www.babbagenet.org**; the software is being developed by Mark P. Line.)

In conclusion, therefore, this book offers a single unified theory for language as well as for other kinds of knowledge, but its various parts need to be evaluated in different ways. I feel relatively confident about the strictly linguistic claims to the extent that I have tested them in my own research (though of course I know that there are plenty of phenomena that I haven't even tried to deal with). But in the areas of overlap with psychology and AI, I am merely offering a new theory. Ideally I would have offered new research evidence to support the new parts of this theory, but I hope the theory already has enough support to justify further evaluation.

2

Morphology

2.1 Outline

WG treats morphology, like the rest of language, as a network, so morphological patterns are represented as a network of relations among words, **morphs**, and sounds or letters. (A number of other morph-like units will be introduced later, but we can ignore them for the time being.) The network approach is relatively uncontroversial in morphology, and indeed WG morphology is quite similar to the theory called 'network morphology' in which the network basis is explicit (Brown, Corbett, Fraser, Hippisley, and Timberlake 1996; Corbett and Fraser 1993). There has recently been a high-profile debate about whether we process regular morphology in the same way as irregular morphology (Pinker 1998), but both sides of the debate agree that we store at least irregularly inflected forms as a network which we exploit by spreading activation. Admittedly the networks in question are generally assumed to be distributed connectionist networks rather than WG-style symbolic networks, but even so this debate shows how easily morphological relations can be visualized as a network. Perhaps the most distinctive characteristic of the WG approach is that it is embedded in a general theory which encompasses the whole of language. Other theories of morphology are typically limited to morphology and are neutral as to the organization of other parts of language such as syntax or the lexicon.

Although the WG theory of morphology tries to cover a wide range of phenomena, I shall only be able to illustrate most of them rather briefly in this survey; but the theory has recently been applied in detail to several challenging areas of morphology:

- Swahili verb morphology (Creider and Hudson 1999; Creider 2002)
- Serbo-Croatian clitics (Camdzic and Hudson 2007)
- English: the morphology and syntax of the contraction *wanna* for *want to* (Hudson 2006*b*)
- English: the morphology of the non-form *amn't* (Hudson 2000*a*).

This section will introduce the main ideas informally via a very straightforward example: the morphology of the word *farmers*.

The challenge for morphology is to relate this particular word—the plural of the lexeme *farmer*—to the pronunciation [fɑːməz]. The example involves both derivational and inflectional morphology:

- **derivational** morphology explains why *farmer* shares the **base** (the lexically specified form, sometimes called the 'stem') of *farm*;
- **inflectional** morphology explains the extra [z].

In WG, words are never related directly to pronunciation. As I shall explain below, this relationship is always mediated by '**forms**', which include traditional roots and suffixes as well as more complex forms. I shall now distinguish forms from other units by enclosing them in {...}, the traditional notation for morphological units. In the case of 'farmers', the derivational pattern relates the forms {farm} and {farmer}, while the inflectional pattern relates {farmer} to {farmers}. This notation will keep forms distinct both from **lexemes** such as FARM (written in capitals throughout) and also from **phonological** structures (which I shall not try to distinguish from phonetic structures) such as [fɑːməz].

The network for this little area of derivational morphology shows not only how FARM is related to FARMER, but also how {farm} is related to {farmer}. These two relations are completely different: FARMER is the 'agent-noun' of FARM, but {farmer} is the 'er-variant' of {farm}. The 'agent-noun' and 'er-variant' relations are quite different and independent:

- The agent-noun of a verb need not be realized by an er-variant (e.g. COOK_{noun} is the agent-noun of COOK_{verb}).
- An er-variant need not belong to an agent-noun; for example, {londoner} is the er-variant of {london}, but LONDONER is not the agent-noun of LONDON.

If words are separate from forms, then word-word relations such as 'agent-noun' are also separate from form-form relations such as 'er-variant'. This network can be seen in Figure 2.1. For present purposes, the relations 'part1' and 'part2' can be taken as primitives, but of course a complete analysis would show that part1 precedes part2 (and so on for higher numbers); for more details see section 2.7.

The dotted line shows that the first part of {farmer} is in some way based on {farm}, but this relation is not simply identity. The detail of this relation is worth exploring as an example of how the logic of networks and default inheritance impacts on the analysis. For convenience, I have called the first part of {farmer} simply X.

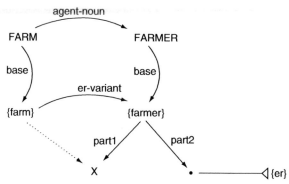

FIGURE 2.1.   The derivational morphology of FARMER

- Simple identity is ruled out because {farm} and X have conflicting properties; for example, {farm} is the base of FARM, but X is the first part of the base of FARMER; and X always precedes {er}, but {farm} does not.
- Another possibility is that X isa {farm}, but this too leads to contradiction. The problem here is that X inherits the properties of {farm}, so it inherits the property of having an er-variant which contains an example of X as its first part; but nothing can be part of itself. Worse still, this analysis leads to an infinite regress because the new inherited first part inherits another er-variant with its own first part, and so on.
- The correct conclusion seems to be that X and {farm} share just one property: how they are realized in pronunciation and spelling. The dotted arrow will stand in for this relation until I have introduced the notion of realization in section 2.3.

In contrast with derivation, inflectional morphology has to explain the relation between the base of FARMER and its 'fully inflected form', or 'fif', which is determined not only by the lexeme but also by the 'inflections' (i.e. the inflectional word-classes such as Plural-noun or Past-verb, which will be discussed more fully in s. 2.2). By default the base and fif are not distinguished, but when FARMER combines with Plural-noun, {s} is added as in Figure 2.2. Here the word that we called 'the plural of FARMER' is named more simply 'FARMER:plural' (the intersection of the lexeme FARMER and the inflection Plural-noun); this is the word whose fif is {farmers}. Once again the dotted line shows that the first part of {farmers} has the same realization as {farmer}.

The difference between derivational and inflectional patterns is entirely located in the relations between the words concerned: relations between a pair

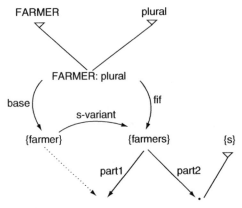

FIGURE 2.2.   The inflectional morphology of *farmers*

of lexemes in one case, and multiple inheritance from a lexeme and an inflection in the other. On the other hand, the morphological structures which signal these relations are much the same in the two patterns, so there will be no distinction between derivational and inflectional morphology as such. Indeed, it would be wrong to think of derivation and inflection as defining the entire world of morphology, because there is at least one import-ant area of morphology which is neither derivational nor inflectional, namely clitics (which I discuss in s. 2.9).

What these simple examples do not of course show is where the specific patterns 'come from'. They are **generated** in the same way as in other con-straint-based theories of grammatical structure such as HPSG (Pollard and Sag 1994) and LFG (Bresnan 2001): the grammar generates X if the elementary patterns that it contains can combine into a complex pattern which matches X. For example, it generates *farmers* if it generates {farmer} and {s} and allows the pattern in which they combine as { {farmer}+{s} }. The basic mechanism for applying a grammar to X is default inheritance, which applies thanks to the Isa relation between X and some stored element S in the grammar. Since X isa S, X automatically inherits from S and then, recursively, from any other elements which S transitive-isa. In our example:

- X is a newly created node which we can call {farmers}, and which has two parts: examples of {farmer} and {s}, which we can call {farmer}' and {s}'.
- {farmers} isa S, the stored node which represents the typical s-variant of any form; S has a two-part structure which (by inheritance) allows {farmers} to have two parts.

- The properties of {farmer}' and {s}' can also be inherited from the two parts of S. In short, if a good match is found between X and S, X is generated by the grammar.

It may be helpful to think of the stored nodes as expressing general 'rules', which generate any items which isa them. The relevant general rules are shown in Figure 2.3. It can be seen that Figure 2.1 inherits the pattern from the left side of this picture, while Figure 2.2 inherits from the right side. The general patterns are, of course, merely the defaults, and can be overridden in exceptional cases such as the agent-noun of COOK and the plural of GOOSE, neither of which has the default suffix.

The main theoretical points that emerge from this analysis of *farmers* are the following:

- Morphology does not relate words directly to phonology (or spelling), but maps them onto an intermediate level of 'forms', some of which are atoms (morphs). This claim unites WG with other theories that recognize an autonomous level of morphology (Aronoff 1994; Sadock 1991), and I shall justify it in section 2.3.
- Morphs (and other forms) have no meaning or syntax in themselves, and indeed are 'invisible' to the syntax because of the number of network links between them and other syntactic objects; in Aronoff's terminology, forms are 'morphomic'. This claim puts WG firmly within the European 'Word and Paradigm' tradition in which word classification is separated cleanly from word structure (Robins 2001).
- Derivation and inflection are sharply distinguished at the level of words, but not at the level of forms (Blevins 2001). The same range of formal

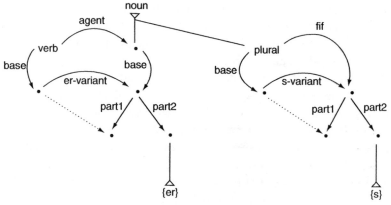

FIGURE 2.3.   The default patterns underlying FARMER and *farmers*

patterns is available for both, and many affixes are used in both—for example, {er} marks not only derived agents but also inhabitants of some towns (e.g. {Londoner}), bank-notes (e.g. {fiver}), and many other relations. This claim follows from the first two: forms which have neither meaning nor syntax can be 'recycled' for many different purposes, including derivation and inflection.

- The power and precision of the grammar lies, as usual, in the classified relations. The analysis of *farmers* required us to postulate the following relations: Agent, Base, Fully inflected form (Fif), Er-variant, S-variant, Part1, Part2. These relations may be subsumed under more general categories (e.g. both Base and Fif isa Realization, Part1 and Part2 isa Part), and may be further subdivided. Many of these relations are quite traditional, but in other theories they are generally not integrated into the theory as they are here.

- These relations allow morphology to be entirely declarative and to dispense with the ordered processes of theories such as 'a-morphous morphology' (Anderson 1992). The real challenge for declarative morphology lies in 'replacive' patterns such as the vowel alternation in {goose} $\sim$ {geese}, but in section 2.7 we shall see that even these (and other apparent processes) can be analysed in declarative terms.

This simple example from English has introduced most of the general machinery of WG morphology. This machinery will allow us to handle a great deal of complexity, but will need some expansion for some special patterns.

2.2 Lexemes, Inflections, and Features

Morphology relates words to their phonological shapes, so it is important to be clear about the 'word' end of this relationship. This section will explain the theory behind the lexemes and inflections invoked in the previous section. The theory is, of course, derived from the basic assumptions of WG about classification and default inheritance.

In principle the distinction between lexemes and inflections is uncontroversial, except perhaps that lexemes are not restricted, as they sometimes are, just to so-called 'lexical' words. Every word (including so-called function words) belongs to some lexeme, and the traditional word-classes are in fact lexeme-classes. As in other theories, a **lexeme** may cover a range of inflected forms of the same word, so the lexeme FARMER includes the word *farmers* as well as *farmer*, the lexeme THIS includes *these*, and the lexeme IF covers just one word. A lexeme is a word with all its default properties—default meaning, syntax, and form—so FARMER refers to one person, is syntactically singular, and is realized as {farmer}. In contrast, **inflections** cover non-default 'variations' on this basic pattern that fit into general patterns; for example, Plural-noun is an inflection whose members refer to sets of individuals, are syntactically plural, and are realized by the base followed by {s}. Of course, these exceptional properties of an inflection may themselves be overridden, so some inflections are 'uninflected' as far as their forms are concerned; for example, some plurals have the same form as the singular (e.g. *deer*). Notice that inflections in WG are simple word-classes with just the same logical status as the lexeme-classes such as Noun; so FARMER:plural inherits (by multiple default inheritance) from both FARMER and Plural-noun. Of course, it inherits quite different properties from each, but the inheritance process is just the same. Thus inflections take their place in the general Isa hierarchy of words alongside lexemes and lexeme-classes.

One of the benefits of this approach is that it allows the logic of default inheritance to capture the notion of **markedness**. The singular *farmer* is unmarked relative to the plural *farmers*, in the sense that the structure of *farmers* includes that of *farmer*, but not vice versa. This asymmetry is not simply a matter of morphology, but also extends to the semantics, where the semantic structure of *farmers* is a set each of whose members isa farmer (Hudson 1990: 139). Clearly the singular noun is basic in meaning as well as in form, so we treat it as the default noun. In this analysis the category 'singular noun' is exactly the same as the category 'noun', so in effect the singular does not exist as a distinct word-class, though the plural does. This analysis works so long as there are no patterns which are restricted to singular nouns; if such patterns did exist, they would be impossible to distinguish from the default, and therefore would be automatically inherited by the plural as well. So far as I know there are no such patterns (apart from agreement phenomena, which I will now discuss briefly), so the analysis is possible.

On the other hand, this outcome is not inevitable, and there are clear cases even in English where a form which is morphologically unmarked nevertheless has to be distinguished from the default. The evidence lies in the verb system, where there are three syntactically and semantically different verb-uses which all require a verb with a bare unmodified base:

- imperative (*Come* in!)
- present plural (They *come* in.)
- infinitive (They will *come* in.)

It may be possible to treat the present plural as the default tensed verb, with Singular and Past as deviations, but imperatives and infinitives are both restricted in ways that prevent them from acting as a default relative to any other inflections. This is most obvious in the case of infinitives, which are required after verbs (such as modals) which do not allow any other forms; this immediately excludes any analysis in which infinitives are (say) the default non-finite verbs, because in such an analysis other non-finite forms would automatically appear wherever the default infinitive was allowed. A tentative classification of English verb forms is shown in Figure 2.4, where both Imperative and Infinitive are treated as distinct categories in spite of their lack of a distinct form.

In comparison with most other approaches (including my own 1990 version of WG), what is probably most striking about this approach to classification is that it makes no use of 'morpho-syntactic features'— attributes such as Number and Tense which have a limited range of possible values, whether these are distinguished by name (e.g. singular/plural) or by simple polarity (+/−). As a basis for classification, features are problematic because they force a major theoretical distinction between two kinds of classification: the hierarchical classification of isa hierarchies, and feature-based classification, found (perhaps) only in morpho-syntax. It would be more parsimonious to avoid this distinction unless it really is essential, and it is much easier to extend Isa classification to morpho-syntax than to extend feature-based classification to other areas. (For example, what is the feature that distinguishes adjectives from adverbs?)

On the other hand, there is one area where features really are indispensable, namely **agreement**. If one word agrees with another in terms of, say, number, then there is no alternative to a feature analysis, because it is impossible to state an agreement rule simply in terms of categories in an Isa hierarchy. Agreement necessarily involves some named parameter or choice to which the agreement applies, so if two words agree in number, the feature Number is

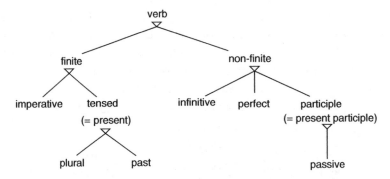

FIGURE 2.4.   The sub-classification of English verb inflections

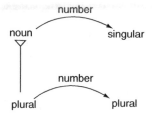

FIGURE 2.5.   The competing values for the feature 'number'

essential. This is not a problem for WG because features can be invoked wherever they are needed. Indeed, every non-primitive relation is a 'feature' in this sense—a named attribute of one node with another node as its argument—and they are commonplace outside language (e.g. sex, nationality, age, ...). Moreover, features can be combined with default inheritance; for example, as shown in Figure 2.5 a typical English noun has the value Singular for the feature Number, whereas a plural noun exceptionally has the value Plural. This is the basis for the WG treatment of subject–verb agreement in English (Hudson 1999). In short, morpho-syntactic features are available when needed (and may only be needed for agreement), but they are not used for classification, the exclusive province of the Isa relation.

Finally, how would this approach to classification work if confronted with a more complex morphological system than English? Take Classical Latin, whose verbs distinguish a large number of non-compound (i.e. single-word) inflectional categories (Griffin 1991: 27):

- six active indicative tenses (present, future, imperfect, perfect, future perfect, pluperfect), each in six subject-forms (i.e. singular/plural, first/second/third person): 36
- four active subjunctive tenses (as for indicative, minus the future and future perfect), each in six subject-forms: 24
- three passive indicative tenses and two passive subjunctive tenses (all but the perfects), each in six subject-forms: 30
- active and passive imperatives, singular or plural: 4
- active and passive infinitives, and active perfect infinitives: 3
- active present and future participles, and passive perfect participles: 3
- active gerund and supine, and passive gerundive: 3

The inflections distinguished in this list number 103, but the participles and the gerundives are inflected like adjectives, so they each also distinguish three genders, two numbers and five cases, giving 30 contrasting categories each; and the gerund is a noun which has 10 inflections (two numbers and five cases).

The grand total, therefore, is 170 inflections for each verb lexeme—a far cry from the six or so inflections of English verbs. However there are a great many general patterns running through the multitude of forms, so the goal is to provide a set of inflectional categories which will permit these generalizations; and thanks to multiple inheritance, this can be done at least as easily in an isa classification as it can in a feature-based system. One possible partial analysis is shown in Figure 2.6. This is meant to be suggestive rather than definitive, and could no doubt be improved. The main point of the example is to suggest how a complex set of intersecting categories can be handled in an Isa hierarchy. It may seem strange to put categories like Passive, Finite, and Future alongside one another, but it must be borne in mind that categories in an Isa hierarchy are not mutually exclusive. They can, and do, intersect, and when they do, their combined properties are inherited by multiple default inheritance. (Incidentally, it should be noticed that in Latin there are no default verbs; every member of a Latin verb paradigm is an inflection, in the sense just defined, because the verb's base is never used on its own.)

In conclusion, then, WG morphology interprets word-level categories which are arranged in an Isa hierarchy. Some of these categories are lexemes, while others are inflections, and categories combine to define inflected forms such as FARMER:plural or (in Latin) AM:Plur,3rd,Passive,Present,Subjunctive— the third-person plural passive present subjunctive of AM, whose form is {amentur}. Features play only a minor role in the classification, as they are invoked only for agreement rules.

2.3 Words, Forms, Phonology, and Realization

The main object of this section is to justify the three-level analysis which distinguishes forms from words on the one hand and from phonological units

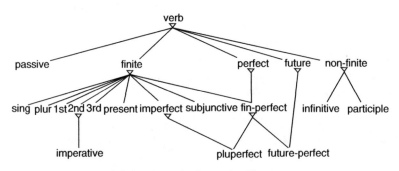

FIGURE 2.6.   The sub-classification of Latin verb inflections

on the other. We already have the notation for distinguishing words such as FARMER:plural from forms like {farmers} and from 'phonological' structures like [fɑ:məz]. In a network, the difference between words and phonological structures is obvious: for example, FARMER:plural is a single unit (in spite of its complex name), with its own network node, whereas the phonological structure may not have a single node for [fɑ:məz], but may have nodes for the grammatically irrelevant units [fɑ:] and [məz]. Such an analysis is sketched in Figure 2.7.

In this analysis it is beyond dispute that the word and its phonology are distinct. What is more debatable is the need for another single unit called {farmers}, lying between the words and the phonological segments. This unit exists on the level of form and, I shall now argue, is distinct from both words (the units of syntax) and phonological units. As before, I shall refer to the smallest forms as 'morphs' (Bauer 2003) in order to avoid confusion with the much more abstract 'morphemes' that are sometimes recognized in syntax, and which are equivalent to syntactic features in other theories or (in my analysis) to inflections. However, not all forms are atomic morphs; for example, I have already introduced two non-atomic forms: {farmer} and {farmers}. Like the corresponding words, each of these has a single node, and indeed the first is recognized as (in some sense) part of the second. However, they are also distinct from the corresponding words because their relevant characteristics are those of forms, not words. To change examples, the form {farms} is exactly the same regardless of which word it realizes—whether the plural of FARM (FARM:plural), or the present singular of the verb FARM_V (FARM_V:singular). Words and forms have quite distinct characteristics: for

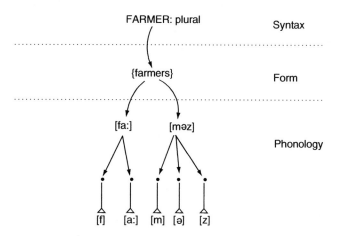

FIGURE 2.7.   A three-level analysis of *farmers*

example, words are classified in terms of word-classes and inflectional contrasts such as number and tense, whereas forms are classified as simple (i.e. morphs) or complex, and if simple as roots or affixes. These differences suggest the need for an internally complex unit which is distinct from the word as well as from the phonological structure—in short, the need for internally **complex forms** such as {farmers}.

The question, therefore, is how to justify not only morphs, but a complete level of systematic analysis including complex units and lying between syntax (the level of words) and phonology. This question is important because there are many theories of language structure which have no place for a level of form. (Indeed, at one time I myself denied that morphs were anything but arbitrary strings of phonemes, so I also denied the existence of a 'morphemic' level of analysis in contrast with a 'phonemic' one—Hudson 1984: 54. Since then, I have gradually moved away from this position through Hudson 1990: 85 and Creider and Hudson 1999.) This rejection of a level between words and sounds is true of any theory in which words are 'signs' which map directly onto semantics and phonology (Pollard and Sag 1994; Chomsky 1995*b*; Langacker 1998; Jackendoff 1997). It is also true of morphological theories in which morphological variation is treated as purely phonological variation which happens to be sensitive to inflectional and other morphosyntactic features of words (Beard 1994; Anderson 1992); and it is equally true of theories which take the converse position, in which morphs are units in the same hierarchy as words and phrases (Halle and Marantz 1993).

On the other hand, my proposed three-way distinction between words, forms, and phonological structures is widely accepted outside WG (Aronoff 1994; Sadock 1991; Levelt, Roelofs, and Meyer 1999). The following is a brief survey of the kind of evidence which seems to support this view.

Autonomy of definition.   Morphs cannot be defined in terms of either meaning or phonology. For example, in spite of their semantic differences the words UNDERSTAND and WITHSTAND must share the same root as STAND, because they all share the same irregular past tense (Aronoff 1976: 14). Similarly, but even more dramatically, the verbs GO, UNDERGO, and FOREGO share the suppletive past tense in *went*. The roots {stand} and {go} bring no meaning or syntax to these very diverse verbs, so they are not words. Nor, on the other hand, are they merely a piece of phonology, because similar pieces of phonology do not share the same characteristics: for instance, a hypothetical verb derived from the noun GO (the name of a Japanese board game), meaning 'play "go"', would certainly have {goed} rather than {went} as its past tense.

Autonomy of mapping.   Mapping to phonology is independent of mapping to words. For example, the form {one} corresponds to at least three quite different words: the numeral ONE_num as in *one book*, the dummy common noun ONE_cn as in *the big one* and the generalized personal pronoun ONE_pp as in *One does one's best*. But regardless of this mapping, {one} also has two alternative pronunciations in the UK: the same as {wan} (the form of the adjective WAN) in the north of England, and the same as {won} (the form of WIN:past) in the south. The morph {one} serves as the meeting point for these two choices, as shown in Figure 2.8. Without {one}, each of the three words would need to be related separately to each of the two pronunciations, entailing a loss not only of elegance but also of psychological plausibility. The question could easily be settled by sociolinguistic research to see whether those (like myself) who use both pronunciations are influenced in this choice by the meaning or grammar. This research remains to be done, but my prediction is that the two contrasts are statistically independent. (This is not to say that meaning and pronunciation are always independent; on the contrary, there has always been good evidence that contrasts of form tend to acquire contrasts of meaning, with irregular and regular past tenses, for example, tending to be associated with different meanings—Kempson and Quirk 1971. The example of {one} is different because it only involves a single form, unlike cases like *hung* and *hanged*, and the different pronunciations are regional so they don't need a semantic explanation.)

Combinational principles.   The principles for arranging morphs and words are different. For example, many languages have more or less free word order, but no language has free morph order (Bresnan 2001: 93). On the contrary, the order of morphemes is rigidly controlled and often arbitrary from a semantic or syntactic point of view (for example, in an Arabic verb form such as {ti-ktib-i}, 'you (fem) wrote', the prefix indicates person while the suffix marks gender). Such structural mismatches between morphology and syntax are commonplace (Sadock 1991).

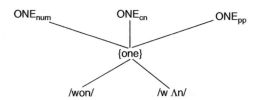

FIGURE 2.8.   A three-level analysis of *one*

Classification of units. Morphological and syntactic classification are distinct. As pointed out earlier, words are classified according to word-class and inflection, whereas forms are simple or complex, roots or affixes, and so on. Moreover, so-called 'irregular verbs' are irregular only in their morphology, and this irregularity never seems to encourage any kind of syntactic irregularity, not even when sub-regularities appear such as the group of verbs like SING, RING, and SWIM which share similar patterns of morphology (Bybee and Moder 1983). Even more striking are languages which have different 'inflection classes' (Carstairs-McCarthy 1992: 231), known in traditional grammar as 'declensions' and 'conjugations'. Traditional grammars of Latin recognize five inflection classes of nouns, each of which distinguishes the same range of inflectional categories but uses a different range of suffixes to do so. For example, the noun AMIC, 'friend', takes the suffix {us} in the nominative singular and {i} in the nominative plural, whereas URB, 'town', takes {s} and {es}. What is striking is that these inflection classes are purely morphological—they have virtually nothing to do with either grammar or meaning. Indeed, they even cut across the main word-classes because the noun distinctions apply to adjectives as well (e.g. BON, 'good', is like AMIC whereas FORT, 'strong', is like URB). If inflection classes were classes of words, this would be strange because one might expect interactions with the other ways of classifying words; but the three-level analysis allows them to be classifications of morphs, not words. Thus it is not the lexemes AMIC and URB but rather the forms {amic} and {urb} that belong to distinct inflection classes.

Morphologically blind syntax. The separation of purely morphological classification from syntactic classification is one aspect of a more general split between syntax and morphology which has led to the important claim that syntax is always blind to morphology (Zwicky 1992*b*). For example, syntactic rules are never sensitive to the presence of a particular morph as such, though they are of course often sensitive to a morpho-syntactic feature which happens always to be signalled by the same morph. This is easy to explain if morphs exist on a different level from syntax, as in the three-level analysis, because this increases the 'topological distance' between syntactic and morphological categories may be equivalent to the 'psychological distance' and which, in theories such as WG, can be modelled in terms of links in networks. For example, according to Figure 2.2, the suffix {s} in *farmers* is no fewer than four links from the syntactic category Plural-noun; consequently the suffix is four links less accessible to any syntactic pattern than the inflection Plural-noun is, and is that much less likely to be mentioned in the pattern.

Mismatches. If words and forms are distinct, we can expect mismatches, and there are many cases where a single form corresponds to two words. This pattern is well known and much discussed under the heading of cliticization, which I shall discuss in section 2.9; so the single English form {you're} corresponds to two separate (but related) words, YOU and BE:present (i.e. *are*). In cliticization, one phonologically weak word 'leans' on a stronger one, but there are other cases where both words seem equally weak, which we might call 'fused words'. The obvious example is the pattern in which a preposition fuses with its complement, a definite article; as I shall show in section 2.8, this is very common across Western Europe, as in French where the words *de le* ('of the') fuse into the single form {du} and *à le* ('to the') merge into {au}, pronounced as a single vowel [o]. The two-word analysis in syntax is (virtually) beyond dispute, so every theory has to provide some mechanism for merging their forms such as the three-level analysis of WG. I shall suggest in section 2.6 that some compounds also require an analysis in which two words share a single form. I shall also propose more controversial fused-word analyses in Chapter 3 for what are often taken as single words—for example, I shall suggest that the form {my} corresponds to ME + 's and that {one} sometimes corresponds to A + ONE.

Psychological reality. Morphological structure is psychologically real. There is massive evidence that ordinary speakers recognize morphological structure, ranging from the famous WUG test with infants (Berko Gleason 1958) to popular etymology. For example, the only plausible explanation for words such as CHEESE-BURGER is that speakers recognized the form {ham} in HAMBURGER, leaving {burger} as residue. If the only psychologically real levels were syntax and phonology this kind of analysis would not be possible. The three-level analysis also explains a wide range of speech-error data (Levelt, Roelofs, and Meyer 1999), such as the different kinds of permutation error in (20) and (21). The first mistake, in which the speaker said *pies* instead of *apples*, can easily be explained in terms of exchanged lexemes ('lemmas' in Levelt's terminology), but *slicely* in (21) makes no sense unless there are morphs which can be used in the wrong word.

(20)   How many pies does it take to make an apple?
(21)   slicely thinned.

Inherent variability. Further behavioural evidence in favour of the three-level analysis comes from the afore mentioned sociolinguistic studies of t/d deletion (Guy 1994), the process whereby words such as *pact* and *packed* are pronounced without a final [t]. Statistical analysis of texts shows that [t] is much more likely to be pronounced in words where it is a suffix, such as *packed,* than in mono-morphs such as *pact.* Once again it is hard to explain this difference without referring to morph boundaries, which presuppose morphs as discrete units.

Recycling. Forms are often 'recycled' to take on different functions. For example, it is common for the same affixes to be used both in inflection and in derivation; thus the suffix {ing} signals present participles and gerunds (which are inflections) but also nouns derived from verbs and even nouns derived from nouns (e.g. *flooring*). More generally, the mismatch between words and forms leads to widespread homonymy, so the level of form is needed even in languages which have little morphology as such.

I believe this list establishes a solid case for the three-level analysis, though there are a few residual doubts which need further research. For example, coordination is generally considered purely syntactic, but examples such as *pre- and post-natal* seem to show that it can apply to forms. More worryingly, intonation may be a case of phonology being related directly to syntax; on the other hand, where words and forms are different (e.g. in clitics), it is always forms rather than words that provide the units of intonation so form may turn out to play a roleeven in intonation.

Supposing that the three-level analysis is right, we are left with a question about the relations between these levels. A popular view is that morphs are parts of words, so the difference is merely a matter of size. This is not my view, and cannot be because I recognize word-sized units at the level of form, such as {farmers}. There is indeed a part–whole relation, but it lies between complex forms and atomic morphs, so it cannot also exist between words and morphs. If morphs were parts of words, then it would be natural to follow the structuralists in seeing them as the smallest units of syntax, but the evidence given above shows clearly that morphs are arranged in quite different ways from words.

In WG, as in many other theories of morphology in the 'Word and Paradigm' tradition, the difference between syntax and form is therefore not one of size but more like the difference between form and phonology: abstractness. Each level has a different vocabulary of units, based on different kinds of abstraction from the linguistic substance, and the levels can be ordered in terms of increasing abstractness from phonology through form to syntax. The following summarizes the differences among the levels:

- Syntax: the basic units are words, which have syntactic and semantic properties, but no phonology. They are realized by forms. Part–whole relations play only a minor part in syntax—they handle coordination and quotations—because the basic relation of syntax is dependency.

- Forms: the basic units are morphs, which are related to meaning and syntax only via the words that they realize. They do have phonology by virtue of being realized by phonological structures; but in a language with an alphabetic writing system they are also realized by written letters—a 'graphological' structure. Smaller forms are organized into larger forms by strict part–whole relations based on rigidly ordered templates, so a smaller form may be part of a larger one.
- Phonology: the basic units are segments, which are realized by phonetic properties and combine into syllables in ways that need not concern us here.
- Graphology: the basic units are letters.

Given that words, forms, and phonological units involve such different kinds of abstraction from speech (or writing), the relation between them cannot be merely a matter of size. This is why I have been using the term 'realization', a difference of abstractness rather than size. For example, as I shall explain in section 5.2, we can think of the form {pet} as a 'redescription' of the sounds [pɛt], so although neither is longer than the other, the sounds realize the form; and similarly, the noun PET is a redescription of the form {pet}, which therefore realizes it. Thus forms realize words, and phonology or graphology realizes forms; for convenience we can give different names to the realization relations between different levels: for phonology and graphology we have the ready-made terms 'pronunciation' and 'spelling', but for realization by form there is no established term, so (reluctantly) I shall use the term 'formation'.

However, even at a given level of analysis, realization relations are not uniform because different lower-level elements can realize higher elements in different ways. For example, we have already distinguished two kinds of formation: bases and fifs (fully inflected forms), which play very different roles in the structure of the word concerned. Similarly, for pronunciation we might distinguish the 'full phonological structure' (fps) from its significant parts—for example, we can pick out the stressed vowel as particularly significant for base-alternating morphology (as with {run} ~ {ran}) and the first and last segments are also highly relevant to allomorphy; so the subdivisions of Formation might include Fps, Vowel, First, and Last. For instance, under this proposal the fps of {sat} would be [sat], its first would be [s], its last would be [t] and its vowel would be [a]. Interestingly, these are the parts of a form which are often most easily accessible in 'tip-of-the-tongue' situations, where a speaker cannot remember a word but knows, say, that it starts with [b] or has [a] as its stressed vowel. A tentative hierarchy of realization relations (excluding spelling) is shown in Figure 2.9.

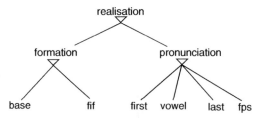

FIGURE 2.9.   Realization relations

We can now add labels to the diagram in Figure 2.7, showing that the inter-level relations are examples of Realization. The result is Figure 2.10, where the two realization relations (Formation and Pronunciation) are distinguished from the part–whole relation of syllable structure. (Of course, it is entirely possible that syllable structure is based, like syntax, on dependency structure; in that case the part relations would be replaced by sideways dependencies between the consonants and vowels.)

We can now return to a question that I raised in section 2.2: what, precisely, is the relation between the first part of {farmer}, which we can call X, and the morph {farm}? I argued that X cannot be {farm} itself, because its properties are different—for example, X is always followed by {er}; nor can X isa {farm}, because this leads to a contradiction and an infinite regress. The dotted line in Figure 2.1 and the next two figures was a stop-gap pending a proper solution. We can now provide that solution: the property that X shares with {farm} is

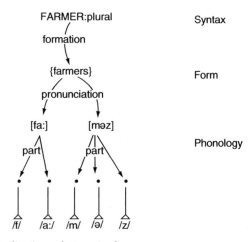

FIGURE 2.10.   Realization relations in *farmers*

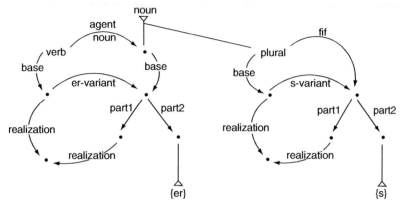

FIGURE 2.11.   Typical derivational and inflectional patterns, including relation labels

its realization. In other words, although its combinatorial properties are different from those of {farm}, it has the same pronunciation. The solution, therefore, is to give each of them the same realization, as in the revised version of Figure 2.3 shown in Figure 2.11.

2.4 Variants and Syncretism

In the analysis of *farmers*, I presented {farmer} as the 'er-variant' of {farm}, and {farmers} as the 's-variant' of {farmer}. These relations encapsulate the idea that morphology (other than compounding) is the analysis of variations on the word's basic form (i.e. its base). Any pair of words which have a distinctive similarity may (in principle) be directly related in our minds, though according to the WG theory of learning (s. 1.8) this similarity has to be learned. The similarity need not be generalizable, so the relation may be unique; for example, the form {female} fairly obviously consists of {male} with {fe} attached, and we can be sure that at least some people associated them mentally because {female} derives from an earlier {femelle} which was changed by analogy with {male}. A cognitively oriented analysis should allow unique relations between two forms—that is, for analogy.

However, at the other end of the scale we also have very general relations such as our er-variant which relates most verb bases to a noun base. What 'variant' relations do is to generalize a similarity between forms, and in this sense they are equivalent to 'morphomic functions' (Aronoff 1994: 24) or 'intermediate bases' (Blevins 2003: 738). To take the simple example of English regular plural nouns shown in Figure 2.3, the fif (fully inflected form) of a plural is the s-variant of its base, and by default the s-variant consists of the base plus {s}. This is an efficient way to define such relations because it allows the formal pattern to be 'recycled' with other functions. Variants often have multiple uses; for example, s-variants are found not only in plural nouns but also in singular present-tense forms such as {goes}. One particularly important case of functional recycling is **syncretism**, where the same form is shared by different inflections of the same lexeme; for example, {wanted} doubles up as the perfect and passive participle as well as the past tense of WANT. Variants capture syncretism efficiently: wherever different words share the same morphological forms, this is because they share the same variant of their bases. I return to this benefit of variants below.

Most of English morphology can be defined quite straightforwardly in terms of bases, fifs, and variants as we did for *farmers*:

- derivation: the base of one lexeme is either the same as the base of another lexeme from which it is derived, or is some variant of it (as, say, its 'agent-noun');
- inflection: the fif of an inflection (say, Plural-noun) is either the same as its base, or some variant of it.

More complex morphology makes more complex demands on variants, which are often reflected in traditional grammatical descriptions. For example, Italian future tenses are normally described as based on the full infinitive (e.g. for the verb FIN, 'finish', they are based on {finire}), with a person/number ending instead of the infinitive's final -e. Thus the fif of FIN:sing,1st,future (meaning 'I shall finish') is {finirò}, based on {finir}, which in turn contains the base {fin}. In this case we might describe {finir} as the r-variant of the base, so the rule for first-person singular futures is to add {ò} to the r-variant of the verb's base—a more complex rule than any found in English.

Even more complex patterns are possible; for example, the Latin word *docuerimus* is the first-person plural future perfect indicative of DOC, 'teach', so it means 'We shall have taught'. Its morphological structure may be analysed as follows:

- {docu} is the perfect-variant of DOC; the perfect-variant is found in all perfect tenses, and is built in different ways by different verbs—for example, the perfect-variant for AM is {amav}.
- {docuer} is the er-variant of {docu}, found in all future-perfect and pluperfect indicatives (and also in perfect subjunctives).
- {docueri} is the i-variant of {docuer}, found in all future-perfect forms.

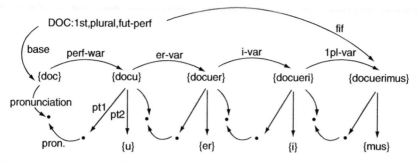

FIGURE 2.12.   The morphological structure of Latin *docuerimus*, 'we will have taught'

- finally, {docuerimus} is the 1pl-variant of {docueri}, containing the suffix which is found in most first-person plural verbs.

The morphological structure is shown, slightly simplified, in Figure 2.12.

Like other relations in language, the different kinds of variant comprise an inheritance hierarchy. Each relation defines a typical pattern which, thanks to default inheritance, allows exceptions—for example, as noted above with the noun COOK, a form's er-variant need not in fact end in {er}, nor need an s-form end in {s}. The names are based on the default pattern, so they should be interpreted with a pinch of salt. The hierarchy of variants is probably broad rather than deep, but some depth is possible. For example, one of the simple generalizations about English verb inflections is that regular bases take {ed} not only in past-tense inflections but also in passive and perfect participles (e.g. {walked} is found in all three inflections); and another is that even irregular verbs have the same form in passive and perfect participles (e.g. {took} in the past and {taken} in both the perfect and passive participles). These generalizations can be captured if the forms used in the perfect and passive participles are both 'en-variants' (even when their actual form contains {ed}), and if 'en-variant' is a sub-case of 'ed-variant' (Hudson 1990: 91). This analysis is shown in Figure 2.13 (over).

The discussion so far has explained how variants are used in WG morphology, but it has not addressed the issue of why they are needed. After all, they introduce an extra link between a word's base and its fif; for example, using variants we say that the fif of a plural noun is the s-variant of its base, and the s-variant consists of the base followed by {s}. Why not simply say that the fif consists of the base followed by {s}? The more complex analysis with variants brings two major advantages.

We have already explored one of these: the possibility of multiple links between a word's base and its fif, as in Figure 2.12 for the Latin verb

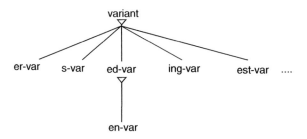

FIGURE 2.13.   Some variants in English

docuerimus. This is important because each of these variant links allows generalizations which would not otherwise be possible because they vary from case to case. For example, while the perfect-variant of {doc} is {docu}, that of {am} is {amav} and of {vinc}, {vic}. It is not possible to subsume all these perfect variants under a single morphological or phonological general-ization, but it is true that every verb has a unique and consistent form which is used as the foundation for all its perfect inflections. The Latin pattern is not at all unusual—it is common for one inflection to be built on the form of a different one (Carstairs-McCarthy 1998).

The second benefit of variant links is in the treatment of syncretism. Again we have already touched on this in the brief discussion of English verb inflections, where every verb, without exception, has exactly the same form in its perfect (as in *has seen*) and passive participles (as in *was seen*). It is important to reveal such regularities rather than to treat them as mere matters of chance, but it is not obvious how to do so. Two options are popular: under-specification and 'rules of referral'.

- Under-specification (Haspelmath 2002: 140) finds a way of classifying the words concerned which unites the homonymous words (and only them) under a single word-class (or feature). In some cases this is possible, but in others it is not. It is generally agreed not to help with the English perfect and passive participle because they do not comprise a natural syntactic class.
- Rules of referral (Stump 1993), on the other hand, do work in this case because they are independent of the classification of words. A referral rule for this case would simply define the realization of one word-class by referring to that of the other; so it might derive the form of a passive participle from that of the same verb's perfect (or vice versa).

Rules of referral are problematic for various reasons (Blevins 2003: 761). One weakness is that they are directional—one form is basic, and the other is derived from it. This is theoretically objectionable for two reasons. First, the choice of direction is often arbitrary, as it is in the case of English perfects and passives. There is no obvious reason to choose one rather than the other as basic, so the theory assumes a directionality for which there is no independent evidence. And second, rules of referral are psychologically implausible. Suppose we treat perfects as basic and derive passives from them; this would imply that it is impossible to recognize a verb as passive without first misanalysing it as a perfect. This is extremely unlikely to be how we actually process passive verbs, because the syntactic context almost always allows only one interpretation—after all, perfects are always preceded by a form of HAVE, as in *have seen*, so the proposed analysis would require a ludicrously circuitous analysis of an example such as *was seen*: first identify *seen* as a perfect, then accept that this is impossible for syntactic reasons, then consult the referral rule for an alternative interpretation, and finally accept the alternative. Surely we can consider both interpretations simultaneously, but if this is so we must be able to recognize the interpretations independently of one another.

WG variants (and their equivalent in other theories) provide an alternative to rules of referral which avoids these problems because variants are not directional. According to the analysis in Figure 2.13, English verb bases have an en-variant, and according to Figure 2.4 their inflections include Perfect and Passive. The syncretism of these two inflections can be captured explicitly by linking them both to the base's en-variant, as in Figure 2.14. The en-variant is defined, including all the irregular variation from verb to verb, elsewhere in the network, so this diagram achieves the same as a rule of referral: it states globally that passives and perfects share the same variant so they are always

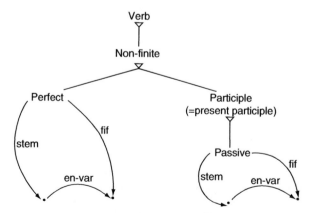

FIGURE 2.14.   The syncretism of Perfect and Passive in English

TABLE 2.1.   Slovene *brat*, 'brother'

	Singular	Dual	Plural
Nominative	1. brat	2. brata	p1. brati
Accusative	2. brata	2. brata	p2. brate
Genitive	2. brata	p3. bratov	p3. bratov
Dative	3. bratu	6. bratoma	p4. bratom
Instrumental	4. bratom	6. bratoma	p5. brati
Locative	5. bratu	p6. bratih	p6. bratih

the same in form, however irregular the verb may be. But unlike rules of referral, there is no question here of directionality, of one form being derived from the other.

The English syncretism is very simple, but the same mechanism can handle much more complex cases, such as that of Slovene. Tables 2.1 and 2.2 show the paradigms for two Slovene nouns. The first (from **www.amebis.si/sklanjanje/**) is a typical regular noun, which shows considerable syncretism. The various forms are distinguished for convenience by numbers; for example, form number 2 is found in two cases of the singular and a different two of the dual. The forms of the plural all have numbers including 'p': p1 in the nominative, p2 in the accusative, and so on. The crucial examples of syncretism are in the genitive and locative, where the dual has the same form as the plural (p. 3 and p. 6 respectively). The second table (from Evans, Brown, and Corbett 2001), shows a highly irregular noun in which the plural is suppletive; but remarkably, even here the pattern of syncretism is just the same, and crucially the dual has the same suppletive form as the plural in the genitive and locative.

At first sight, the Slovene data appear to provide very strong evidence for a rule of referral, because the dual is obviously parasitic on the plural rather than vice versa. However even this asymmetry can be expressed in terms of

TABLE 2.2.   Slovene *člóvek*, 'person'

	Singular	Dual	Plural
Nominative	1. člóvek	2. slovéka	p1. ljudê
Accusative	2. slovéka	2. slovéka	p2. ljudî
Genitive	2. slovéka	p3. ljudí	p3. ljudí
Dative	3. slovéku	6. slovékoma	p4. ljudêm
Instrumental	4. slovékom	6. slovékoma	p5. ljudmí
Locative	5. slovéku	p6. ljudéh	p6. ljudéh

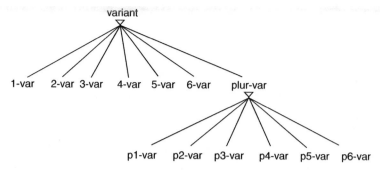

FIGURE 2.15. Variants for the Slovene noun explaining syncretism

variants, provided the variants are organized in an Isa hierarchy which unites all the plural variants. Suppose we have the variants of Figure 2.15, whose names follow the numbers in the paradigm tables. The crucial syncretism involves two variants, p3 and p6, so for example *ljudí*, the p3 variant of *člóvek*, doubles as the fif of the genitive in the genitive as well as in the plural. The proposed classification associates these two variants with plurality by default, and by default dual forms are like the singular, not the plural; so the two dual cases which have variants p3 and p6 stand out as exceptions, reflecting the intuition that these are basically plural forms which are doubling as duals rather than the other way round. However, this asymmetry is in the system rather than in the processing. For example, any p3 variant such as *bratov* or *ljudí* is associated just as directly with the dual genitive as with the plural. The example shows how WG variants (interpreted through default inheritance) have the same explanatory power as rules of referral, but without the dubious psycholinguistic implications of directionality.

2.5 Derivation and Inflection

The traditional division of morphology into derivational and inflectional is respected in WG by the basic distinction between inter- and intra-lexeme rules which we considered in the discussion of *farmers* in section 2.2. Derivational morphology relates different lexemes (e.g. FARM and FARMER), whereas inflectional morphology relates a single lexeme's base to the fif (fully inflected form) of one of its inflections. At the same time, however, I have stressed that both kinds of morphology make use of the same mechanisms for defining morphological structure—that is the system of variants defined in section 2.4, and the mechanisms for combining morphs into complex forms which will be explained in section 2.7. The traditional distinction follows automatically from the distinction between lexemes and inflections: given that morphology relates different words to each other and that words can be classified either in terms of lexemes or inflections, it can relate one lexeme either to another lexeme or to an inflection of itself. This being so, there is no need to decide which morphological patterns are derivational and which are inflectional—to the extent that the distinction is important it will emerge naturally from the network.

It is fortunate that this distinction is not important in WG, because there are cases where it is less than clear. For example, consider the patterns in which one lexeme is derived from an inflected form of another lexeme, as in English adjectives that are derived from passive verbs—adjectives such as TIRED, WELL-DRIVEN, and HAND-MADE. It is clear that these are adjectives rather than verbs; for example, unlike the verb TIRE, the adjective TIRED can combine with VERY (*very tired*); there is no verb WELL-DRIVE; nor can WELL generally be used before DRIVE (as in *He well drove the car*). Consequently these must be distinct lexemes from the corresponding verbs TIRE, DRIVE, and MAKE, but their base is in each case the en-variant of the verb's base—just the same form as is found in the verb's passive inflection. This is clearly no coincidence, because they also have passive syntax, in that the adjective's subject corresponds to the verb's object. It is at least tempting to conclude that the adjective is derived from the verb's passive inflection—another logical possibility for cross-lexeme relations, but one which fits uneasily into the traditional derivation/inflection contrast. Similar problems arise with mixed categories such as gerunds and participles; for example, *reading* in the following example is a gerund.

(22)   He did badly through not reading many books.

Traditionally, a gerund such as *reading* is both a verb and a noun, so it must belong to a different word class from READ, and therefore constitutes a distinct lexeme READING; but at least one analysis (presented in ch. 4) also recognizes it as an inflection of READ.

In spite of these uncertain borderline cases, the WG treatment of morphology accounts well for the differences traditionally associated with the contrast between derivation and inflection; the following list is taken from Haspelmath 2002:71, with slight rewording. The comments are mine.

Difference 1: inflection, but not derivation, is relevant to the syntax.

Inflections (in the WG sense) are syntactic in the sense that they are mentioned by rules of syntax and semantics, whereas no rules of syntax refer to derivational classes such as agent-nouns. Seen from syntax, a derived lexeme (e.g. FARMER) has just the same syntax as any other member of the same lexeme class (e.g. MAN). Moreover, even if the derived lexeme preserves some of the valency (dependency requirements) of the source lexeme, this valency must be adapted to the normal syntactic rules of the derived word's class; for example: the verb DISCOVER takes a bare object (*discover the route*) but the derived noun DISCOVERER has to express this dependent as a possessor (*discoverer of the route* or *the route's discoverer*).

Difference 2: inflection is obligatory but derivation is optional.

Derivational relations are optional in the obvious sense that a lexeme which is a potential 'source' for another can in fact be used in its own right. In contrast, inflections (in the WG sense) are obligatory because they are demanded by the syntax; so for example a verb cannot depend on CAN unless it isa Infinitive. Since the inflection itself is obligatory, its morphological consequences are also obligatory.

Difference 3: derived words, but not inflections, can be replaced by simple words.

Since morphological structure is irrelevant to syntax, a derived lexeme with morphologically complex base can usually be replaced by a simpler one without loss of grammaticality; for example, as already observed FARMER is syntactically indistinguishable from MAN. In contrast morphological structure due to inflections is not optional, so complex and simple words are generally not interchangeable.

Difference 4: inflection does not change the sense but derivation may do.

Inflections have to combine with lexemes in such a way that multiple inheritance is possible; consequently, the properties which inflections contribute have to be totally compatible with those of the lexeme. One of the lexeme's properties is its sense, so the inflection cannot change this. If an inflection does affect the meaning, it is generally the referent rather than the sense that is affected; for example, Plural-noun defines the referent as a set rather than as the usual individual (so *dogs* refers to a set each of whose members isa dog). In contrast, derivation is a relation between distinct lexemes, neither of which inherits from the other, so changes are normal. Thus FARMER has not only a different base but also a different sense from its source lexeme, FARM.

Difference 5: inflection involves more abstract meanings than derivation.

As just mentioned, the meanings which inflections add to those of their basic lexemes are sufficiently different from those of the basic sense to be compatible with it. Typically they are 'abstract' in the sense of being tied to syntax, and more generally to the needs of communication, rather than to everyday classification of the world (the province of lexical semantics). For example, inflections express purely syntactic relations (case) or deictic relations (tense) as well as logical subtleties such as number. In contrast, a derived lexeme is just an ordinary lexeme with a sense that may differ in any way from that of its source; for example, the sense of FARMER is a person, so if anything it is more concrete than that of FARM.

Difference 6: inflection is semantically regular, but derivation may be irregular.

Inflectional meanings generally do not interact with those of the lexemes with which they combine, and there is strong pressure to avoid interactions in order to minimize inheritance clashes between inflections and the lexemes they combine with. However this is just a tendency; for example, the verb BE has an irregular meaning ('go') when it combines with the inflection Perfect as in 'I have been to Paris'. In contrast, such idiosyncratic meaning changes are commonplace in derivation because a derived lexeme exists as an ordinary lexeme subject to the normal possibilities for semantic change; compare the relatively regular FARMER with irregular SPEAKER (as applied to audio equipment).

Difference 7: inflection is less relevant than derivation to the base meaning of the lexeme.

This difference is closely related to the previous ones. Inflectional meanings have to be independent of the lexical senses with which they combine because they are combined by default inheritance. Consequently they have to avoid a conflict. In contrast, derivation builds the meaning of one lexeme into that of another so the derived meaning has to interact with the base meaning and is often very different.

Difference 8: there is less base allomorphy in inflection than in derivation.

Haspelmath's examples of this tendency include the English adjective BROAD, whose inflections are regular (*broader, broadest*) but whose derived noun is BREADTH, with a changed base. This tendency naturally has exceptions—for example, the irregularly inflected verb SING has a completely regular derived noun SINGER—but to the extent that it is true, its explanation is the same as for the semantic differences just noted. Lexemes, whether derived or not, are typically listed and memorized items which undergo phonological changes such as the one that presumably changed BROADTH to BREADTH. In contrast, most inflected forms are computed rather than stored, so except for very frequent items phonological variation tends to be corrected quickly.

Difference 9: the applicability of patterns is unlimited for inflection, but limited for derivation.

This difference arises from the logic of the analysis. Inflections are word-types which combine freely with lexemes, so any lexeme may combine

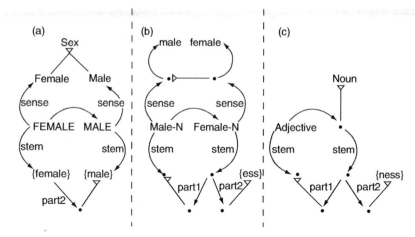

FIGURE 2.16.   Three degrees of generality in derivation

with any inflection of the same word-class and inflections are all 'fully productive' (applying freely to all potential candidate words). (There are exceptions, such as the English inflectional distinction between *was* and *were* which applies to just one lexeme, BE.) In contrast, derivation may be of any degree of generality, from the unique relation between MALE and FEMALE mentioned in 2.4 through frequent but unproductive patterns such as PRINCE—PRINCESS to completely productive patterns such as NICE—NICENESS. This variation is possible because there are at least three logically possible patterns, illustrated in Figure 2.16. Pattern (*a*) is unique to the two listed adjectives, FEMALE and MALE, whose semantic similarity has come to be reflected in a clear but ungeneralizable formal similarity; pattern (*b*) relates two ad-hoc subclasses of Noun called 'Male-N' and 'Female-N', in which the female's form and meaning are both derived from the male's. The members of these classes (not shown in the diagram) are simply listed, so they include PRINCE and PRINCESS. Pattern (*c*) applies to the typical adjective, so it is automatically inherited by every adjective, even if some adjectives override the default morphology (as {size} overrides the predicted {bigness}). No doubt other intermediate patterns are possible.

Difference 10: inflection is expressed at the edge of the word, while derivation is expressed close to its base.

This difference follows automatically from the fact that inflectional affixes are added to bases (which may or may not have been affected by derivational morphology). As might be expected, there are exceptions even to this principle—for example, the German noun *kinderlein*, 'little children', in which the usual inflected plural of KIND ({kinder}) is followed by the derivational suffix {lein}. Moreover, Semitic-type 'interdigitation' integrates inflectional morphology even more closely than derivational morphology with the base (the two or three radical consonants). For example, in the North Cushitic language Beja, causative derivation is expressed by {s} added just before the radical consonants, but inflection is expressed by the interdigitated vowels as well as by a mixture of prefixes and suffixes (Hudson 1974). For example, the following two forms are both based on the radical {d-b-l}, meaning 'collect':

(23)   ti.s.daabil.a
       you.caus.collect-past.you-masc
       you (masc. sing.) caused to collect
(24)   ti.s.diibal.a
       you.caus.collect-imperf.you-masc
       you (masc. sing.) used to cause to collect

In such cases the expressions of derivation and inflection are thoroughly mixed up together.

Difference 11: inflection, but not derivation, allows cumulative expression.

Typical inflectional languages allow one morph to express a combination of inflections; for example, Latin *vincam*, 'I shall conquer', contains the affix {am} which expresses first-person, singular, and future tense. Such cumulative expression is less common in derivation because derivational relations apply to the morphology one at a time, each time producing a pronounceable lexeme. In contrast, multiple inflections in highly inflected languages apply simultaneously, so it is natural for several inflections to share a single morph.

Difference 12: derivation, but not inflection, may be iteratable.

Haspelmath's examples include *post-post-modern* and the German *Ur-ur-ur-grossvater*, 'great great great grandfather'. Iteration is impossible in inflection because this has a single goal: to predict the word's fully inflected form (fif). Once this has been predicted, it cannot be used as the basis for further fifs because fifs are based on bases, not on other fifs. In contrast, derivation relates one base to another, so there is no reason why a derived base should not serve in turn as the base for a further derivation.

Difference 13: derivation always changes word-class, but inflection never does.

Haspelmath mentions this popular criterion for distinguishing inflection from derivation, but rejects it as untrue. I agree. It is too easy to find exceptions in both directions. As Haspelmath points out, Gerund is a verb inflection but, as I shall assume in Chapter 4, it is also a noun, so this inflection does change word-class. Moreover there are plenty of derivations which do not change word-class, such as Haspelmath's earlier examples (*post-modern, Ur-grossvater*) and negative derivations such as *untidy*. It would be most surprising if this contrast did hold, because it would imply strange restrictions on both derivation (the related lexemes must belong to different word-classes) and inflection (inflections can never inherit from more than one word-class).

In short, the WG account of derivation and inflection explains all the observed differences between the two.

2.6 Compounding

Compounding falls clearly within the domain of derivational morphology, and by definition it relates a single lexeme—the compound word—to two other lexemes; for example, the lexeme MATCHBOX is related to the lexemes MATCH and BOX. However, there are at least three ways in which one lexeme may be related to two others:

1 It may simply share their forms—for example, the base of MATCHBOX is {matchbox}, which consists of (instances of) {match} and {box}.
2 It may be a combination of the two lexemes themselves—so MATCHBOX is actually a syntactic combination of MATCH$_{box}$ and BOX$_{match}$, stored as a combination just like any idiom, but each contributing just its ordinary form.
3 These two analyses may be combined, so that BOX$_{match}$ is stored with the unique form {matchbox}.

It seems likely that each of the three analyses is correct for some kinds of compound but not for others.

Analaysis A. This could be called the 'one-word' analysis because MATCHBOX is a single word in both syntax and form, and its links to MATCH and BOX are merely a matter of shared forms. The structure is shown in Figure 2.17.

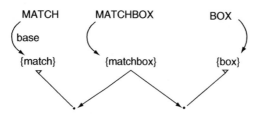

FIGURE 2.17.   The one-word analysis of MATCHBOX

The one-word, non-syntactic, analysis is clearly appropriate where two conditions are met:

(i) where the parts are combined in ways which are not allowed in ordinary syntactic word-combinations. The classic examples here are 'dvandva' compounds such as *Alsace-Lorraine*, where the parts are simply juxtaposed on equal terms (Bauer 2003: 31).

(ii) where the phonology follows the pattern of single words rather than of word combinations (as in, for example, BLACKBIRD but not in *black bird*).

Analysis B. The 'two-word' pattern recognizes each part of the compound as a separate word with its own separate word-form, just like any other combination of words; but the combination may be stored as a whole. Under this analysis, MATCHBOX is two separate words, but each word is a distinct sub-lexeme which is always associated with the other. We can call these sub-lexemes BOX$_{match}$ (i.e. BOX as used with MATCH) and MATCH$_{box}$, (MATCH as used with BOX). The two-word pattern is shown in Figure 2.18.

The two-word analysis has the great advantage of applying the ordinary rules of syntax so that they explain the order of the constituents. It is indistinguishable from the analysis of two-word idioms, which are syntactically and phonologically like ordinary syntactic combinations except for their unpredictable meaning. This meaning is attached to the head word so that it overrides the default meanings of either word. This is an appropriate analysis if:

(i) the pair is idiomatic but phonologically like two separate words, as in NARROW SQUEAK and CLOSE SHAVE (both meaning a situation in which an accident almost happened),

(ii) the pair forms a collocation, such as BLIND DRUNK,

(iii) there is any other reason for believing that the two-word combination is stored as a single unit. To take a simple example, the names of roads usually consist of a distinguisher and a word such as ROAD or AVENUE, but the two have to be memorized as single units.

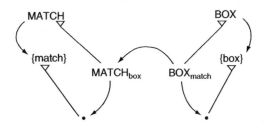

FIGURE 2.18.   The two-word analysis of MATCH BOX

Analysis C. The 'two-word, one-form' analysis combines features of the first two analyses. In this analysis, MATCHBOX consists of two separate words, but these two words share a single fused form, {matchbox} (whose parts are, once again, examples of {match} and of {box}), as in Figure 2.19.

This analysis recognizes the ordinary syntactic relation between the parts, which explains their order and at least part of their meaning, while also recognizing that their combined forms look to the phonology like a single word-form. In short, it recognizes two words in the syntax and one word-sized form. This is appropriate if:

(i) the phonology suggests a single word, as in the case of the single word-stress on MATCHBOX, BOOKSHOP, or OXFORD STREET,

(ii) the morphology is that of a single word rather than two separate words, as in German compounds where an adjective shows no agreement with its head noun (e.g. GROSSMUTTER, 'grandmother', contrasting with *grosse Mutter*, 'large mother').

The point of this discussion is to show that the theoretical framework of WG allows a wide range of different analyses for items which might informally be called 'compounds', each appropriate to a different combination of characteristics. Consequently, WG could be said to contain not just one 'theory of compounds', but at least three different theories. This provides welcome flexibility for analysis, but it also provides a theoretical explanation for the uncertainty that we all face over the spelling of English compounds: should we write a word-space (or wordspace or word space), a hyphen, or nothing at all between the parts? In many cases usage seems quite arbitrary, and even authoritative dictionaries do not always help with a clear verdict—for example, should we write *bookplate*, *book-plate*, or *book plate*? Longman recognizes just the first of the three options, and Collins Cobuild just the second

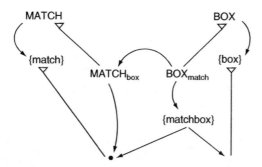

FIGURE 2.19.   The two-word, one-form analysis of MATCH-BOX

and third. This is a type C, 'two-word, one-form' structure so our spelling could reflect the syntax (*book plate*) or the form (*bookplate*); but the hyphen offers an intermediate position of uncertainty (as it were, half a word-space). Even more importantly, the range of alternative analyses explains why linguists have always had such difficulty in finding watertight criteria for recognizing single-word compounds.

2.7 Morphological Structure

Morphological structure is the structure of complex forms; for example, we have seen that {farmers} contains {farmer} and {s}, where {farmer} consists of {farm} followed by {er}. This is the simplest kind of structure, which is easily described in terms of parts and wholes—in other words, constituent structure. However there is a great deal of morphology which cannot be described in such a simple way, so I shall now show how WG can handle more complex patterns. The preceding discussion provides a conceptual framework for this discussion in which all the forms concerned are embedded in a web or relationships; for example,

- {farmer} is the base of FARMER:plural.
- {farmers} is its fif (fully inflected form).
- FARMER is the agent-noun of FARM.
- {farm} is the base of FARM.
- {farmer} is the base of FARMER.

In each case there is a generalizable pattern in which a relatively simple form is 'involved in' a relatively complicated one. This involvement could be described in procedural terms such as 'adding {s}', but we shall see that the machinery of inheritance networks provides a satisfactory declarative account of all such cases.

If two forms are related morphologically, the relation between them is some version of the 'variant' relation (s. 2.4), so {farmer} is the er-variant of {farm} and {farmers} is the s-variant of {farmer}. It will also be helpful to be able to refer to the converse of this relation, '**source**', with {farm} as the source of {farmer}, and {farmer} of {farmers}. What we have to explore in this section is the variety of ways in which the variant may differ from its source, starting with simple concatenation as in {farm} + {er} = {farmer}. We have already shown how this kind of structure can be described in terms of Part1 and Part2 (see Fig. 2.1 and Fig. 2.2), very general relations which no doubt apply to many different kinds of knowledge. Most of morphology seems to consist of purely binary structures which can be defined in this way, and the recursive 'variant' system ensures that this is so even when the result is a long string of morphemes. For example, Figure 2.12 shows how the five morphemes of Latin *docuerimus* are combined in a series of binary steps whereby {docu} is the perfect-variant of DOC, {docuer} is the er-variant of {docu}, and so on.

However, at least in principle, concatenative morphology does allow **non-binary** relations, and it remains to be seen whether they are ever needed. The strongest case can probably be made for them in inflectional patterns which involve both a prefix and a suffix, such as the German past participle (25) or the Semitic-type second-person gender and number contrasts found for example in the Beja example (26) (Hudson 1974).

(25) a   {ge}{frag}{t}, 'asked'
      b   {ge}{jag}{t}, 'hunted'
(26) a   {a}{ktib}, 'I wrote'
      b   {ti}{ktib}{a}, 'you (masc. sing.) wrote'
      c   {ti}{ktib}{i}, 'you (fem. sing.) wrote'
      d   {ti}{ktib}{na}, 'you (plural) wrote'

Figure 2.20 is a grammar for German past participles, in which the number of parts has risen to three. According to this grammar, the 'ge-variant' of {frag} (the base of FRAGEN, 'ask') is {gefragt}, with three parts: {ge}, {frag} and {t}, in that order.

Somewhat more interesting are cases where there are changes within the base, such as the **vowel-alternations** familiar from Indo-European languages. In English these are all irregular, but they have the same morphological function as suffixes so, for example, we can analyse {men} as the s-variant of {man} and {rang} as the ed-variant of {ring}. The real challenge lies in their morphological structure: how to show the difference in the vowels without obscuring the similarities in the consonants. These partial similarities mean that it would be quite wrong to treat these cases as examples of suppletion

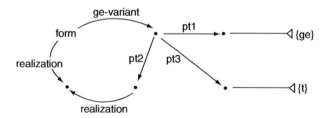

FIGURE 2.20.   A three-part structure for German past participles

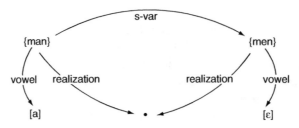

FIGURE 2.21.   The vowel change in {men}

(alongside {go}—{went}), and of course in some languages internal changes can be generalized. The solution lies in the types of Realization relations introduced in section 2.3. A form has a Realization relation not only to its full phonological structure, but also to parts of this structure including the stressed vowel, the former via the Fps relation and the latter via Vowel. If we can pick out the vowel then we can say (in a network) that the s-variant of {man} has the same realization as {man} except that its vowel is [ɛ] instead of [a]. This very simple analysis is shown in Figure 2.21. (Note that default inheritance ensures that [ɛ] overrides the default [a] because Vowel isa Realization.)

The semitic **interdigitation** pattern mentioned earlier builds on the same mechanism, except that instead of varying a single vowel it varies two, which we can distinguish as V1 and V2. For example, Figure 2.22 shows that the plural of the Arabic noun for 'book', whose base is {kita:b}, is realized as {kutub}.

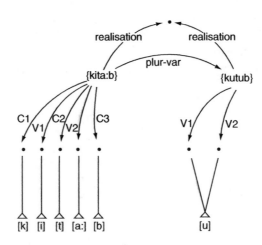

FIGURE 2.22.   Vowel alternation in Arabic

TABLE 2.3.   Ponapean reduplication

root	progressive	meaning
duhp	du–duhp	dive
mihk	mi–mihk	suck
wehk	we–wehk	confess

Once again the two forms have the same realization by default, but specified parts of the realization are overridden.

I have shown how WG handles not only affixation but also internal changes in the base. Another common type of morphological process is **reduplication**, in which the whole or part of the base is doubled. For example, in Ponapean the first consonant and vowel of a verb base are reduplicated to form the progressive, as illustrated by the words in Table 2.3 (Haspelmath 2002: 24). A WG analysis is shown in Figure 2.23; no doubt this analysis would be better if it referred to syllables rather than single segments.

The last type of morphological process for consideration is 'deletion', where a variant is shorter than its source. The obvious language for examples is French, where masculine adjectives and nouns are often considered to be derived by deletion of the last consonant; for instance, *petit*, 'small', is [ptit] in the feminine and [pti] in the masculine. Here too a declarative analysis is possible thanks to the possibility of picking out one part of the base—its final consonant ('Cf'). By default, Cf is the lexically specified consonant, but in the 'short variant' it is zero. A WG analysis can be seen in Figure 2.24.

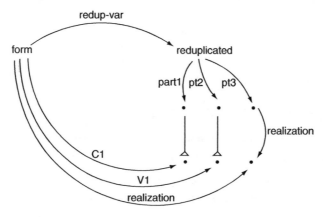

FIGURE 2.23.   Reduplication in Ponapean

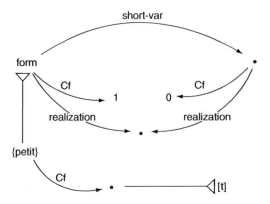

FIGURE 2.24.   Final consonant loss in French

The main conclusion of this brief survey of morphological processes is that a declarative system such as WG has all the power that is needed for handling complexities which are often assumed to need procedures such as copying and deletion rules. Most of this power comes from two parts of the WG apparatus:

1 default inheritance, which allows some relations to override others.
2 the hierarchy of realization relations, which allows forms to be related directly to specific parts of their phonological structures.

2.8 Fused Words

Fused words are very common, but are rarely discussed—indeed, it is hard to find any accepted name for them. The phenomenon is very familiar in Western European languages which have prepositions that 'fuse' with a dependent definite article, as exemplified in the following list:

(27) du (= *de le) village 'from the village'   (French)
      au (= *à le) village 'to the village'   (French)
      al (= *a el) cine 'to the cinema'   (Spanish)
      del (= *de el) cine 'from the cinema'   (Spanish)
      do (= *de o) campo 'from the countryside'   (Portuguese)
      na (= *em a) casa 'in the house'   (Portuguese)
      pelo (= *por o) parque 'through the park'   (Portuguese)
      nella (= *in la) scatola 'in the box'   (Italian)

im (= in dem) Dorf 'in the village'   (German)

sto (= *se to) trapezi 'on the table'   (Greek)

yn (= yn y) ty 'in the house'   (Welsh)

bhon (= bho an) 'from the'   (Gaelic)

leis an (= le an) 'with the'   (Gaelic)

The point about these examples is that in each case two words are 'fused' into a single form. To take an extreme case, the spelling *au* in French is syntactically indistinguishable from the preposition *à*, 'to' or 'at', followed by a dependent definite article (which would normally be written *le*), but phonologically it is just a single segment which jointly realizes the two words.

It is not obvious how to analyse such examples in a three-level analysis of words because the fusion could be either above or below the level of form; for example, the two words *à* and *le* could be realized by a single form, or they could by realized by distinct forms which share a single phonological structure. The two alternatives are shown in Figure 2.25, where À$_{le}$ and LE$_{à}$ distinguish the cases of *à* and *le* that occur together from the default uses of these words.

There is in fact some evidence in favour of the second of these analyses, in which the fusion is at the level of form. The relevant data are shown in (28).

(28) a à la maison 'to the house' (fem)
      b à l'heure 'to the hour' (fem)
      c au livre 'to the book' (masc)
      d à l'homme 'to the man' (masc)

As these examples show, the definite article is always written *l'* (and pronounced [l]) if the next word begins with a vowel, so distinct masculine and feminine forms are only found before a consonant. However, in the

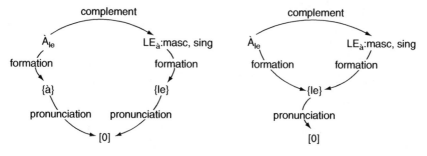

FIGURE 2.25.   Two outline analyses of French *au*

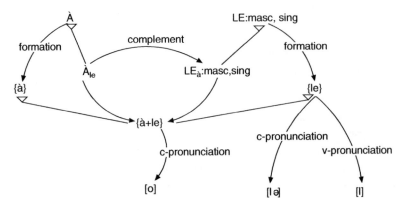

FIGURE 2.26.   A complete analysis of French *au*

case of *au livre* the following consonant is relevant to the pronunciation not only of *le* but also of *à*, so the fusion must apply at a level where the phonological environment can apply to both words. In a procedural model, it would be possible to change the default [alə] in two steps ([lə] to [o] before a consonant, then delete [a] before [o]), but in a declarative model this is not possible. Instead, the two forms must already be merged into a single form which can be affected as a whole by the phonological context—in other words, {à}+{le} must have been fused into {à+le}, as shown in Figure 2.26. In this diagram, the effect of phonological context is shown by the distinction between 'c-pronunciation' and 'v-pronunciation', the pronunciations found respectively before a consonant and a vowel. Thus just as the c-pronunciation of {le} is [lə], that of {à+le} is [o].

As I mentioned earlier, fused words are common. The following is a list of some examples from English; many of these are analysed in some detail in (Rosta 1997). In each case there is some evidence that what looks (and sounds) like a single word is in fact two words at the level of syntax, so the realizations of these two words must be fused either at the level of form (as for French *au*) or (perhaps) only at the level of phonology.

- *per = for each. Per* must 'contain' a determiner to explain the apparent lack of one before the noun:

(29) a   He paid two pounds per litre.
      b   *He paid two pounds per each litre.
      c   *He paid two pounds for litre.

- *my* = **me's*, *his* = **him's*, etc. *My* must have the same syntactic structure as *John's* because anaphoric binding applies in just the same way in both cases, and in both cases the determiner on its own can refer to the possessed.

(30) a John's mother loves him/*himself.
     b His mother loves him/*himself.
     c John's loves him and Jane's loves her.
     d His loves him and hers loves her.

- *better* = *had better*, *got* = *have got*. The finite verb must be present in the syntax whether or not it is pronounced. Since this suppression only occurs in the company of specific words (e.g. *better*, *got*) it can be treated as a case of lexically specified fusion.
- *one* = **a one*. This fusion is needed to explain why *a* can generally combine with *one*, but not if they are immediately next to one another:

(31) a the big one
     b a big one
     c the one with long ears
     d (*a) one with long ears

- *another* = **a more*. This fusion explains why *another* is ambiguous between the ordinary meaning of *other* (as in *Don't choose the same one—choose another one!*) and the same meaning as the *more* which means 'extra' (as in *once more* or *some more beer*); and it also explains why it only has this meaning with singular countable common nouns which ordinarily require *a*:

(32) a (some) more beer
     b *a more cup
     c *(some) more cup
     d another cup

- *today* = *this day*, *tonight* = *this night*, *yesterday* = *last day*, *tomorrow* = *next day*. These fusions explain the gaps in Table 2.4.
- *once* = *one time*, *twice* = *two times*. Higher numbers do combine freely with *times*, so it is strange that the same is not true of *one* and *two* (and used not to be true of *three*). The fusion analysis removes the oddity.
- *bigger* = *more big*, etc. The syntactic similarity between analytic and inflected comparatives is well known and obvious.

In each of these cases a fusion analysis turns what appears to be a strange restriction on syntax into a simple fact of morphology.

TABLE 2.4.   Lexical gaps in this/last/next + morning/evening/night etc.

this morning	this evening	*this night	*this day	this week
*last morning	?last evening	last night	*last day	last week
*next morning	*next evening	*next night	*next day	next week

2.9 Clitics

Clitics are an important challenge for any theory of morphology because, like fused words, they depart from the usual simple mapping between words and forms; but unlike fused words, the clitic generally has a separate phonological realization. A typical word has its own fully inflected form (fif), which is a full word-form. In contrast, a clitic is a word which is realized by a mere affix rather than by a separate word-form. For example, the shortened form of an English auxiliary such as _'s (for *is* or *has*) is a clitic because:

(a) it must be a separate word in the syntax because syntactically it is indistinguishable from the full form *is*, but

(b) its realization must be an affix because a typical non-affix is at least one syllable long, and {_'s} must attach to a preceding word.

The last two decades have seen a great deal of work on the theory of clitics (e.g. Anderson 1996; Borer 1992; Sproat 1988; Zwicky 1992a, 1977), but not much agreement on how they should be accommodated in a general theory of language structure. Clearly the answer to this question depends on more general questions about the structure of language, so the following account will rest heavily on the WG assumptions outlined above.

Clitics are complicated, but they are not surprising. Indeed, given what we know about grammaticization, together with the three-level analysis of words, we could predict the existence of clitics as steps on the route from separate words to single words. Here are some well-known steps on this route:

- typical word: a separate word realized by a full word-form
- clitic: a separate word realized only by an affix
- fused word (s. 2.8): a separate word whose realization is inseparable from that of a neighbour
- word-part: a mere affix realizing some property of the containing word.

As we might expect, therefore, clitics themselves may have different degrees of deviance from the typical word, ranging from the so-called 'simple' clitics of

English to the 'special clitics' (Zwicky 1977) of languages like French and Serbo/Croatian. In this brief introduction to the WG treatment of clitics I shall explain how simple clitics can be handled and then list various extra bits of theoretical apparatus that are needed for more complicated systems. There is also a detailed WG analysis of clitics in Serbo/Croatian (Camdzic and Hudson 2007).

For all their simplicity, English words show several different kinds of clitic-like patterns. The typical word has a base form which is realized at least by a stressed syllable, so any word shorter than this is deviant and might be called a clitic; by this criterion, clitics would include a wide range of 'function' words such as *a, the, to, and, in, you,* and so on. As with clitics, there is generally a choice between a full pronunciation (with a stressed vowel) and an abbreviated one, and in some cases there are even syntactic constraints on the abbreviation. For example, *I've got you* can be abbreviated to *gotcha,* but only given a specific structure; the abbreviation is not possible in an example like (33).

(33)   In the pictures I've got you look great.

A spectacular example of fusion is found in *what are you* which can fuse to *whatcha* in examples like (34).

(34)   What are you [wɒtʃə] doing?

However, these examples probably require no more apparatus than the fusion examples discussed in section 2.8. In addition, all these reduced forms need a phonetic form in which they are part of a larger 'phonological word', though in the absence of a proper analysis of phonological structure it is hard to take this claim any further. However, none of these examples merits the name 'clitic' if, as I suggested at the start of this section, clitics are words whose realization is an affix.

On the other hand, reduced auxiliaries such as _'s ~ *is* (or *has*) and _'m ~ *am* probably do qualify as real clitics, because they have to attach to a preceding word. For example, although *am* normally loses its vowel after *I,* this does not happen before *I* (although ordinary phonetic reduction to schwa is possible there). The easiest way to apply this restriction is to classify these reduced forms as suffixes which seek a 'host'—a preceding strong form. If they are suffixes, then they are affixes; but since they are the word's full inflected form (fif), the word qualifies as a clitic. Moreover, the affix is subject to the well-known syntactic constraint that it can only be used as the realization of a verb that has a following overt complement.

(35)   *a*   I'm not sure whether Bill is American, but I know Ed is/'s Canadian.
       b   I'm not sure whether Bill is American, but I know Ed is/*'s.

Furthermore, there is a striking similarity between the reduced _'s and the inflectional suffix {s}, which shows just the same range of allomorphs (including voiced [z] after a vowel and the epenthetic vowel after a sibilant). The obvious explanation for this similarity is that the two forms are examples of the same morph, and since the inflectional {s} is obviously a suffix, the same must be true of the reduced verb form. These considerations all support the conclusion that the reduced verb is a clitic, realized by a mere affix. This analysis is shown in Figure 2.27, where the properties of _'s are inherited from the more general category 'Reduced-auxiliary'.

The general characteristic of clitics that emerges from this analysis is that their pronunciation is an affix, and as an affix it requires a 'host', a larger form of which it is a part. For most affixes the host is defined by the morphology; for example, the host of {s} in the plural of DOG is the form {dogs}. However, clitics are different because they provide their own host, a form which exists solely to accommodate the clitic; for example, in (36) it is {you's}, which clearly has no status at all in syntax.

(36)   That picture of you's nice.

This adhoc form consists of the clitic plus the immediately preceding form, which in this case happens to be {you}, and is recognized as a special

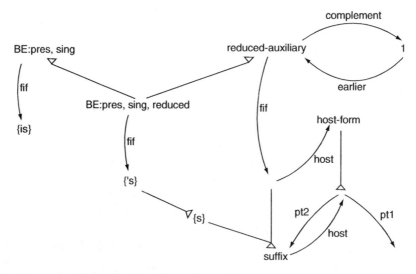

FIGURE 2.27.   The reduced auxiliary _'s as a clitic

kind of form, a 'host-form'. Host-forms are the key to analysing clitics, though (as we shall see) some clitic systems require further complexities as well.

In some cases, of course, the host-form is stored rather than newly created. This happens when a clitic combines frequently with a particular form, and the tell-tale evidence for storage is a special fused form; so for example, when reduced *are* follows its subject *you*, the two fuse as [jɔː] (written *you're*). However, fusion here (as elsewhere) is syntactically limited, so it is not possible if *you* and *are* just happen to occur next to one another, even though the normal reduced auxiliary is possible.

(37) a You're [jɔː] lovely.
      b The pictures of you are *[jɔː] lovely.

The special pronunciation of *you're* is shown in Figure 2.28, in which 'BE:pres, red.$_{you}$' is *are* as found with *you* (i.e. YOU$_{are}$) as its subject.

Host-forms are responsible for a great deal of apparent complexity in the syntax, as they impose their own ordering which often conflicts with the

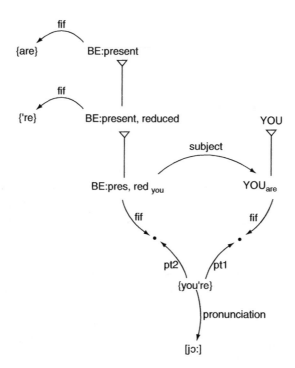

FIGURE 2.28. *You're* as a clitic with fused host-form

normal word-order rules and give rise to Zwicky's 'special' clitics. My examples are from Beja, a North Cushitic language of the Sudan and Eritrea which I studied for my Ph.D. (Hudson 1964, 1973, 1974, 1976*b*). Beja is strongly head-final so the object of a verb normally precedes it, but if it is a clitic pronoun, it is attached to the verb as a suffix (e.g. {ho:k}, 'you'). (In the annotation, N and A stand for nominative and accusative, the only two cases, and S and P stand for singular and plural.)

(38) a   u:-tak   o:-gaw   rih-ia
          the(NS)-man   the(AS)-house   see-past,3sing
          'The man saw the house.'

      b   u:-tak   rih-ia-ho:k
          the(Ns)-man   see-past,3sing-you
          'The man saw you.'

Similarly, a possessor pronoun is attached as a suffix to the possessed noun, whereas a full noun possessor may be on either side of it:

(39) a   o-tak-i   gaw
          the(AS)-man-'s   house
          'a house of the man'

      b   gaw   o-tak-i
          house   the(AS)-man-_'s(NS)
          'a house of the man'

      c   gaw-u:-k
          house-NS-you
          'a house of yours'

As can be seen, clitic pronouns are realized by suffixes in the word they depend on. Furthermore, when attached to a noun, they bring with them an inflectional suffix which shows the latter's case and number; for example, the nominative singular *gaw-u:k* contrasts with *gaw-o:k* (accusative singular), *gawa-a:k* (nominative plural), and *gawa-e:k* (accusative plural), so generalizing across these various alternatives, the realization of 'your' is {V:k}. This case/number suffix only appears before a clitic pronoun, so it is an example of rather a rare category: an inflected clitic, that is, a clitic which is realized not just by one affix, but by two. We shall see later further evidence that the case/number suffix is part of the realization of the pronoun rather than of the noun, although it is the noun that it agrees with.

The examples given so far are relatively straightforward but the analysis needs to recognize the following elements, which we can illustrate with the word *gaw-u:k*, the nominative of 'your house':

- the syntactic words GAW and 2S (second person singular), a noun with its dependent possessor.
- the forms {gaw} and {u:k}, which are respectively the fif of GAW and of 2S.
- the parts of {u:k}: the case/number agreement {u:} and {k}, the unique signal of 2S.
- the host-form {gaw-u:k}, consisting of {gaw} and {u:k}.
- the relation 'host' from the clitic affixes {u:k} to the host-form.
- the relation 'anchor' from the host-form to {gaw}, showing that the host-form takes its position from (or is anchored to) {gaw}; this relation may be symbolized in diagrams as '@' (since the host-form is 'at' the head word).

Figure 2.29 shows both the structure of example (39*b*) and the general pattern for clitics from which it is inherited.

The examples so far have shown how host-words can override the demands of ordinary syntax. However the mismatch between syntax and forms can be much greater than this (Sadock 1991). What makes Beja clitics complicated is that several clitic suffixes may combine in the same host-form, and when they do their order is determined by the host-form, not by the syntax. We have already seen one example of this mismatch between morphology and syntax in the case/number suffix {u:} which is part of the pronoun suffix but agrees with the possessed noun. The complications multiply when we consider another suffix, {i}. This is the 'possessive marker' in *o-tak-i gaw*, 'the man's house' (example (39)). The function of {i} is similar to that of the English possessive _'s*, but {i} turns a noun into a 'possessive adjective' which inflects for gender, number, and case in agreement with the noun that it modifies. For example, *o-tak-i*, "the man's", becomes *o-tak-i-:b* when it modifies an accusative

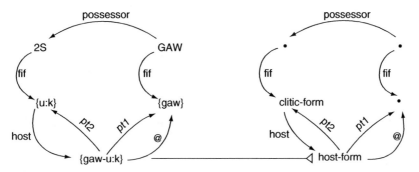

FIGURE 2.29.   Beja possessive and other clitics

noun. This agreeing case is quite separate from the case of the possessor noun, which is always accusative, so the obvious conclusion is that {i} is the realization of an adjective which has the usual range of possible inflections for an adjective but which takes an accusative noun as its dependent (just as English _'s does, according to Hudson 1990: 276). The adjective means 'possessed by X', where X is the referent of the dependent noun, but I shall call it simply ADJ for reasons that will emerge later. Since its fif {i} is a suffix, it follows that ADJ is a clitic.

We now have two clitics, {i} and {V:k}, both of which can attach to a noun. The question now is what happens in a phrase such as 'your man's house', where both clitics attach to the same noun. Here the syntax and morphology pull in different directions; to bring out the conflict, let us assume that 'house' is nominative, whereas 'man', as the possessor, must be accusative. Syntactically, {V:k} modifies 'man', so we might expect the accusative singular agreement {o:k}; and since 'your man' depends as a whole on ADJ, {o:k} should be closer than {i} to 'man'. The predicted form is therefore as in (40).

(40)   *tak-o:k-i   gaw
       man-your(A)-_'s   house(N)
       'your man's house'

But this is impossible. The only possible order is {i}{V:k}, shown in (41).

(41)   tak-i-u:k   gaw
       man-_'s-your(N)   house(N)

Moreover, {V:k} agrees with 'house', not 'man'. This shows particularly clearly that the agreement suffix {u:} is not part of the realization of 'man'; but in this example, the suffix must realize two words: the pronoun (without which it would not be possible) and ADJ, whose number and gender it signals. The proposed structure for *takiu:k gaw* is shown in Figure 2.30.

The order of {i} and {V:k} is determined by the rules that order the parts of the host-form (shown in the diagram as 'pt1', and so on). These rules are very general and go beyond possessive adjectives. ADJ can also be used to form object relative clauses (though in this use the form is {e}, which also realizes ADJ when the dependent noun is plural—e.g. *gawa-e-u:k*, 'of your houses'). ADJ once again acts as a dummy adjective with the usual adjective inflections, but this time its dependent is a verb rather than a noun; so given a verb such as *tam-i:ni*, 'he eats', we form an object-relative clause by adding {e}, giving *tam-i:ni-e*, 'which he eats'. Once again we find that ADJ can combine with clitic pronouns, this time acting as object of the verb; and once again we find that the pronoun has to follow the {e} of ADJ, contrary to the demands of

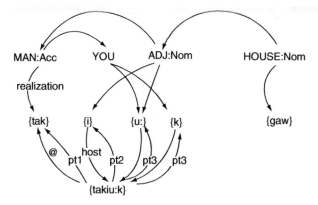

FIGURE 2.30.   The syntax and morphology of Beja "your man's house"

syntax. The following example uses a causative verb in order to allow a second object inside an object-relative clause:

(42)   rih-s-an-e-u:k   tak
       see-cause-past, 1sing- {e}-you(N)   man(N)
       'a man who I showed you'

As in the earlier example, the form of {V:k} shows the case of the modified noun rather than reflecting the function of the pronoun itself, which is always the object.

Beja illustrates two kinds of mismatch between syntax and morphology that can be found in clitic systems: an anti-syntactic order of elements, and clitics doubling as inflectional affixes. Of course, other languages offer other kinds of complication. We shall now briefly consider two of these:

(i)   complex host-forms, with places for a large number of clitics;
(ii) 'second-position' clitics, which are suffixed to the first element of their clause.

For complex host-forms we need look no further than the Romance languages such as French. The following account draws on a fuller analysis (Hudson 2001a) which contains a great deal more detail and justification.

French host-forms normally treat all the clitics as prefixes to the verb, though positive imperatives turn most of their clitics into suffixes. In the following examples, the clitics are italicized, as French orthography treats the prefixes as independent words. (I mark morpheme boundaries in these examples with a full-stop because hyphens are part of the orthography of French.)

(43)   a   *Je   ne   les   leur*   donn.er.ai   pas.
           I   not   them   to-them   give.future.1sing   not
           'I shall not give them to them.'

b Jean *me*   *les*   *y*   env.err.a.
   John for-me them   there   send.future.3sing
   'John will send them there for me.'
c Donn.ez   *-les*   *-moi*!
   Give.imperative them   to-me
   'Give me them!'

As usual in morphology, the order of elements is absolutely rigid. The order for prefixed clitics is as follows, moving from earlier to later:

- subject pronoun: JE, TU, IL, ELLE, NOUS, VOUS, ILS, ELLES (I, thou, he, she, we, you, they-masculine, they-feminine)
- negative marker NE
- object pronouns:
  - ME, TE, SE, NOUS, VOUS (me/myself, thou/thyself, himself/herself, us/ourselves, you/yourselves)
  - LE, LA, LES (him, her, them)
  - LUI, LEUR (to him/her, to them)
- Y (a fused preposition phrase containing the preposition À, 'to, at' and any third-person pronoun with inanimate referent: 'to/at it/them' or simply 'there')
- EN (like Y, but containing DE, 'of, from')

From a syntactic point of view, this ordering reflects an apparently arbitrary mixture of grammatical function (subject—direct object—indirect object) and reference (first, second, and third person, reflexive or non-reflexive); and NE, Y, and EN sit uncomfortably alongside the personal pronouns. The easiest assumption is that each position is associated with a stipulated list of forms; the only price to be paid for this simplicity is the need to distinguish the forms {nous} and {vous} according to whether they are subjects or objects. The relevant part of a grammar of French is shown in Figure 2.31. This diagram should be self-explanatory (except that for simplicity I have omitted all but one 'host' link).

Needless to say, this 'grammar' is intended to capture just one characteristic of French clitics: their position relative to the verb and to each other. It is not meant to show how these forms realize syntactic structures, but it does explain some otherwise odd gaps in syntactic structure. The numbered parts cannot be repeated, which means that they define 'slots' which can be filled only once. This excludes some syntactically well-formed sentences such as sentence b in the pair in (44).

(44) a Je   me   lui   présent.er.ai.
         I   myself to-him   introduce.future.1sing
         'I shall introduce myself to him.'
      b *Je me   vous   présent.er.ai.
         I   myself to-you   introduce.future.1sing
         'I shall introduce myself to you.'

Sentence b is ungrammatical simply because the forms {me} and {vous} belong to the same group, so they compete for the same position (Part 3).

We now turn to the other kind of complexity, 'second-position' clitics. These are interesting because cliticization interacts with syntax much more than in any of the other examples that I have discussed so far. In English, clitics simply attach to whatever happens to be the next word thanks to the ordinary rules of syntax. In French, most clitic pronouns are tied to the verb on which they depend, but follow special positioning rules which can all be located in the morphology of a host-form. But in a second-position language such as Serbo-Croatian, clitics migrate from their syntactic parent to the second position in their clause. For example, in (45) the italicized clitics may follow any word provided it is the first in the sentence; no other position is permitted.

(45) a Ivan   *ga* *je* htjeo   vidjeti.
         Ivan   *him* is   wanted   see
         'Ivan wanted to see him.'
      b Htjeo   *ga* *je* Ivan   vidjeti.
      c Vidjeti *ga* *je* Ivan   htjeo.

Second-position clitics are a challenge for any theory which rejects clauses and 'positions', as WG does. If we cannot refer to 'the second position in a clause',

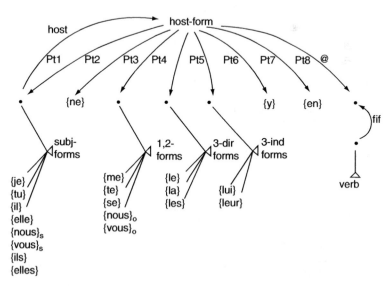

FIGURE 2.31.   A grammar for French host-forms

how can we handle second-position clitics? The WG solution (in Camdzic and Hudson 2007) is to accept a slightly more complicated analysis for these clitics than for French. Whereas French clitics demand a host-form in the morphology, but no special structure in the syntax, Serbo-Croatian clitics need a syntactic 'host-word' as well as a host-form. In the example above, the host-word is *Ivan ga je*, that is, a word containing the clitics and also the word to which they are attached. This is realized in a straightforward way by the host-form {Ivan-ga-je}, which has the same analysis as the host-forms in French; but there would be no point in recognizing a host-word in French because it would contribute nothing to the syntax. In Serbo-Croatian, on the other hand, the host-word is vital for the syntax because it defines the notion 'second position in the clause'. It is clause based because it is anchored to the clause's root verb, and it guarantees second position because all the other dependents of this root verb also depend on it, and any word which depends on the host-word must also follow it. Consequently, the host-word must be in the 'first position', that is, at the start of the clause, and because the clitics are suffixed to a non-clitic form, within the host-word, they are in what could be called the 'second position'.

The structure of example (45a) is shown in Figure 2.32, but the details of the analysis, and of how it handles a range of other complications in the clitic system, can be found in Camdzic and Hudson 2007. The main point of this rather complex diagram is the host-word which I have

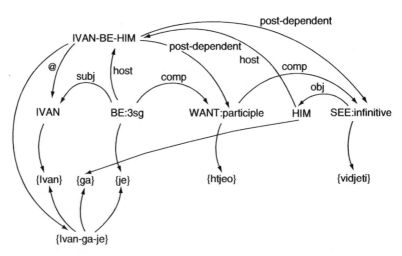

FIGURE 2.32.   Serbo-Croatian second-position clitics

labelled (arbitrarily) 'IVAN-BE-HIM'. This is sanctioned by the two clitics of which it is Host, it is anchored to the word IVAN, and it forces the words WANT:participle and SEE:infinitive into a later position thanks to the post-dependent links. The morphology is very similar to the French host-forms.

The general conclusion that I draw from this little survey of cliticization phenomena is that they include a range of very different types, each of which requires a different kind of structural treatment. However, it does seem possible to range them on a scale of structural complexity or deviance, with English abbreviations at one end and Serbo-Croatian clitics at the other.

2.10 A Summary of Morphological Categories

This chapter has surveyed a wide range of morphological issues and phenomena, including:

- the separation of the level of form from both syntax and phonology
- derivation versus inflection
- morphosyntactic classification by inflections and by features
- multiple affixation and affix order
- other morphological processes such as vowel change and reduplication
- syncretism and intermediate bases
- compounding
- fused words
- clitics.

The list covers most of the familiar territory of morphological theory, though there are important gaps such as incorporation and allomorphic processes which presuppose a developed theory of phonology (e.g. tone-change).

The analyses offered have all stayed within the basic framework of ideas that I outlined in the first chapter, and have made use of some very general categories such as the relation Part (with its sub-types Part1, Part2, and so on). But of course some of the analytical categories are peculiar to morphology. We can divide these categories into relations and entities.

- Relations:
  - **Realization,** with its sub-types:
    - Formation, divided into:
      - Base
      - Fif (fully inflected form)

- Pronunciation, divided into:
  - First segment
  - Last segment
  - Vowel
  - Fps (full phonological structure)
  - Spelling.
- **Variant**, with many parochial sub-types (er-variant, s-variant, en-variant, perfect-variant, etc.):
  - relations between host-forms and clitics or words:
    - host
    - anchor
- Entities:
  - **Form**, with sub-types:
    - Morph
    - Affix
    - Root
    - Complex form
    - Word-form
    - Host-form
    - **Clitic**, a sub-type of word whose formation is an affix.

The WG claim is that these categories are sufficiently general to cover a significant proportion of the known morphological phenomena of the world's languages. However there is no point in aiming at an exhaustive list because there is no 'universal grammar' which defines all the possibilities and which we might one day finish exploring. Every one of these categories has presumably arisen historically in response to functional pressures, and, just like most of the other categories of cognition, the categories are quite concrete and easy to learn inductively. Not all of them are needed by all languages; some languages need very few of them; and no doubt there are morphologies that go beyond this list. But there is no reason at present to doubt the general claim that morphology can be analysed successfully as an inheritance network.

3

Syntax

3.1 Dependency Structure, not Phrase Structure

By far the most controversial characteristic of WG syntax has always been the adoption of **dependencies** rather than phrases as the basis for sentence structure (Hudson 1984: 75). Most theories of syntax have followed the American tradition of phrase-structure analysis which started with the Immediate-Constituent Analysis of the Bloomfieldians (Bloomfield 1933; Wells 1947; Harris 1951) and which was formally defined by Chomsky (Chomsky 1957). This gives a part–whole analysis in which sentences are divided into successively smaller phrases until the parts are syntactic atoms—morphemes in some theories and words in others. In contrast, the dependency tradition is much older, with roots in Paninian grammar (Bharati, Chaitanya, and Sangal 1995) and in the ancient grammars of Greek, Latin (Covington 1984; Percival 1990), and Arabic (Owens 1988). In this tradition, the main unit of syntax is the word, and all grammatical relations relate one word to another; these relations have had various names such as 'connection' (Tesnière 1959) but the term 'dependency' has a respectable ancestry and the great advantage of alluding to the asymmetrical relationship between a superordinate and subordinate word.

The contrast between the two approaches can be seen in Figure 3.1, which makes the rather obvious point that dependency structures (like the lower one) are very much simpler than phrase structures. Of course, this is not in itself evidence for or against either theory, but other things being equal we should presumably prefer the simpler analysis. Since the early 1980s my view has been that the extra nodes are not only unnecessary, but undesirable because they make certain kinds of generalization harder to state. Since 1990, this view has been confirmed by other kinds of evidence—statistical and psychological—which I shall report later.

It will be helpful to prepare for the following discussion by highlighting the formal similarities and differences between the two theories—or more precisely, between the 'classical' (X-bar) version of phrase structure, PS theory

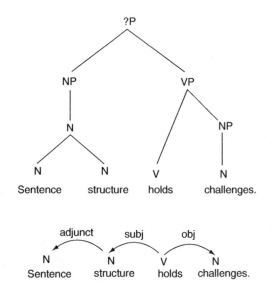

FIGURE 3.1.   Phrase structure compared with dependency structure

(Jackendoff 1977), and the WG version of dependency structure. This quali-
fication is important because there are a great many different formal interpretations of dependency grammar (Bröker 2001), and, of course, an even
larger number of variations on the basic idea of phrase structure. A thorough
survey of all the alternatives on either side would probably be neither relevant
nor helpful. I shall call these theories PS and DS for short.

The main **similarities** between PS and DS are the following assumptions:

- Words are grouped into **phrases** that have an abstract structure that goes
  well beyond mere linear order and linear adjacency. The phrases are
  generally agreed to reflect **dependencies** between words, with every
  phrase built around a **head** word on which all the other parts depend;
  in dependency terms, every word (except the sentence-root) has a **parent**
  on which it depends, so the head of a phrase is the parent of the heads of
  all the other phrases inside it. These dependencies are oriented not only
  towards meaning but also towards linear order, so a phrase is both a unit
  of meaning and also (by default) an uninterrupted string of words. Of
  course, as its name implies, PS treats phrases as basic and therefore
  provides a separate node for each phrase, but even a WG dependency
  structure can be interpreted in terms of phrases: each word that has at
  least one dependent is the head of a phrase which consists of that word
  plus (the phrases of) all its dependents.

- Every phrase is endocentric—i.e. every phrase contains one word which is its head, and whose classification determines the distribution of the whole phrase. In PS the head has the same class-label as the whole phrase (e.g. N inside NP), while in DS the arrows point away from the head.
- Every word or phrase has a grammatical function which can be classified in terms of a system of general categories such as 'head', 'complement', 'subject', 'adjunct' and so on (though I shall later question this particular set of contrasts). This system distinguishes heads or parents from dependents (i.e. all the other functions), and shows how the dependents relate either to the whole phrase (PS) or to the head word (DS). In spite of disagreements over detail—for example, I have never seen the need for 'specifier' in spite of its popularity in other theories—there is general agreement, even if only implicit, that these relations form a hierarchy from the most general (dependent) to the most specific (e.g. indirect object), with intermediate categories such as complement and object. This hierarchy is particularly clear evidence for the hierarchical classification of relations, which is one of the main tenets of WG.
- A phrase's internal structure is independent of the phrase's external relations. In PS, the internal relations are shown below the relevant XP node, while DS shows them by the arrows which point away from the head word.
- The parts of one phrase may double up as parts of another phrase. At least in 'classical' PS this is shown either by movements and traces (Chomsky, passim) or by 'structure-sharing' (Pollard and Sag 1994). In DS it is shown by arrows connecting one word to two (or more) other words. Figure 3.2 shows the two PS systems (A and B) alongside the DS system (C); the dotted lines in the first two diagrams show that in each case *John* functions as the subject of *working* as well as *is*. In the DS analysis this double relation is explicit in the dependency arrows.

Alongside these important similarities, however, DS and PS rest on very different assumptions about sentence structure. In each case, the difference can be explained in terms of the network postulate of section 1.1.

The first difference involves the treatment of grammatical relations—the traditional 'grammatical functions'. In DS, the grammatical functions are **basic**, and are distinguished as different types of dependency; this is as expected in a network, where relations are always expressed directly by links between nodes. In contrast, in 'pure' PS, the grammatical functions are merely implied by the phrase structure, and even then the implied functions (head, complement, adjunct, specifier) are stipulated rather than 'native' to PS

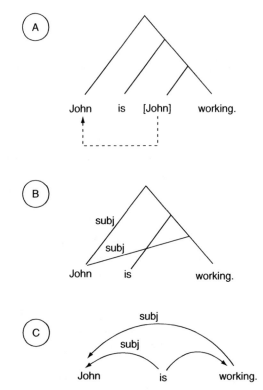

FIGURE 3.2.   'John' belongs to two phrases in 'John is working': 3 analyses

(Chametzky 2003). However, it is important to remember the many variations on PS that do label grammatical functions explicitly—Head-driven Phrase-Structure Grammar (Pollard and Sag 1994), Lexical Functional Grammar (Bresnan 2001), Relational Grammar (Blake 1990), Functional Grammar (Siewierska 1991), Systemic Functional Grammar (Halliday 1985), and Role and Reference Grammar (Van Valin 1993). The challenge for these theories is to explain why PS is needed in addition to these function labels.

The second difference follows from this one: DS has no **phrasal nodes**. Phrases and dependencies are alternative ways of showing how words interrelate and one of the reasons why DS has been widely ignored in syntactic theory is precisely that DS and PS are virtually interchangeable, to the extent that they are widely believed to be notational variants (Gaifman 1965; Robinson 1970). It is true that versions of phrase structure and dependency structure can be defined which are weakly equivalent, but even these versions imply very different structures and the relatively sophisticated versions that

I am calling PS and DS are certainly not equivalent. On the other hand, the two theories are not sufficiently different to be complementary; so we cannot argue for combining both PS and DS into a single structure (though a case might possibly be made for combining a rudimentary phrase structure with a rudimentary dependency structure—Rosta 1997: 31). We have to choose between DS, where dependency relations between words are basic, and PS, where they are merely implied by the relations of parts to (hypothetical) wholes. Given the network postulate, we have to choose DS because relations are basic. If there is a relation between two entities, it must, by definition, be a link between them; relations cannot be implied.

Of course, the force of this argument depends on whether the 'vertical' relations of a word to its phrase are in fact more or less real than its 'horizontal' relations to other words; e.g. whether *holds* in Figure 3.1 is more closely related to its phrase *Sentence structure holds challenges* or to its subject *structure* and its object *challenges*. In other words, is it more revealing to relate *holds* directly to *structure* and *challenges*, or indirectly via the whole phrase? The answer is obvious. It is encouraging to see some convergence in the direction of DS: a variation on the Minimalist Program has been proposed by Collins in which 'a representation is a set of lexical items, and the relations between them.... [This view] is closely related to that of dependency-based grammars' (quoted in Chametzky 2003). Furthermore, Collins draws two conclusions in an unpublished presentation:

(i) The theory of movement does not need to refer to phrase structure.
(ii) All syntactic relations are head–head relations.

However it takes more than one swallow to signal spring and this remains a minority view in PS.

The third difference between DS and PS is that in DS a word is always represented by a single node. Again, this has to be so if sentence structure is part of a network, because a network identifies entities only by the nodes that represent them so no entity can be represented by more than one node. This immediately rules out not only 'movement' from one node to another, but also '**unary branching**', in which a single unit receives two distinct analyses. For example, in Figure 3.1 the single item *challenges* is represented by two nodes, one classified as a noun and the other as a noun phrase; and similarly for *sentence structure*. Unary branching plays an essential role in classical X-bar theory (and also in other kinds of phrase structure), but it is impossible in DS. Interestingly, Chomsky too now rejects unary branching (Chomsky 1995a: 246), which again reduces the difference between DS and his version of PS.

Fourthly, and finally, if DS allows only one node per word, the traditional subject–predicate (or NP–VP) analysis is at least unnatural, and may even be impossible (depending on what other assumptions one makes). Take a simple example: *John loves Mary*. If the word-token *loves* has only one node, this must support both the dependents; so there can be no node which is linked to *Mary* but not to *John*, so there is no VP. Consequently, there can be no geometrical asymmetry between subjects and objects, and no c-**command** relation—or at least, no c-command relation defined, as in other theories, in purely geometrical terms. C-command plays a central role in some PS theories, so this difference clearly lays DS open to criticism, or even refutation if c-command were to turn out to be indispensable. Advocates of DS can react in two different ways to this challenge.

1 One strategy is to duplicate c-command in DS by dividing verbs into two 'words', an inflectional element and a lexical one (e.g. *loves* = Present + LOVE—see Rosta 1997: 297; Kreps 1997: 134). In this analysis, the subject depends on the inflectional element and the object on the lexical one, so if the lexical element depends on the inflectional element, the subject does in some sense 'command' the object. (More generally, X c-commands Y if X depends directly on Z and Y depends on Z only indirectly.) Unfortunately this analysis also assumes a very different view of morphology, in which morphology is driven much more than in WG by the needs of syntax.

2 The other strategy is to replace c-command by some other analytical tool. In HPSG this is obliqueness (Pollard and Sag 1994: 238), but obliqueness is no easier to match in WG than c-command is. The most promising candidate in WG is semantic phrasing—the hierarchical structure which is created in semantics if dependents contribute their meanings one at a time (Hudson 1990: 146–51). For example, in *John loves Mary*, the object contributes before the subject, giving 'loves Mary' and 'John loves Mary', but no: 'John loves'. However, this is simply a promising line of research, and the work remains to be done.

These differences are real and important, and any grammarian must choose between the alternatives. Even if it is hard to choose, the choice is certainly not a question of mere notation, nor is it one that can be based simply on a head-count of practitioners, because the dependency tradition is alive and well in established theories such as Categorial Grammar (Steedman 2000), Tree-Adjoining Grammar (Joshi and Rambow 2003; Rambow and Joshi 1994), Functional-Generative Description (Sgall, Hajičova, and Panevova 1986), and Meaning-Text Theory (Mel'cuk 1997). In short, dependency theory has come to be recognized in theoretical, descriptive, and applied linguistics as a serious alternative to phrase structure.

But this is not all. Dependency has attracted interest in other areas of language study as well. It has maintained the popularity it has always enjoyed in computational linguistics; for example, 'a recent evaluation of parsers for practical applications has shown that the majority of the evaluated parsers were dependency-based' (Mollá, Schneider, Schwitter, and Hess 2000, quoting Sutcliffe, Koch, and McElligott 1996). Again:

> There are compelling reasons to reconsider unsupervised dependency parsing. First, most state-of-the-art supervised parsers make use of specific lexical information in addition to word-class level information—perhaps lexical information could be a useful source of information for unsupervised methods. Second, a central motivation for using tree structures in computational linguistics is to enable the extraction of dependencies—function-argument and modification structures—and it might be more advantageous to induce such structures directly. Third, ... for languages such as Chinese, which have few function words, and for which the definition of lexical categories is much less clear, dependency structures may be easier to detect. (Klein and Manning 2004)

'Treebanks' of corpora with a dependency analysis are now available in a wide variety of languages (Abeillé 2004, in particular Carroll, Minnen, and Briscoe 2004; Lin 2004). One research avenue that is being explored is to allow a parser to use a dependency treebank as its 'memory' to help it to build analyses incrementally, without backtracking or revision (Nivre, Hall, and Nilsson 2004; Nivre 2004). One of the attractions of dependency analysis for computational work is the relatively small amount of disagreement over analyses compared with the considerable variation found in phrase-structure analysis (Carroll, Minnen, and Briscoe 2004). Moreover, one of the most widely used practical parsing systems is the Helsinki Constraint Grammar (Karlsson 1995), and another is Link Grammar (Mollá, Schneider, Schwitter, and Hess 2000); both of these systems use a version of dependency grammar rather than phrase structure.

Meanwhile, dependency structures have revealed interesting mathematical properties. Recent work in graph theory has studied the mathematical properties of dependency networks in various languages and discovered, *inter alia,* that they are all 'scale-free' (Ferrer i Cancho, Solé, and Köhler 2004), which means that they tend to have very richly connected 'hub' nodes rather than a random distribution of links among nodes. The same is true of many other human institutions such as the internet and airline routes, so again language turns out to be like other networks that are derived from human cognition (Barabási 2003).

There have also been particularly interesting developments in the study of corpus statistics which tend to confirm the psychological reality of syntactic dependencies rather than phrase structure. The work that I shall now discuss uses both adult and child usage statistics to draw conclusions about how language is processed and learned. It is important to recognize that the figures are seriously affected by the analyst's assumptions about the grammar of the language concerned, and especially as far as frequent patterns such as determiners are concerned. However, such uncertainty affects only a minority of constructions, so it does make sense to compare the figures from different projects.

The most interesting figures concern 'dependency distance', the number of words that separate a word from its parent (a measure first recognized, so far as I know, in 1980: Heringer, Strecker, and Wimmer 1980: 187). If the two words are next to each other, the distance is 0; if they are separated by one word it is 1; and so on. This figure is related in an obvious way to processing difficulty, because both words need to be, or to be made, active in working memory at the point when the dependency between them is established. This is normally the point where the second of the words is being processed, i.e. has just been heard or read (or is just being spoken or written), so the distance measures either the time for which the first word has to be kept active, or the extra activation needed to reactivate it. Either way, the greater the dependency distance, the harder the processing.

To see the effects of distance, consider the following difficult sentence.

(46)   John gave the child of the man who lives in the house to his right sweets.

The structure is shown in Figure 3.3, which shows that *sweets* depends on *gave* and is separated from it by 13 other words. In order to understand this sentence, we have to remember that *gave* needs a direct object throughout the time when these 13 words are being processed, and if we fail to keep this information active, we have to reconstruct it from the stored memory of the sentence's meaning. Either way, the extended distance puts an extra burden on processing resources: if we do keep the syntactic information the effort of

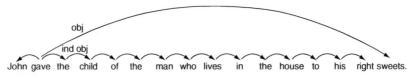

FIGURE 3.3.   A very long dependency distance

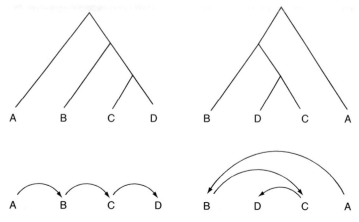

FIGURE 3.4. Two competing orders in PS and DS

doing so takes away from the resources available for processing the intervening words; and if we forget the syntax, it takes extra resources to reconstruct it
at the point where it is needed. (In s. 1.7, I defined working memory as the
currently active area of long-term memory, whose capacity is limited by the
total amount of available activation.) There is a great deal of experimental
evidence that such sentences are indeed hard to process (Frazier 1985; Gibson
1998), and even some persuasive evidence that the difficulty is much easier to
explain in terms of dependencies than in terms of phrases (Pickering and
Barry 1991).

The evidence from processing is relevant to the choice between DS and PS
because the only relevant units seem to be words. If PS were right, we might
expect phrases, as such, to need processing resources, but in fact this appears
not to be so. There is no evidence that the number of phrasal nodes makes a
contribution which can be separated from the number of words. Moreover,
PS would suggest that the order of words inside a phrase is relevant only to the
processing of that phrase, whereas DS predicts that phrases will be organized
'globally' so as to minimize overall dependency distance. To take an abstract
example (Fig. 3.4), PS gives no reason for preferring the order A B C D to B D
C A, other than symmetry and generality, whereas DS favours the first order
because it minimizes dependency distance.

A great deal of recent work has confirmed the relevance of dependency
distance as measured here in terms of intervening words.

– Work on syntactic processing has shown that difficulty increases with
  dependency distance. In particular, '(1) the longer a predicted category

must be kept in memory before the prediction is satisfied, the greater is the cost for maintaining that prediction; and (2) the greater the distance between an incoming word and the most local head or dependent to which it attaches, the greater the integration cost' (Gibson 1998). These two generalizations both consider the length of a dependency, measured from the head (1) or from the dependent (2). Unsurprisingly, perhaps, it turns out that the difficulty of a dependency is affected not only by the number of intervening words (its 'distance' in my terms) but also by the processing demands of these individual words. One factor which influences these demands is whether the referent is 'given' or 'new' in the discourse (Gibson 2002), but no doubt other factors should be considered as well. Dependency distance (counted in words) must eventually be integrated into a more sophisticated model of processing such as Gibson's.

— In typology there turns out to be a strong tendency for languages to organize their grammars so as to minimize the 'processing domain' (which roughly corresponds to dependency distance) of words (Hawkins 2001). For example, the optionality of dependents in Japanese seems to compensate for the consistent head-final order which would otherwise make the average dependency distance higher than in a mixed-order language such as English; the result of this optionality is that Japanese uses fewer dependents per word than English does, so the average dependency distance in casual conversation is very similar to that of English (Hiranuma 1999; the mean distances for English and Japanese were 0.39 and 0.36 respectively). On the other hand, there is also evidence that some languages tolerate very different degrees of difficulty in free conversation; e.g. dependency distance is much higher in German than in English (Eppler 2004: 155; the mean distances for English and German were 0.49 and 0.87); and in Chinese news bulletins, the distance is a very surprising 1.81 (Liu and Hudson 2006), although the figures for news bulletins are not directly comparable with those for free conversation in the other languages. The differences between Chinese, German and English suggest that the pressure to minimize distance may conflict with other functional pressures.

— At least one language (Welsh) seems to have explicit markers of dependency distance. Soft mutation (which applies various phonological changes to a word's first consonant) applies to verb dependents under complex conditions (Borsley and Tallerman 1996) which may reduce to being separated from the verb. For example, the VSO order means that objects are normally separated from the verb by the subject as in (47):

(47) a Gweles   (i)   **gi.**
       saw-1SG (I)   dog
       'I saw a dog.'

    b Prynodd   y   ddynes **feic.**
       bought:3sg the woman bike
       'The woman bought a bike.'

    c Roedd   y   ddynes yn prynu beic.
       was:3sg the woman in buy   bike
       'The woman was buying a bike.'

    d Mae ci   yn yr ardd.
       is   dog in the garden
       'A dog is in the garden.'

    e Mae yn yr ardd **gi.**

(All the Welsh examples are from Tallerman (p.c.)).

In (a), *gi* is the mutated form of *ci*, 'dog', whose form shows it to be object rather than subject; interestingly, this is true even when the subject *i* is unrealized, which is as we might expect if missing subjects are syntactically present but unrealized (see the later discussion in s. 3.7). Similarly in (b), *feic* is the mutated form of *beic*, as expected since it is separated from the verb by the subject phrase *y ddynes*; but in (c), *beic* is unmutated because it is directly next to its non-finite parent verb *prynu*, the subject being shared and therefore not present as a separator even in the syntax. Moreover, just like objects, subjects are mutated if they are delayed, as in (d). In sentence (d), *ci* is in the unmutated form expected of a subject, but it is mutated in (d) because it has been separated from the verb *mae*. As a rule, therefore, a subject or object dependent is mutated if it is separated from the verb.

However, the rule must be a little more complicated because of the apparent counter-examples in (48).

(48) a y ddynes werthodd **feic**
      the woman sold:3sg bike
      'It was the woman who sold a bike.'

    b Fedr Sioned ddim gyrru bws.
       can   Sioned not   drive bus
       'Sioned can't drive a bus.'

    c Fedr Sioned ddim gyrru bws.
       can   Sioned not   drive bus
       'Sioned can't drive a bus.'

The main problem is that extracted subjects seem to behave like unrealized pronouns separating the object from the verb. An example is (48*a*), where *feic* is the mutated form of *beic*. This pattern contrasts strikingly with the one in

(47c), *Roedd y ddynes yn prynu beic,* where sharing has moved the subject of *prynu* before it so that it does not trigger mutation. Maybe further research will be able to explain why sharing and extraction have such different effects. Another area where research is needed is the effect of the negative particle *ddim*. The unmutated gyrru in c shows that this blocks the mutation which otherwise occurs on the dependent non-finite verb, as shown in b, where *yrru* is the mutated form of *gyrru*.

- A number of monolingual corpus studies have shown a very strong tendency for dependency distance to be low. In the PEN Treebank, 74.2 percent of words had a distance of zero, and for 95.6% the distance was 4 or less (Collins 1996); and a selection of adult speakers from the CHILDES database showed 63 percent at zero and 99 percent at 4 or less (Pake 1998). Moreover, mathematical studies have shown that the networks of syntax are examples of 'small worlds', meaning that the average number of links between nodes is small (Ferrer i Cancho, Solé, and Köhler 2004)—in fact, a great deal smaller than if it had been left to chance (Ferrer i Cancho 2004). This has important implications for the theory of language acquisition. Suppose the child starts with a very small working memory which can only hold the current word and the immediately preceding one. Computer modelling has shown that a short memory span actually improves initial learning because it screens out a lot of irrelevant patterning (Elman 1993). The observations about dependency distance explain this finding: most adjacent pairs of words are in fact related, so non-adjacent pairs are much less likely to represent a pattern that is worth learning. Indeed, so far as English is concerned every syntactic dependency can be found between adjacent words, so concentrating on adjacent pairs would be an excellent learning strategy for English.
- Child language also shows the same tendency to minimize dependency distance, but (as expected) more sharply. Children learning both English and Hebrew have been shown to combine three words much more easily when dependency distance is zero than when one word is separated from the word on which it depends (Ninio 1994, 1996, 1998). For example, a phrase such as *this glass* is much more likely to be used as object than as subject, whereas for *big glass* the reverse is true. This is very hard to explain in terms of PS, but exactly as predicted by WG, on the assumption that *glass* depends on the determiner *this* whereas *big* depends on *glass*. For example, *take this glass* is easier than *this glass broke* because in the latter *broke* is separated from its dependent *this* by *glass*; conversely, *big glass broke* is easier than *want big glass* because *big* separates *want*

from its dependent *glass*. Generalizing, once children start to produce three-word utterances, they pass through the three stages shown in Figure 3.5. This generalization is all the more impressive because it cuts across a range of constructions that express different semantic relations, which confirms that the relation 'syntactic dependent' is a real mental category for children. (As noted above, this notion can easily be learned by children on the basis of words which are physically next to each other as well as semantically related, so there is no need to assume that it is innate.)

Dependency distance is not the only consideration that makes child language relevant to the choice between PS and DS. A number of other researchers have argued that DS is more appropriate than PS for the analysis of children's language (Robinson 1986; Van Langendonck 1987; Macwhinney 1989; Pake 1998). For one thing, it is easier to learn DS than PS because the objects of learning are just words and their dependency relations; there are no abstract phrasal categories. Equally important, however, is the fact that children's first syntactic patterns seem to consist of lexically specific pairs of words (Tomasello 2000, 2003). For example, Tomasello's daughter used the verb *cut* only with an object, but used *draw* in a much wider range of patterns, with no transfer from one verb to others. This kind of learning is as expected if children acquire DS by learning it, since dependencies are primarily dependencies between individual words. Moreover, it fits well with the WG claim that all relations, including syntactic dependencies, are classified in an Isa hierarchy (s. 1.2). If the hierarchy of word-classes can be learned by induction (s. 1.8), then so can the hierarchy of dependency types. In short, DS

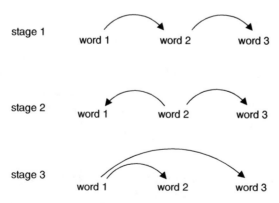

FIGURE 3.5.   Three stages in children's three-word utterances

is suitable for child language because it is suitable for lexically specific constructions; but of course exactly the same reasons show that it is suitable for adult language as well.

3.2 Word Order, Landmarks, Precedence Agreement

Syntactic dependencies are often thought of as primarily a matter of meaning, with little to do with such superficial issues as word order (e.g. Bröker 1998, 2000); but this has never been my view. Like all other concepts, dependencies bring together a cluster of properties, and meaning is only one such property along with word order, agreement, case choice, and so on. The established dependency relations such as subject and object are primarily concerned with these more superficial grammatical features, and only secondarily with meaning; indeed, the subject or object of a verb need not have any semantic relation to that verb at all. This is true of so-called 'raising' verbs such as SEEM and EXPECT (as in *It seems to be raining* and *I expect it to rain*, where *it* is the subject of *seems* and the object of *expect*). This being so, it is natural to extend the notion 'syntactic dependency' to relations which involve word order but which never involve meaning, such as the 'extraposee' relation in examples like (49), where the position of *which* shows that it must depend on *has* although the semantics links it only to *book* (and indeed justifies a second dependency on this word).

(49) A book has been published which will cause a sensation.

Word order, then, is one of the main properties which can be predicted from syntactic dependencies; so the question for this section is precisely how this is done.

One of the main topics for debate among dependency grammarians is whether dependency structures should be '**projective**'. Standard dependency structures (following Tesnière 1959) are tree-like 'stemmas' containing one node for each word, and a stemma is projective if each word can 'project' (by a straight line) up to its node without crossing the line from any other word. In other words, a projective stemma is one in which all phrases are continuous, as in a standard Phrase-structure tree. WG has always assumed **strict projectivity**, and this still seems correct because most phrases do, in fact, have to be continuous. It seems that apparent exceptions always involve some kind of special pattern for which a special kind of structure is needed. In the absence of such a special structure, it is always ungrammatical to put part of one phrase inside another. For example, we cannot take the phrases *very big* and *a book*, and splice them together to give **very a big book* because each phrase is interrupted by part of the other.

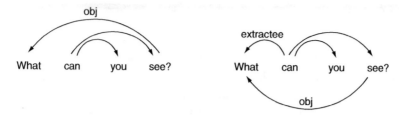

FIGURE 3.6.   Projective and non-projective analyses

The price paid for this very simple principle is that special structures are needed for all the apparent counter-examples, and in every case the special structure involves at least one extra dependency. The basic idea is that the extra dependency makes the overall structure projective. For instance, take extraction as in (50).

(50)   What can you see?

Here *what* is the object of *see*, but the phrase *what . . . see* is interrupted by *can you*, neither of which is part of it. If we assume the usual kind of dependency structure in which each word depends on only one other word, we have the first structure in Figure 3.6, which is non-projective. However, if we assume an extra dependency (called 'extractee') linking *what* to *can*, then at least part of the structure is projective, even if one dependency indicates an interrupted phrase. The second diagram in Figure 3.6 shows the projective dependencies above the words and the one non-projective one below—a useful convention which has been used in WG for some years.

It goes without saying that each of the extra dependencies must be justified in the usual way; for example, Extractee carries the well-known properties of extracted elements—standing just before the subject and verb, allowing recursive long-distance dependencies, and so on (Hudson 1990: 354–403). However, it is clear that such dependencies are concerned with very little but word order, and have little claim to semantic justification; this is why it is so important to be clear, as I explained above, that dependencies need no semantic justification. WG has been applied successfully to a wide range of discontinuous patterns, and the very simple projective structures allow an equally simple algorithm for parsing (Hudson 2000b): given a word w_n at the end of a string $w_1 \ldots w_m$,

(a) Try to 'capture' the nearest independent word so that it depends on w_n, and if that succeeds, do the same for the next nearest independent word and so on recursively.

(b) Then try to 'submit' w_n to w_m so that w_n depends on w_m; if this fails, try the word on which w_m depends, and so on recursively to the root of the sentence.

However, a number of research questions have arisen.

The first concerns the basic mechanism for expressing simple word-order restrictions, such as 'a word follows its parent'. How should this be expressed in a network, given that networks have no built-in left/right or before/after dimension? In earlier work I used the general concept Position, with Before and After as special cases (Hudson 1990: 18), and invoked these concepts not only for word order but also for semantic ordering of events; for example, the meaning of past tense locates the time of the referent Before the time of the utterance (ibid. 222). I still believe that this analysis was on the right lines because it treated the ordering of words as a special case of the ordering of events in time. In the absence of evidence to the contrary, we can assume (with Jackendoff 2002: 248) that the mental processes involved in ordering words are the same as those for other events, so we should use the same analytical apparatus.

However, I now think we can improve the analysis by importing the notion 'landmark' from Cognitive Grammar (e.g. Langacker 1998) as the relation between an object to be located (a 'trajector') and the object from which it takes its position. This relation is purely a matter of ordering, in contrast with syntactic dependencies which are more abstract and are based on a variety of simpler relations which can therefore be predicted from dependencies. One of the predictable relations is word order, so there is a very simple default mapping from syntactic dependencies to landmarks:

(51)   **Parents are landmarks**: a word's parent is its landmark.

In short, a word typically takes its position from its parent (i.e. the word on which it depends). For example, if *small* depends on *children*, then by far the most efficient way to predict the position of *small* is to say that it stands just before *children* (wherever that may be). This is exactly the same policy as the one we follow in giving spatial descriptions such as 'The book is on the table' (rather than 'The table is under the book'), taking larger or more permanent objects, whose position is more likely to be known, as the landmark for smaller or more movable objects. The 'structure dependence' which is claimed to be a distinctive characteristic of language (Smith 1999: 134) is actually a special case of a much more general mental tendency to locate 'dependent' objects or events in relation to more fixed ones so that the two are located as a single unit. Thus, just as we expect the book to move if we move the table which it is on, so we expect a word to 'move' along with the word which it depends on.

Having introduced Landmark as a relation, we now have an option which is not available in Cognitive Grammar: to subclassify it. This allows us to kill

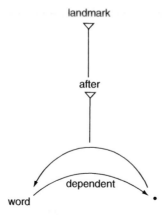

FIGURE 3.7. A word's dependents follow it

two birds with one stone: to identify not only the landmark but also the dependent's position in relation to the landmark. We therefore treat Before and After as sub-types of Landmark, so if X is in the Before relation to its landmark Y, then X is before Y. We can now express the generalization about words following their parents in Figure 3.7. For clarity, I shall show landmark relations as dotted lines so as to distinguish them from dependencies.

This very simple generalization defines the default order even in a mixed-order language such as English (where most word-tokens follow their parent), but there are many exceptions which override it. Many of these can be covered by recognizing 'pre-dependent' as a sub-type of Dependent (as I have since 1990), and then identifying particular dependency types (such as Subject) as pre-dependents. This extension is shown in Figure 3.8. Further exceptions can then be defined in terms of the related words; for example, although subjects are always pre-dependents, the subject of an 'inverting' auxiliary verb (e.g. in an interrogative clause) follows it. As with many other grammatical categories, Pre-dependent is needed for the grammars of some languages—those like English which systematically put some, but not all, kinds of dependents before their parents—but is certainly not universal. For example, a language such as Japanese has no use for the distinction because virtually all dependents precede their parents, so Dependent and Pre-dependent would be the same thing.

The relation Landmark and its sub-types provide a good basis for indicating word order in a network. However, we must distinguish between the 'partial' ordering imposed by the grammar and the full ordering found in any given utterance. At one extreme, a language that has 'free word order' allows

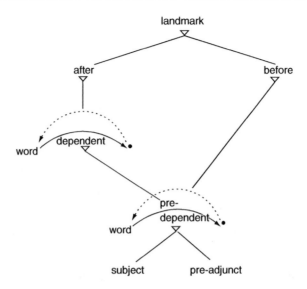

FIGURE 3.8.   Pre-dependents precede

dependents to stand either before or after their parents, so the grammar says nothing at all about 'before' and 'after'; all it needs to say is that parents are also landmarks (Tzanidaki 1996, 1998). However, the words in an utterance have to be in some linear order, so the sentence structure will include 'before' or 'after' according to the actual order. Similarly, co-dependents may be free in the grammar to organize themselves in any order, but in any particular sentence their order will inevitably be fixed. For instance, in *a holiday in France with Mary*, the co-dependents *in* and *with* occur in that order, so the sentence structure will show *in* as not only 'after *holiday*', but also 'before *with*'. These details are not inherited from the grammar, because the grammar does not fix the order of such co-dependents, but are properties of the word tokens. The alternative ordering (*a holiday with Mary in France*) would have been equally grammatical, but structurally different.

It seems, therefore, that a word may have more than one landmark. Apart from its parent, it has at least those of its co-dependents which are next to it. In some cases, these landmark relations are fixed by the grammar—for example, an indirect object in English must be not only after the verb, but also before the direct object, as in (52) but not in (53).

(52)   He gave his students good marks.
(53)   *He gave good marks his students.

In cases such as *a holiday with Mary in France*, however, the ordering of co-dependents is free, so we must assume that a general principle, called 'sister-ordering', introduces a landmark relation between each dependent and the one next to it. (I explore 'sister-ordering' later).

Now that we have a mechanism for defining the before/after relation, we are ready to consider projectivity. How can we guarantee that phrases are continuous? Or in dependency terms, how can we guarantee that dependents of different words do not get mixed up together? We might look for a specifically syntactic solution to this problem, but landmarks are part of general cognition so we should look for a much more general solution. The problem of ruling out ungrammatical sentences like (54) is just the same as the problem of ruling out misinterpretations of sentences like (55).

(54)   *Good read books.
(55)   The circle is to the left of the diamond which is to the right of the square.

The natural interpretation of (55) has the circle between the diamond (its own landmark) and the square (the diamond's landmark), as in the diagram on the left of Figure 3.9. However, the circle would, strictly speaking, still be in front of the diamond even if it was also in front of the square as in the right-hand diagram. Similarly, the natural position of *good* is between its landmark and the latter's landmark.

What the verbal and non-verbal examples have in common is that a landmark relation applies not only to the object that has that relation in its own right, but also any other object that takes this object as its own landmark. In other words, landmark relations are 'transitive' (in the logical sense), so the basic landmark relations imply others. The next figure, Figure 3.10, shows the

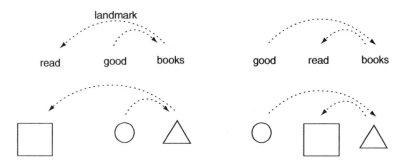

FIGURE 3.9.   Verbal and non-verbal sequences both avoid 'discontinuity'

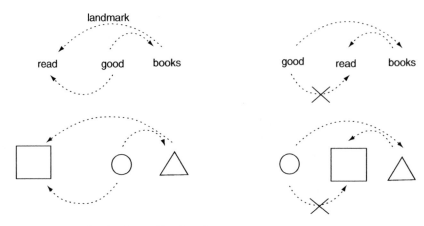

<small>FIGURE 3.10.   Illegal inherited landmarks</small>

implicit relations below the objects. As can be seen, the right-hand structures are illegal because the inherited landmark relations point in the opposite direction from the relation from which they are inherited.

In these examples, an object shares its landmark relations with its 'subordinates', that is to say with the objects that take it as their landmark. We can call this kind of transferred landmark 'subordinate transitivity' to distinguish it from the second kind, 'sister transitivity', which is based on the sister-ordering already introduced. Both kinds of transitivity involve three nodes A, B, and C, where B is the landmark of A and either A or B is the landmark of C; thinking in terms of a triangle joining A, B, and C, we start with the side AB plus either BC or AC. What transitivity supplies is the missing side. The two possibilities are shown schematically in Figure 3.11, where the solid landmark lines are given and the dotted one can be inferred by transitivity.

In sister transitivity, sister dependents automatically take each other as landmark, though once again these relations are merely potential. Taking the

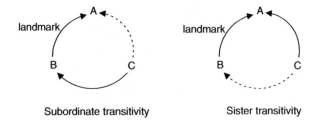

<small>FIGURE 3.11.   Subordinate and sister transitivity</small>

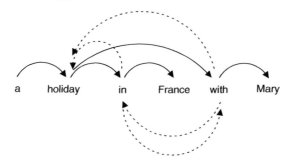

FIGURE 3.12.   Landmarks in *a holiday in France with Mary*

example discussed on p. 135, *a holiday in France with Mary*, both *in* and *with* depend on *holiday*, so each of them takes *holiday* as its landmark; but they must be in some order, so *in* takes *with* as its 'before' landmark and vice versa. The structure is shown in Figure 3.12, with the inferred relations once again drawn below the line.

Sister transitivity is important because it blocks discontinuities where the dependents of two sisters are mixed up together as in (56) and in (57), contrasting with (57) (from Rosta 2005: 190).

(56)   *a holiday in with Mary France
(57)   *Give students tulips of linguistics.
(58)   Give students of linguistics tulips.

As Rosta points out, the difference between (57) and its paraphrase (58) cannot be explained in terms of landmark relations inherited by a dependent from its parent. His explanation focuses on the crossing dependencies in (57) which are circled in Figure 3.13, and uses this as evidence for the general ban on tangling dependency arrows that I invoked in earlier work.

In contrast, I would now explain the difference in terms of the inherited landmark relations below the line. The logic is as follows:

Step 1. The words *students* and *tulips* both depend on *give*, so by (51) they each have *give* as their landmark 'in their own right'.

Step 2. Since they are sisters, by sister transitivity they also have each other as landmarks.

Step 3. Since *of* depends on *students*, it has *students* as its landmark in its own right.

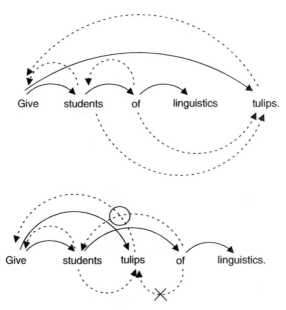

FIGURE 3.13.   Legal and illegal sister dependents

Step 4. Since *students* has *tulips* as its landmark (thanks to Step 2), and *of* has *students* as its landmark (Step 3), *of* must also have *tulips* as its landmark by subordinate transitivity.

Step 5. More specifically than Step 4, *of* must inherit a 'before' relation to *tulips* from *students*; this is true in (58) but not in (57)—hence the difference between these two examples.

This explanation gives the correct result, but it could be objected that the price is an implausible theory of sentence structure in which virtually every word has a landmark relation to every other word.

This theory is surely not likely to be true of the mental representations that we actually build in real time—after all, what would be the point of all this structure and inferential activity, and would it not mean a very sharp increase in the number of landmark relations with increasing sentence length? However exactly the same objection applies more generally to all inference, so we can invoke the general solution that I suggested in section 1.7 whereby we only inherit properties that are active and therefore relevant. In other words, the theory of transitivity does not in fact require all these landmark relations to be inherited—it merely allows them.

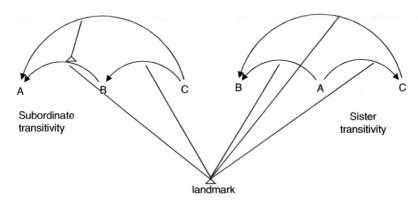

FIGURE 3.14.   Landmark transitivity

In short, we can derive the syntactic principle of projectivity from a much more general cognitive principle for selecting landmarks. This principle can be translated into a static formal definition of what makes a structure 'natural':

(59)   **Landmark transitivity**

        If A is a landmark, of sub-type L, for B, and:

- B is a landmark for C (subordinate transitivity),
  then A is also a type L landmark for C.
- A is also a landmark for C (sister transitivity),
  then B is also some type of landmark for C.

The very general principle of landmark transitivity is displayed in Figure 3.14, with subordinate transitivity on the left and sister transitivity on the right.

One of the benefits of this approach is that it applies smoothly to coordinate structures, which in WG are treated in terms of 'word strings'—strings of words which otherwise have no structure other than their dependency relations. For example, the brackets in (60) enclose the coordination and its parts, the conjuncts:

(60)   I went to [[Edinburgh yesterday] [and Birmingham on Thursday]].

The main point to notice about the structure in Figure 3.15 is that the tangling of dependency arrows does not affect grammaticality, which is odd if tangling is ungrammatical. In the earlier approach to word order I had to make a special exception for coordination (Hudson 1998: 29): in general tangling is

FIGURE 3.15.   Legal tangling in coordination

banned, but coordinate structures allow it. In contrast, landmark transitivity applies to coordinate structures in just the same way as to all other structures.

To summarize, I have explained projectivity in terms of landmarks and landmark transitivity. This is a relatively new solution in the WG literature (where I have also called it variously 'precedence concord' and 'order concord'), so I shall now compare it briefly with two earlier WG solutions:?

Analysis A. The Adjacency Principle (Hudson 1990: 114) requires every word to be separated from its parent P only by other words which are also subordinate to P. This principles faces two problems:

   (i) It does not generalize beyond syntax, so it misses the similarities between syntactic projectivity and non-linguistic ordering.
  (ii) It wrongly rules out sentences like (61), where *John* depends on *died* (as well as on *has*), but is separated from it by *has*, a word which is not subordinate to it.

  (61)   John has died.

Analysis B. The No-tangling Principle (Hudson 1998: 20) requires every word to have at least one parent to which it is linked by an arrow which does not tangle with any other arrow. For all its intuitive attractiveness, this principle fails because:

  (a) Like the Adjacency Principle, it does not generalize beyond syntax.
  (b) It does not explain the badness of examples like *Red drink wine* (meaning: *Drink red wine*) unless we assume an otherwise unmotivated arrow pointing at the root word, *drink*.
  (c) It does not apply to coordinate structures such as Figure 3.15.

The analysis in terms of landmark transitivity avoids all these problems.

The next research question is how to distinguish dependencies which are relevant to word order from those that are not. This question arises when a word has more than one parent, as in (61) above (*John has died*) where both *has* and *died* are parents of *John*. The analysis is hardly controversial, since it reflects the structure-sharing associated in most syntactic theories with

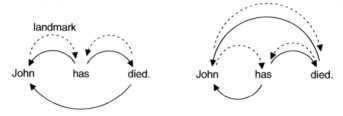

FIGURE 3.16.   Correct and incorrect analyses of a raising structure

'raising' structures. The structure I assume is shown in the first diagram in Figure 3.16, where the link to *John's* 'higher' parent, *has,* is taken as the one which defines its landmark. In contrast, the second diagram shows an analysis which is impossible because the landmarks defy landmark transitivity: *John* precedes *has,* but its landmark *died* follows it. Although they both have the same order of words, the first structure is the only possibility.

Examples like this suggest a very general principle which I have called the Raising Principle (Hudson 2000*b*) and which roughly speaking claims that 'raising' is possible, but 'lowering' is not—a very familiar idea from generative grammar (Richards 2004). We shall see later that this can in fact be expressed as an ordinary network 'rule' with the usual possibility of exceptions.

(62)   The **Raising Principle**. If a word has more than one parent, then its landmark is the parent which is superordinate to all the other parents.

Thus in *John has died,* the two verbs are both parents of *John,* but *has* is chosen as its landmark because it is superordinate to *died.* (X is **superordinate** to Y if Y depends on X or if Y depends on a subordinate of X—in other words, if Y is lower in a chain of dependencies than X.) The Raising Principle explains, for example, the difference between (63) and (64).

(63)   Finished John has.
(64)   *John finished has.

In (63), *John* takes its usual position before *has,* its highest parent, even though its lowest parent (*finished*) has been displaced to the left; but in (64), it is from the lowest parent that *John* takes its position. The Raising Principle predicts correctly that this is impossible. The relevant structures are shown in Figure 3.17, in which the first two diagrams take *has* as the landmark of *John,* as required by the Raising Principle, while the third diagram incorrectly has *finished* as landmark of *John.*

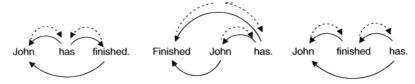

FIGURE 3.17.   Subjects may be raised but not lowered

The Raising Principle also predicts that when two parents are interdependent, either may act as the landmark. This situation is fairly rare, but is found in English WH questions (Hudson 2003*d*), where the wh-pronoun and finite verb depend on each other. For example, in *Who came?*, *who* depends on *came* by virtue of its subject link, but *came* depends on *who* because an interrogative pronoun has a tensed verb as its complement—a dependency which is particularly clear when the tensed verb is elided, as in (65).

(65)   A   Somebody came.
        B   Who?

Because the wh-pronoun depends on the finite verb, it may be preceded by a front-shifted adjunct as in (66).

(66)   Tomorrow, what shall we do?

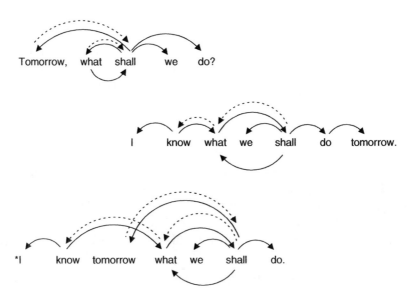

FIGURE 3.18.   Why adverb-fronting is impossible in dependent WH interrogatives

In this case, both *tomorrow* and *what* take *shall* as their landmark. However, in subordinate wh-interrogatives, this structure is ruled out because *what* has to follow *shall* so landmark transitivity requires *tomorrow* to do likewise.

(67)   I know what we shall do tomorrow.
(68)   *I know tomorrow what we shall do.

Figure 3.18 only shows the relevant dependencies and landmarks. In the first diagram, *shall* is the landmark for *what*, which explains why *tomorrow* can also have *shall* as its landmark; in contrast, the second diagram has to show *what* as the landmark for *shall* in order to explain why *what* in turn has *know* as its landmark; but the third diagram shows that these landmarks prevent *tomorrow* from having *shall* as its landmark.

The Raising Principle is well motivated by examples such as these. Unfortunately, there are also reasons for believing that it does not apply to every structure in every language. The clearest counter-evidence comes from so-called 'partial VP fronting' in German, where structures like the ungrammatical (64), **John finished has*, are in fact grammatical. I start with some background information about German clause structure.

(69)   Eine Concorde ist hier nie   gelandet.
      A   Concord   is   here   never   landed
      'A Concord has never landed here.'
(70)   Hier ist eine Concorde nie gelandet.
(71)   *Hier eine Concorde ist nie gelandet.

Example (70) is an ordinary example of a verb-second German sentence in which the finite verb (the auxiliary *ist*) follows just one of its dependents (*hier*). The pre-verbal dependent need not be the subject but only one such dependent is allowed, so (71) is absolutely ungrammatical. The pre-verbal dependent may be a participle, as in (72), and the pre-verbal participle may bring some of its dependents forward with it, as in (73).

(72)   Gelandet ist eine Concorde hier nie.
(73)   Hier gelandet ist eine Concorde nie.

The crucial examples here (from Haider 1990) are (74) and (75), in which the participle is accompanied by its subject.

(74)   Eine Concorde gelandet ist hier nie.
(75)   Zwei Concordes gelandet sind hier nie.
      two Concords landed are here never
      'Two Concords have never landed here.'

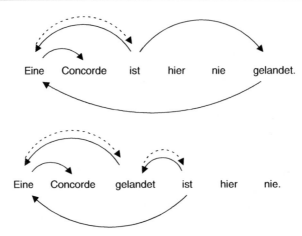

FIGURE 3.19.   German partial VP fronting

Examples like these are crucial because the shared subject (e.g. *eine Concorde*) clearly takes its position from the participle, rather than from the finite auxiliary; notice how the verb agreement shows unambiguously that the first noun phrase really is the subject of the finite verb (*ist* or *sind*).

These examples contradict the Raising Principle because the shared subject takes its position from the lower of its two parents; consequently, the subject must have 'lowered' from the auxiliary to the participle. The relevant dependencies of (69) and (74) are shown in Figure 3.19, contrasting the raising pattern in *eine Concorde ist … gelandet* with the lowering one in *eine Concorde gelandet ist…*.

The conclusion that I draw from the German data is that although raising is normal, exceptions are possible. As Haider points out, even German generally forbids lowering, and only allows it in exceptional circumstances—for example, with verbs that have 'very low transitivity', with meanings such as 'land'—so by default, word order does follow the Raising Principle. This conclusion suggests that raising is a default pattern, so it is learned from experience but can be overridden. Perhaps the name 'Raising Principle' is misleading because it is not a 'principle' in the sense of (say) Chomsky's theory of 'Principles and Parameters', where principles are outside the grammar but control the way in which the grammar is applied. It would be more accurate to describe Raising as a 'rule' just like the other generalizations in the grammar. This is reassuring because WG has no way to express 'principles', whereas rules are easy; so we can replace the Raising Principle (62) by rule (76):

(76) **Subordinate parents are not landmarks.** If a word has more than one parent, then its lower parents do not act as its landmarks.

This rule can be built into a network as in Figure 3.20, where as usual the dotted arrows are landmark relations, the solid arrows are dependencies, and the lower triangle of dependencies defines a particular kind of dependency in which a word depends on a co-dependent. This diagram in effect allows lower dependents to inherit the landmark relation, but then suppresses this by giving it the zero quantity allowed in section 1.3. German Partial VP is an exception to the rule of Raising, so it must be stipulated as such by a rule which overrides the sub-default at the bottom of Figure 3.20 by turning the o back into a default 1.

I should draw attention to an unresolved problem where the newly formulated Raising rule may be helpful. It concerns the syntactic relation between determiners and common nouns such as *this book*. I have argued that these words depend on each other in just the same way as we saw above for *Who came?* (Hudson 2004a); for example, the head word is the common noun in phrases like *last night* (which are allowed to occur as adjuncts without a preposition), but it is the determiner in phrases where the common noun may be elided (e.g. *I liked this (book)*). However, word order shows none of the flexibility that we saw in interrogative clauses, and consistently treats the determiner as head: if *book* takes *this* as its preceding landmark, any dependent of *book* must do the same, hence the badness of **big this book*. If the

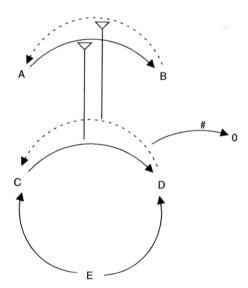

FIGURE 3.20. The Raising rule as a network

Raising rule allows stipulated exceptions, then at least we can stipulate that determiners never take their complement common nouns as landmark. However I have to admit that this stipulation is quite unsatisfying because the same seems to be true of determiners in so many other languages. I hope future research will be able to produce a better solution.

To summarize the WG theory of word order described so far, it has the following components:

- **Ordinary dependencies,** which typically (but not always) carry meaning and other inter-word relations such as selection and agreement.
- A 'landmark' relation, which is subdivided into 'before' and 'after' and is transitive; it is this transitivity that keeps all the words in a phrase together.
  - A '**Parents are landmarks**' rule (51): a word's parent (the word on which it depends) is its landmark.
  - A '**Subordinate parents are not landmarks**' rule (76) which handles most cases where a word has two or more parents by blocking the landmark role on lower parents—i.e. which favours raising rather than lowering. This rule takes priority over the first rule but may itself be overridden by specific rules for lowering.
- Some **extra dependencies** such as Extractee and Extraposee which always combine with 'ordinary' dependencies and have the effect of 'raising' a word so that it depends on its grandparent (or higher ancestor) as well as on its own parent.

There is just one more element in the current theory. This is another kind of extra dependency, which allows a word (as it were) to delegate its grammatical function to its parent—another kind of raising in which a word functions in a higher construction than it otherwise would. Most of the work in this area of WG has been done by Rosta, who has introduced a number of suggestive terms such as '**proxy**' or 'surrogate' (Rosta 1997, 2006) to complement the term 'projection' which I introduced (Hudson 1990: 367). A good example of this 'delegating' dependency is the dependency which allows the prepositional pied-piping in (77):

(77)   The person with whom she works is a tyrant.

The challenge is to explain why *with* stands at the start of the relative clause just as though it were a relative pronoun, and the explanation obviously builds on the fact that its complement is in fact a relative pronoun, *whom*. The WG solution is to recognize *with* as the 'proxy' of *whom*, the word to which *whom* 'delegates' its role as relative pronoun. In other words, the

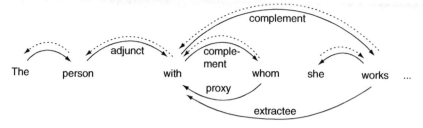

FIGURE 3.21.   A proxy in prepositional pied-piping

extractee in a relative clause is either a relative pronoun (e.g. *whom*) or the proxy of a relative pronoun (as in *with whom*). The relevant part of (77) is shown in Figure 3.21.

I should like to finish by applying the WG analytical system to a particularly challenging set of data from the Mexican language Zapotec which Broadwell has presented as evidence for Optimality Theory (Broadwell 1999). I have already offered one WG account of these data (Hudson 2003c), but I can now offer a much simpler one which uses just the relations Proxy and Landmark. The challenge lies in the details of Zapotec prepositional pied-piping, but first we must consider some background facts; all the examples are from Broadwell's article.

The language is head-initial, with basic V S O clause order:

(78)   Ù-díny Juàny bè'cw cùn   yàg.
       C-hit   John   dog   with stick
       'John hit the dog with a stick.'

('C' is a comitative prefix which is irrelevant here.) The structure for this sentence is presumably self-evident. The head-initial order is summarized in rule (79):

(79)   A word's parent is its After—i.e. it follows its parent.

As in English, interrogative pronouns are front-shifted, so we can assume that as in English they receive an Extractee dependency which requires exceptional pre-head order. An example is (80), whose structure can be assumed to be as

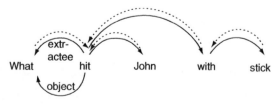

FIGURE 3.22.   Zapotec extraction

in Figure 3.22 (where I replace Zapotec words by their English translation equivalents).

(80) Tú   ù-díny Juàny cùn yàg?
      what C-hit   John   with stick
      'What did John hit with a stick?'

So far Zapotec fits easily into the patterns familiar from other languages. What makes it especially interesting is the treatment of more complex front-shifted phrases, illustrated by the following examples:

(81) a <u>Xhí</u>   <u>cùn</u>   ù-díny   Juàny bè'cw?
        what   with   com-hit   John   dog
        'What did John hit the dog with?'
     b <u>Tú</u>   <u>x-pè'cw</u> cù'à   Juàny?
        who   poss-dog   com-grab John
        'Whose dog did John grab?'
     c <u>Tú</u>   <u>bè'cw</u>   cù'à   Juàny?
        which   dog   com-grab John
        'Which dog did John grab?'

(The two interrogative words Xhí and Tú are distinguished by animacy rather than word-class.) In each case the order given is the only one possible within the fronted phrase (which is underlined), but in each case this is the reverse of the normal phrasal order, where prepositions usually precede their complement and possessors and demonstratives follow the head noun. It is easy to see a functional advantage of this pattern: as in its English equivalent, it allows pied-piping, in which the whole of the questioned element is fronted, rather than merely the question word itself; but unlike English, it also keeps the wh-word at the start of the clause so that the hearer knows immediately that the coming clause is a question. On the other hand, the Zapotec pattern involves a double disruption of the normal order, so it is not surprising that it is so unusual.

The WG analysis of the data given so far is quite straightforward. As in English, a proxy rule applies, though the details are slightly different from English:

(82) If an interrogative word's parent is a noun or preposition, then it is the
      interrogative word's proxy.

(Zapotec does not allow stranded prepositions, so this rule is obligatory.)

(83) The extractee of a verb may be either an interrogative pronoun or the proxy of one.

For example, in (81a), 'what' depends on 'with' but the latter is its proxy and therefore acts as extractee of 'hit'; this is why the preposition is front-shifted along with its interrogative complement. Unlike English, however, the order of the question word and its proxy is reversed: the default head-initial order of (79) is overridden by Before. This reversed word order is expressed in the crucial rule in (84):

(84) A word's proxy is its Before—i.e. the word is positioned before its proxy.

In the examples considered so far, the interrogative word has caused the fronting of a single word: a preposition ('what with') or a noun ('what stick'). The really interesting data are sentences in which these possibilities combine, so that the fronted phrase means 'with what stick'. In this case, of course, there is no direct dependency between the interrogative 'what' and the preposition 'with', so the usual rule for assigning Proxy in (82) does not apply; and yet (as in English) the preposition may in fact be fronted as well. Consequently, the proxy rule needs to be expanded:

(85) If an interrogative word's parent, or its proxy's parent, is a noun or preposition, then it is the interrogative word's proxy.

In other words, 'what' may have two proxies at the same time: its own parent 'stick', and also the latter's parent, 'with'.

With this proxy analysis in place, we can now turn to the word-order facts in these examples. How does rule (84) apply to a word that has not one proxy but two? The answer depends on whether we interpret it as applying to both proxies or just to one of them. If the word precedes both the proxies, we have just one order: 'what with stick'. But if it precedes either of them, we have two possible word orders: 'what with stick' and 'with what stick'—which is, in fact, exactly what Zapotec allows. 'Which' may precede 'with':

(86) Xhí   cùn   yàg   ù-díny Juàny bè'cw?
      which with   stick hit   John   dog
      'With which stick did John hit the dog?'

Or it may precede 'stick':

(87) Cùn   xhí   yàg   ù-díny Juàny bè'cw?
      with   which stick hit   John   dog
      'With which stick did John hit the dog?'

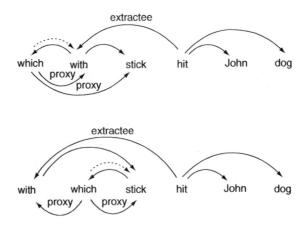

FIGURE 3.23.   Multiple proxies in Zapotec

No other order is possible, which confirms that this analysis is probably on the right lines. The relevant dependencies in these two structures are shown in Figure 3.23.

This section has focused mostly on the strengths of the WG account of word order, but there are also research questions that I cannot yet answer. One question is whether the ordering should apply to words or to forms. In this section I have assumed that it applies to the words themselves, so each word takes another word as its landmark. However, there are two reasons for considering an alternative analysis in which ordering is a property of forms rather than the words they realize.

1 The discussion of clitics in section 2.9 showed that the special position of some clitics is best explained by morphological rules which locate them inside a larger host-form. Morphological rules apply to forms rather than to words, so at least these order rules apply to forms, and maybe more generally they all do.
2 I shall suggest in section 3.7 that ellipsis involves words that have no form to realize them. One of the potential problems of this kind of analysis is to decide whether inaudible and invisible words have a position and if they do, how to identify it; the freer the word order, the more serious this problem becomes. But if it is forms rather than words that have a position, this problem disappears.

A more demanding question is how best to account for the 'sister-ordering' discussed earlier in relation to examples such as (52) and (53). For example, why does a verb's subject have to precede its 'pre-adjuncts' (non-extracted adverbs)?

(88)   John never smokes.

(89)   *Never John smokes.

This question goes to the heart of the difference between dependency and phrase structure, and it might appear to favour phrase structure. A typical PS answer will involve some kind of VP node, to which *never* attaches (by adjunction) before it is combined (by predication) with the subject; so in terms of landmarks, we would say that the landmark of *John* was *never smokes* whereas for *never* it was just *smokes*. This offers an explanation for the order which is not available in a dependency analysis, where *John* and *never* both have the same landmark. The only option in a dependency analysis is to stipulate the order. However, it would be wrong to see this as a choice between explanation and stipulation because the PS answer simply postpones the stipulation. Why should *never* be attached to VP rather than to the whole sentence? This cannot be predicted from the semantics because the scope is the whole sentence, and in any case the position varies from language to language; so the grammar of English must stipulate that adverbs such as *never* are adjoined before a VP. Moreover, the more hierarchical the structure is, the harder it is to handle free order (which of course is very easy in a flat dependency structure). In short, a phrase-structure treatment of word order has its own problems.

It is easy to stipulate sister-ordering, but stipulation does not deepen our understanding so it is always important to seek more general explanations. This is certainly an area where WG needs a great deal more research.

3.3 Selection and Constructions

One of the main developments during the 1990s was the sharpened contrast in views over the status of 'constructions'. On the one hand, Chomsky and his followers rejected the traditional focus in grammar on constructions in which

each language is a rich and intricate system of rules that are, typically, construction-particular and language-particular: the rules forming verb phrases or passives or relative clauses in English, for example, are specific to *these* constructions in *this* language ... The more recent principles-and-parameters (P&P) approach, assumed here, breaks radically with this tradition, ... The notion of grammatical construction is eliminated, and with it, construction-particular rules. Constructions such as verb phrase, relative clause and passive remain only as taxonomic artefacts, collections of phenomena explained through the interaction of the principles of UG, with the values of parameters fixed. (Chomsky 1995*b*: 170).

On the other hand, most cognitive linguists (Bates 1998; Croft 2001; Fillmore, Kay, and O'Connor 1988; Goldberg 1995; Kay and Fillmore 1999; Kay 2002;

Kuzar 1998; Michaelis and Lambrecht 1996; Tomasello 1998) put increasing emphasis on the study of constructions as the basic units of syntax: 'basic sentences of English are instances of *constructions*—form-meaning correspondences that exist independently of particular verbs' (Goldberg 1995: 1). In this view, constructions are more general than individual lexical items, but much less general than the very abstract parameters and patterns that Chomsky envisages.

I believe that this disagreement is a matter of substance rather than mere terminology or taste. The opposing sides are using the word *construction* with much the same meaning: a combination of syntactic and semantic patterning, such as 'relative clause' or 'passive'. And although they may have different interests, they both recognize the need, in the long run, to account for detail and generalization in the same theoretical package. The question is whether a grammar of English (or any other language) recognizes such specific categories as relative clauses and passive verbs. Moreover, since both camps are trying to model linguistic competence, this question must translate into a question about cognitive structures: do native speakers of English recognize relative clauses, passive verbs, and so on as distinct concepts? Ultimately, then, it should be possible to resolve the argument by psychological experiments, but meanwhile we can make some progress by combining psychological theory with linguistic observation.

In terms of psychological theory, the disagreement boils down to the question of how grammar is acquired—do we inherit it genetically, as Chomsky claims, or do we learn it inductively, as assumed by cognitive linguists? If we learn it (as I believe we do—see s. 1.8), then constructions are an inevitable by-product of the learning, even if we then abstract even more general patterns. (For example, I assume that we recognize passive verbs as a subclass of 'participle', which isa 'non-finite'.)

In terms of linguistic facts, it is very easy to demonstrate that constructions have peculiarities that must be stored in the mind. For example, English relative clauses have a distribution which is slightly different from that of French relative clauses. On the one hand, ordinary English relative clauses may modify the word *everything* as in (90), whereas the French equivalent in (91) can only be modified by a free relative introduced by *ce* as well as the usual relative pronoun.

(90)   Everything that I bought was dear.

(91)   Tout   *(ce)   que   j'   ai   acheté   était   cher
       All   that   what I   have bought   was   dear
       'Everything I bought was dear.'

On the other hand, French is more liberal than English in its use of relative clauses after verbs of perception, where French uses full finite relative clauses (92) but English only allows reduced participial relative clauses (93).

(92) Je l'   ai   vu   qui   sortait.
      I   him   have   seen   who   was going out
      'I saw him going out.'
(93) I saw him (*who was) going out.

The question is whether such details as these can be shown to follow either from more general differences between the languages, or from lexical idio-syncracies. At this point the outcome is simply a matter of faith, and my personal belief is that no such explanation will be possible. Moreover, the facts are very easy to learn from experience—indeed, they are precisely the kind of facts that would be expected in a usage-based theory of learning—so they support the view of learning which is associated with constructions.

In short, I believe that the syntax of a language does in fact consist of a very large number of constructions, each with its own peculiar interactions with other constructions and with lexical items. This means that the syntax is basically a rather messy collection of inductive generalizations on which we impose some order by generalization, rather than a small set of very simple, very abstract, and very elegantly interacting patterns on which the imperfections of language have imposed some mess. Since we obviously cope with a great deal of mess in the rest of cognition, I see no reason not to assume the same for language. Seen from this standpoint, we can admire the degree to which language is orderly; whereas those who expect perfection struggle with reality.

Sem	CAUSE-RECEIVE	< agt	rec	pat >
R: instance, means	PRED	<		>
Syn	V	SUBJ	OBJ	OBJ$_2$

Sem	CAUSE-RECEIVE	< agt	rec	pat >
R: instance, means	HAND	<hander	handee	handed>
Syn	V	SUBJ	OBJ	OBJ$_2$

FIGURE 3.24. The ditransitive construction in Construction Grammar

The obvious question for Word Grammar is how it can accommodate constructions, given that these tend to be thought of in terms of phrase structure. For example, in Construction Grammar a construction is a frame which contains two or more syntactic elements (e.g. a verb and its subject and object) each of which is paired with an element of semantic structure. Figure 3.24 is taken from Goldberg 1995: 50–1. The top box is the ditransitive construction, with a row at the bottom for the construction's syntactic parts, another row at the top for the general semantic roles of these parts, and a middle row waiting to be filled in with more specific semantic roles. The lower box shows the result of adding the details for the lexical item *hand*, which is an instance of V and whose meaning is an instance of PRED.

This analysis is very easily matched in WG, where the absence of phrase structure is an advantage rather than a disadvantage. If we stick tightly to the spirit of Goldberg's diagrams, we get the frighteningly complicated WG network in Figure 3.25. However, thanks to inheritance, the WG network could be very much simpler than this. As soon as we classify HAND as an example of a ditransitive verb, all its syntactic and semantic dependencies may be inherited. Moreover, ditransitive verbs inherit the default mapping between subject and agent from the entry for Verb; and if we classify Ditransitive as a subclass of Transitive, it inherits objects and their default mapping to

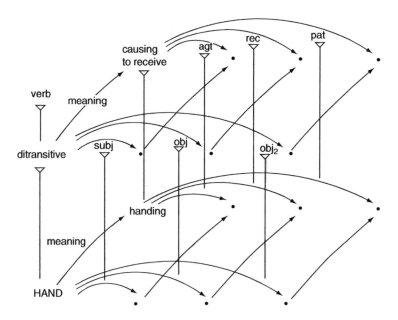

FIGURE 3.25.   A WG analysis of ditransitive HAND

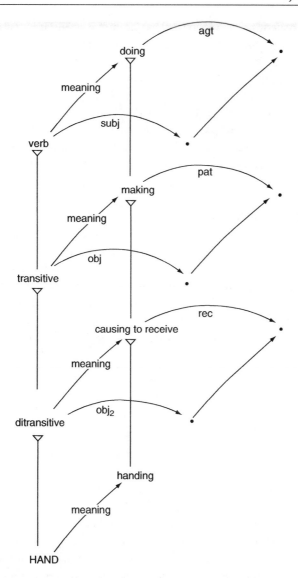

FIGURE 3.26.   An improved WG analysis of ditransitive HAND

patients. With these changes, the WG network now looks like Figure 3.26.
Notice that the ditransitive construction has been analysed into three different
constructions, each consisting of one verb class and one dependency. There is
no single 'frame' which holds them all together into a single construction
because there is no need for one. What holds the three parts together is
inheritance, not phrase structure.

The constructions of Construction Grammar translate easily into WG dependency structures, as can be seen in great detail in Holmes 2005. A typical dependency type is defined in relation to some relatively general word-class; for example, it is verbs that have a subject and transitive verbs that have an object. In 1984, I argued against word-classes such as 'transitive verb' on the grounds that they are only united by a single property, so the class of verbs that happen to have an object is no more useful than the class of things that happen to be red (Hudson 1984: 110). I still believe that categories are justified by their ability to reflect correlated properties, so every category must combine at least two properties; but I no longer think that 'transitive verb' breaks this principle. The reason is that transitive verbs not only have an object, but they also map this object onto a particular semantic role. In relation to constructions, therefore, the WG claim is that every construction consists of a particular configuration of words related by dependencies defined in terms of more or less specific types of word and dependency.

Another tenet of Construction Grammar is that constructions can be extremely selective in terms of the lexical items which they tolerate. For example, Kay and Fillmore 1999 give a detailed analysis of a construction which they call *What's X doing Y?* (or WXDY for short), as found in examples like (94) to (95):

(94)   What is this scratch doing on the table?
(95)   What do you think your name is doing in my book?
(96)   What is it doing raining?

As they point out, the syntax of these examples follows very general patterns, but the lexical meaning of the construction itself is limited to the words *what*, BE, and *doing*. On the other hand, X and Y are completely free.

Kay and Fillmore offer an analysis in terms of Construction Grammar, but their analysis translates easily into WG (Holmes and Hudson 2006). Indeed, a dependency analysis is far more appropriate where one word selects another word lexically because all the relations are between single words; in contrast, phrasal nodes simply get in the way. For example, in WG the word *rely* is directly linked to the preposition that it selects, *on*, whereas phrase structure separates them with a prepositional-phrase node. Similarly, the WG analysis of WXDY links the head word *what* directly to its dependent BE and the latter directly to *doing*. The semantic peculiarity is due to the fact that each of these words is a special sub-case of the general lexeme, with a special meaning; for example, WHAT$_{wxdy}$ has the peculiarity of taking BE$_{wxdy}$ as its complement, as well as the peculiarity of meaning what Kay and Fillmore call 'incongruity-judgement'. A WG analysis is shown in Figure 3.27.

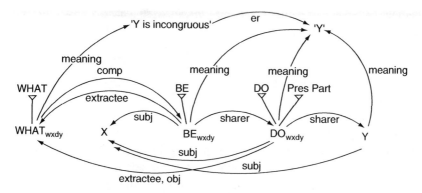

FIGURE 3.27.   A WG analysis of the What's X doing Y construction

The main point of this section has been to show how WG can accommodate both the generalizations and the idiosyncratic behaviour which have
been subjected to detailed discussion in Construction Grammar. I return to
the analysis of constructions in section 3.5; more detailed discussion of a wider
range of examples can be found in Holmes and Hudson 2006.

3.4 Agreement and Features

Agreement rules are important for the theory of classification, because they
are the best evidence we have for morphosyntactic **features** such as gender
and number. As I explained in section 2.2, features are a kind of relation which
has no special status in WG; a person's sex and nationality (which might be
called features) are among their properties alongside their name, their job,
and their mother. The same is true in language, where a word's gender or
number (traditionally called features) are treated in much the same way as its
meaning, its form, and its syntactic valents. But what features are **not** used for
in WG (in contrast with most other theories) is classification; for this we use
Isa links. For example, past and present verbs can be distinguished satisfactorily in the Isa hierarchy of word-types so there is no need to invoke a
separate contrast of 'tense'.

What role does this leave for features? Consider the case of how we classify
physical objects. Some dimensions of classification emerge as salient, and can
be expressed in terms of distinctive adjectives such as *big, round, red, expen-
sive,* and *nice;* and some of these are arranged neatly in contrast-sets—that is,
features—which are named by nouns such as *size, shape,* and *colour.* But not
all contrast-sets have convenient established names (as opposed to nonce
creations with {ness} such as *expensiveness* and *niceness*), and not all adjectives

belong to convenient contrast-sets (e.g. *linguistic, shadowy, chunky*). In short, features are a convenient mental construct that we create for some sets of contrasting characteristics, but not for all. The same seems to be true in language. Features are real mental constructs for which there is good evidence, but by no means all contrastive characteristics are organized in terms of features.

As I asserted at the start of this section, the best evidence that we have for features in syntax is agreement; indeed, I believe this may be the only evidence that we have. Consider the agreement rule in English which requires a determiner to agree in number with its complement common noun, giving *this book* and *these books*, but ruling out **these book* and **this books*. If we can assume that the feature Number contrasts the values Singular and Plural, then the rule is easy to formulate:

(97) A pronoun and its complement must have the same (value for the feature) number.

But without this feature, the rule is at best difficult to formulate, and at worst impossible—especially if we hope for a revealing analysis. The main point of agreement rules is the identity of values, so it is essential to have an analysis which reveals this identity (rather than one which, say, stipulates that singular in one place requires singular in the other). Identity is easy to express in a network, and we already have many precedents for it in syntax—for example, the rule that the subject of a verb such as WILL is identical to the subject of its 'sharer' complement. This rule is diagrammed in Figure 3.28, alongside the diagram for rule (97). However, identity presupposes some set of relations which have non-identical arguments but identical values. In the case of the agreement rule, this relation is the feature Number, without which the rule could not be expressed.

The conclusion so far, therefore, is that a feature is a relation between some entity and a value, fully comparable with other relations such as Subject. However, there is one respect in which features are special: the range of possible values is restricted to a short list defined in the network, in contrast, for example, with the relation Subject, whose values are open-ended.

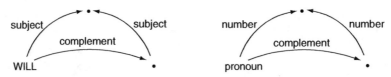

FIGURE 3.28. Structure sharing and agreement are similar

Feature-like relations occur outside language, of course, with sex as a classic example of a two-valued opposition; and multi-valued features are found in language, with Bantu gender and Finno-Ugric case systems as the classic examples. Consequently it would be hard to argue that the formal properties of feature systems are peculiar to language so we can assume that the cognitive mechanism for handling them is freely available to any language learner.

This mechanism must list a number of alternative values, which can be achieved in WG by treating the alternatives as a set. (We shall consider the theoretical basis for sets in a little more detail in s. 5.5.) A set has members which may be defined either extensionally, by listing all the members, or intensionally, by providing properties of the typical member; in the case of feature values, we clearly need an extensional definition (e.g. the members of Number-set are Singular and Plural). The value for a noun's number is one or the other of these: Singular by default, and Plural if it is a plural noun. Figure 3.29 adds these links to the morphosyntactic analysis in Figure 2.5.

This analysis not only lists the possible values, but also maps them onto the Isa hierarchy and does so in such a way as to reveal their markedness relations. Since these feature-values only have one role in the grammar—handling agreement—they can be assigned entirely according to the needs of agreement. For example, English subject-verb agreement does not exactly follow the singular-plural contrast, because singular *I* and *you* take verb forms that are otherwise reserved for plural nouns (*I/you/we/they go*, but *he/she goes*). In a detailed analysis of these and other facts (Hudson 1999) I argue that the best

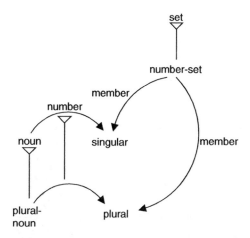

FIGURE 3.29.   A noun's number is singular or plural

way to accommodate these two pronouns is to assign them plural number (as exceptional nouns alongside the general subcategory Plural-noun). As I point out there, there is no real conflict between this number and their other properties precisely because number carries no properties of its own.

To summarize this section, features are available in WG when needed, but in grammar they are only needed for agreement rules. (I have said nothing about phonology, but since this is where the notion of features started in modern linguistics, it seems more than likely that they play some role there too.) A feature can be modelled quite straightforwardly as a relation between some entity and one member of a fixed set of values. However, features are not a mechanism for classification, as such; rather, they are properties which contribute to a classification on just the same footing as other properties.

3.5 Dependency Types and Constructions

Much of the complexity in syntax is handled in terms of default inheritance, which allows 'marked' constructions to be treated as partial exceptions to the 'unmarked' defaults (Hudson 2003c). This mechanism allows WG to dispense with both movement rules and rich feature structures. Default inheritance has the great attraction of being well attested outside language, so I believe it is the right mechanism to invoke if we can get away with it. The fact is that syntactic structure is complicated, and this complexity has to be accommodated by any serious theory of syntactic structure. In WG, the complexity lies in the rich network of dependencies that shows all the syntactic relations between the words in a sentence. One of the complications in this structure is the rather elaborate classification of dependencies in a hierarchy of 'types' (e.g. 'subject', 'object'); and another is that two or more dependencies may converge on the same word. The main focus of the present section is the classification of dependency types but we shall consider some convergent patterns as well.

In broad outline I still favour the analysis of dependency types that I presented in 1990 (Hudson 1990: 208), but more recent work allows it to be developed somewhat. For convenience, the 1990 analysis is shown in Figure 3.30, with small changes of terminology ('visitor' is replaced by 'extractee' and 'pre-dependent' and 'post-dependent' now have a hyphen).

I should like to start by clarifying the status of this analysis. First, the distinction between pre-dependents and post-dependents is not meant to be universal. As with virtually everything else in WG, this analysis is meant to model what any native speaker can learn, so every category has to be learnable from the evidence in the language concerned. The categories Pre-dependent and Post-dependent only apply to a language such as English

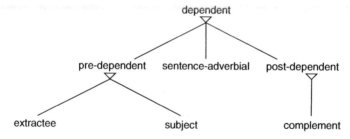

FIGURE 3.30. The main dependency types in 1990

where some dependents point in one direction but a significant proportion point in the other direction; as I commented in 3.2, this distinction is not needed for consistently head-initial or head-final languages.

Moreover, the fact that this contrast appears at the top of the hierarchy reflects accurately an interesting fact about English (which, I guess, may be true of many other languages as well): that it is 'consistently mixed'. What I mean by this apparently contradictory term is that the pre-/post-dependent contrast applies to almost every word-class. It is easy to imagine a language in which words of one class always follow their dependents while those in another always precede them. The result would be a mixed-order language, but so far as I know this is not a common typological pattern. In languages such as English, not only verbs but at least some words of every major word-class allow both pre– and post-dependents, as can be seen from Table 3.5. As noted in section 3.1, there is a strong tendency to minimize dependency distance in order to reduce the memory load on hearers; but consistently head-final or initial orders work against this because every dependent but one must be separated from the head word by the other dependents. In contrast, a mixed order such as SVO allows two dependents both to be immediately next to the

TABLE 3.5. pre- and post-dependents across word classes in English

Word class of head	Example		
	Pre-dependent	Head	Post-dependent
verb	John	saw	Mary
common noun	big	book	about linguistics
adjective	very	happy	to see you
adverb	very	soon	afterwards
preposition	*just*	*before*	Christmas

head word (though another solution, noted in s. 3.1, is to allow dependents to be freely suppressed). It is striking that languages which adopt the mixed solution for one word class often apply it to other word classes as well.

To return to the analysis in Figure 3.30, one of its more controversial characteristics is the absence of a distinct category of 'adjuncts'. In this analysis, adjuncts are simply default dependents. This conclusion was based (Hudson 1990: 208) on the fact that almost all of the criteria for distinguishing adjuncts from complements involve some peculiarity of complements (e.g. complements are limited in number or have a form selected by the head word); in contrast, adjuncts are dependents that lack these peculiarities, which means that they only have default properties. The peculiarities of complements that I listed in 1990 are as follows:

- The possibility of a complement varies with the lexical item acting as head: with some head words a complement may be obligatory, with others optional and with yet others impossible.
- Only one complement of a particular type is permitted for each head word.
- The head word may select the complement either lexically (as when a verb selects a particular preposition) or inflectionally (as when a verb selects a particular case).
- A word's complements are closer to it (in terms of word order) than its adjuncts are.
- A word generally determines the semantic role of each complement (e.g. the objects of LIKE and EAT have different semantic roles), whereas default dependents determine their own semantic role (e.g. AFTER and BEFORE have similar but contrasting semantic roles).
- Complements are typically nouns, which give very little information about their semantic role.
- A word's complements are integrated semantically with it before other dependents are added; e.g. *He wrote the book quickly* refers to a quick example of writing a book (quicker than the norm for book-writing) rather than to an example of writing quickly (such as speed-typing) applied to a book.

The prototypical complement is the direct object, so *saw Mary* shows nearly all these characteristics:

- The complement *Mary* is obligatory.
- It is unrepeatable.
- It is closer than any potential adjuncts (e.g. *saw Mary yesterday*, not *saw yesterday Mary*).
- It fills a semantic role provided by *saw*.

- It is a noun.
- It is integrated into the semantic structure before any potential adjunct is added.

The only missing complement feature is lexical or inflectional selection.

More generally, as I pointed out in 1990: 206, 'the form and function of the complement are fixed by the head (whether idiosyncratically or by general rule), but the adjunct fixes its own form and function'. Expressed more elegantly in terms of inheritance, this means that it is from the head word that a complement dependency is inherited; for example, the object relation between *saw* and *Mary* in *John saw Mary* is inherited from *saw*, not from *Mary*. In contrast, an adjunct dependency is inherited from the dependent word; for example, in *left recently*, the dependency is entirely inherited from *recently*, which:

- needs a parent,
- requires its parent to be a non-adjective,
- provides a time for its parent's semantics.

The first of these characteristics is simply that of a typical word, since the default word needs a parent (but not a dependent). Consequently, in the absence of any extra restrictions, the default word is an adjunct of some other word, so the default dependent must also be an adjunct. If '(default) dependent' and 'adjunct' are the same thing, we can—indeed, must—do without one of them, so I have discarded 'adjunct'. This conclusion is of course diametrically opposed to more familiar analyses in which adjuncts have a more complex structure than complements.

One reasonable objection to my 1990 analysis is that the peculiarities of complements are simply an automatic consequence of the way a grammar is organized. Given a dependency relation R between two words H (the head word) and D (the dependent), R is a property of both H and D so it must be generated by the grammar along with all the other properties of H and D (such as their meaning, their realization, and so on); in other words, the grammar must say that R is possible between H and D. The only mechanism for generating properties is by inheritance (combined, as needed, with spreading activation and binding), so R must be inherited as a property of H alone, of D alone, or of both H and D. Since every word requires a parent, at least some aspects of R must be inherited by D, but this might be all—R need not be one of H's inheritable properties at all. In this case, R is entirely inherited by D, and this is what we call an adjunct. The other possibility, of course, is that H does make some contribution, but since this may range from very little to very much (the most typical complement) we may expect either some kind of a continuum of 'complement-hood', or even a more or less random patterning of the features listed above. In either case, the category 'complement' adds nothing to the facts which are already available from the grammar.

This objection seems to receive support from the well-known problems of distinguishing complements from adjuncts (Allerton 1994; Somers 1984). For example, 'obligatory adjuncts' such as (98) and (99) lie half-way between the two.

(98)   She treated him *well*.
(99)   I put it *there*.

As complements, they are obligatory and they fill a semantic role provided by the head, but as adjuncts they themselves define this semantic role and their position is just the same as if they had been ordinary adjuncts. Conversely, there are what we might call 'non-selected complements' as in (100) and (101).

(100)   I lifted *up* my arms.
(101)   They beamed *up* the space ship.

These are ordinary 'particles', with just the same syntactic properties as the *up* in idiomatic examples like *give up smoking* or *look up the word*; in particular, they have a very special position in clause structure between the verb and its object, which are normally inseparable. Moreover, in all these examples an alternative position for the particle is after the object (*lifted my arms up, gave smoking up*, and so on). Presumably *up* is a complement in *give up smoking*, because it is selected by the verb GIVE when this means 'renounce'; so in such cases the particle is obligatory. But when it is used, with exactly the same syntax, after *lift* or *beam*, it looks much more like an adjunct because it is entirely optional and defines its own semantic role. Given the lack of syntactic differences, the two cases should presumably have the same syntactic structure, but the choice between adjunct and complement seems to oblige us to give different structures. One possible conclusion, therefore, is that the category 'complement' is just an informal idea from traditional grammar (comparable with, say, 'article'), and the only reality we need to recognize consists of the specific grammatical functions such as 'particle' or 'direct object'.

However, this is not my conclusion. 'This empirical diagnostic "problem" is, in fact, precisely what we should expect to find in natural language, when a proper understanding of the adjunct/complement distinction is achieved' (Dowty 2000). My explanation (though not Dowty's) is that 'complement' is in fact needed in a grammar, as a cover term for a number of more specific categories such as 'direct object', 'indirect object', and 'particle'. Each of these has typical members which have most, or all, of the default complement properties listed above, so these properties can be generalized across all complements; for example, the maximum number of a complement is one, so if 'object' isa complement, only one object is permitted per word. However, the logic of default inheritance allows exceptions—the borderline cases in which one or more of the defaults have been overridden. Indeed, it would be surprising if there were no exceptions, and it is very easy to see why the typical cases are extended as 'grammatical metaphors' (Halliday 2002: 345) to provide extra flexibility in the grammatical system. For example, once *up* is available as a selected particle, it would be very odd not to exploit it creatively; and similarly for all the constructions such as the direct object and resultative constructions which have recently been discussed so interestingly (Goldberg 1995; Levin and Rappaport Hovav 1991; Holmes 2005; Holmes and Hudson 2006).

In general, then, I still believe the 1990 analysis is correct, including the category Complement. However, it has a number of weaknesses, not least the treatment of Complement and Subject as unrelated categories. Subjects have all the characteristics of a typical complement—selected by the head, only one allowed per head word, and so on; so subjects and complements should have a special relation in the classification. Since 1990 I have started to use the term **Valent** (a dependent which is part of a word's 'valency') to cover both, distinguishing them lower down the hierarchy as pre-dependents (for subjects) and post-dependents (for complements). In the revised hierarchy, therefore, a specific relation such as Direct object isa Complement, which isa Valent and Post-dependent, each of which isa Dependent—a somewhat richer hierarchy than in the 1990 analysis. This richness may be seen in Figure 3.31, which also shows another growth-point: the development of non-valent

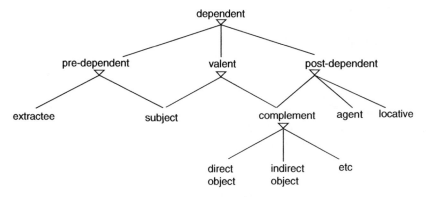

FIGURE 3.31. A revised hierarchy of dependency types

dependency types such as 'agent' and 'locative' which are needed for sentences such as (102) and (103).

(102)   He was run over *by* a bus.
(103)   *In* the garden stands an old shed.

Dependency types are highly relevant to the movement called 'construction grammar' which I discussed in section 3.3. This movement, with its emphasis on (possibly) idiosyncratic syntactic 'constructions', has raised the question of what kind of syntactic unit is best suited to describing such patterns as well as the more canonical ones. In general, the discussion has assumed the phrase-structure tradition of American linguistics, with the result that constructions are treated as phrase-types such as 'transitive verb phrase', but WG offers a promising alternative. Five characteristics seem particularly relevant:

1 Dependency structures are ideal for relating individual words (rather than whole phrases) directly to each other; for example, the idiom KICK THE BUCKET requires the lexeme KICK to be related directly to THE, and THE to BUCKET. In stating such relations, the apparatus of phrase structure is unhelpful because it obscures the word-to-word relations.

2 Dependency structures also avoid the problem of classifying non-canonical phrases such as *Off with his head! Oh for a bit of sunshine!* or *How about a cup of tea?* Part of the challenge is to explain why they can occur, without a verb, as complete sentences; but the solution is simply to stipulate that their head words (*with, for, about*) need no parent (contrary to the default rule).

3 A WG-style network of dependencies accommodates complex constructions such as the *What's X doing Y* construction (e.g. *What's your towel doing on the floor?*) discussed in section 3.3, where *what* is extracted and X is raised.

4 Default inheritance is ideal for handling the exceptional behaviour which characterizes so many constructions. For example, the archaic word orders of *come what may* or *come September* (meaning 'in September') can be stipulated while still recognizing the ordinary subject relation.

5 Richly classified dependency types help to relate these patterns to more general patterns. For example, in the *What's X doing Y* construction, all the dependencies belong to types which can be found in more general patterns, but each one is specialized in some way: so *what* is the object of *doing* but has the special property of being obligatorily extracted and lexically restricted to *what*. Moreover, the meaning of this object is quite different from the usual object of the verb DO. Classified dependencies combined

with default inheritance allow us to have the best of both worlds: to recognize similarities to regular patterns while also recognizing differences.

In short, WG offers just the right degree of flexibility for handling the messy fringe of idiosyncratic constructions as well as the central core of regularity (Holmes and Hudson 2006).

Having said this, however, a great deal of research remains to be done on dependency types. For example, I have assumed for some time that a passive subject is also the object of the passive verb; so in *He was chosen, he* is both the subject and the object of *chosen* (Hudson 1990: 336–53). This is important because it shows that a dependent's relation to its parent may involve two distinct dependency types. But if this is possible for passive subjects, what about other cases? Gisborne has argued persuasively that the ordinary dependency called 'subject' may in fact be decomposable into at least two separate dependencies which typically converge but which can be prised apart (Gisborne 2006). The crucial evidence comes from sentences like (104) (from Bresnan 1994).

(104)   It's in these villages that we all believe (*that) are found the best examples of this cuisine.

This example seems to contain two phrases which both qualify as subject of *are found*, represented respectively by *in these villages* and *the best examples of this cuisine*; but each is a different kind of subject. The former is the one that is sensitive to that-trace effects, which prevent it from being extracted across *that*; while the latter is the one with which the verb agrees. The former we might call 'topic' or 'first valent' and the latter 'pivot' or 'agreement valent', but whatever we call them, they seem to be different. If this is so, then the analysis of subjects needs a great deal of rethinking.

3.6 Mixed Categories

Since the logic of WG is multiple default inheritance (see 1.4), we should expect that some words will inherit from more than one word-class—in other words, we should predict the existence of 'mixed categories' (Malouf 2000). These are actually surprisingly easy to find in English. For example, the words MUCH and MANY (which may of course be singular and plural inflections of a single super-lexeme) seem to be both adjectives and nouns:

- Like adjectives, but not nouns, they may be modified by degree adverbs such as *very* and *surprisingly: very many* (but* *very quantity*), *surprisingly much* (but: *surprisingly quantity*).
- Like some adjectives, but unlike all nouns, they may be modified by *not*: *not *(many) people came.*
- Like adjectives, but not nouns, they have comparative and superlative inflections: *more, most.*
- Like nouns, but not adjectives, they may occur, without a following common noun, wherever a dependent noun is possible, e.g. as object of any transitive verb or preposition: *I didn't find many/*numerous, We didn't talk about much.* Notice that at least in the last example there is no anaphoric ellipsis, so it would be difficult to justify an unrealized common noun after *much.*
- Like determiners (which are nouns), but not adjectives, *much* excludes any other determiner: **the much beer,* *his much money;* and *many* is very selective in its choice of accompanying determiners (e.g. *his many friends* but not **those many friends*).

It might be thought that the evidence points to a case of syntactic ambiguity, where a single word-form may be associated either with an adjective or with a noun—as in for example, the form {other}, which realizes an adjective in *the other people,* but a noun in *the others.* However, the **much/many** case is different because here the noun and adjective properties must belong to the same word, in the same interpretation; the evidence lies in examples like (105), where the noun and adjective properties combine in the same word token.

(105)   Not very much happened.

Similar comments seem to apply to LITTLE (as in *He said very little*) and also to both ALL and EVERY, both of which allow degree modifiers such as *almost* and *absolutely* even when in other respects they are clear determiners (*almost every house*).

I discussed these cases in some detail in 1990, but had to leave them as an unsolved problem (Hudson 1990: 307–8). Thanks to multiple inheritance we can now solve the problem by classifying these words as both adjectives and nouns at the same time. However we have to be more precise than this in order to explain some differences from more straightforward nouns; for example, if MANY is a noun, why is **big many* impossible? The answer builds on the system of word-classes for nouns. Not all nouns take adjectives as modifiers; those that do are common nouns and (to some extent) proper nouns, but pronouns (which in WG are also nouns) do not (e.g. **big them, *big who*); so maybe MANY is a pronoun. This analysis suggests solutions to two problems:

1 The badness of *big many*: just like THEM, MANY cannot combine with modifying adjectives because it is not a common noun.
2 The goodness of *many people*: just like THIS (and other determiners), MANY allows a following common noun as a dependent.

Consequently I assume that MANY is not just a noun, but more precisely a pronoun. There is a somewhat similar problem on the adjective side, where we find that MUCH and MANY cannot be used predicatively (**His money is much*, **His sons were many*) except in archaic phrases such as *His sins were many*. The obvious solution is a distinction between attributive and predicative adjectives, where most adjectives may be either and are classified simply as 'adjectives'. The proposed analysis is shown in Figure 3.32.

If these arguments are correct, then Chomsky's feature analysis of word-classes (Chomsky 1970) is wrong. In this system, nouns are [−V,+N] while adjectives are [+V,+N] so it is logically impossible to be both a noun and an adjective since the feature [V] cannot have both a negative and a positive value at the same time. More generally, since mixed categories are bound to require conflicting values for at least some features, they are a fundamental threat to the idea that word-classes can be defined by means of feature-matrices where each class excludes all the others. On the other hand, as explained at the start of this section, mixed categories are exactly what we expect in a system that allows multiple inheritance in an inheritance hierarchy. This difference provides another reason for not using features to classify words (cf. s. 3.4).

Multiple inheritance is not just permitted in WG: it is essential for the treatment of inflection. As I explained in section 2.2, inflectional categories such as Plural-noun are word-classes which combine with lexemes such as DOG to define inflected lexemes such as DOG:plural, whose properties are inherited

FIGURE 3.32.   *Many* is both a noun and an adjective

from both the lexeme and the inflection. It would be misleading to describe inflected lexemes as mixed categories because the lexeme and the inflection complement each other—they are designed to go together, as it were. This is partly because the inflections and lexemes are members of the same class of words; for example, DOG and Plural-noun both isa Noun. However, some inflections are mixed categories because they isa two different word-classes. English gerunds are a very clear case of this; I give a detailed analysis of these in Chapter 4. However adjectival participles make the same point well, because they are both adjectives and verbs at the same time. (Etymologically, participles 'participate' in these two categories.) This is not obvious in English because adjectives are relatively hard to identify with confidence, but in more highly inflected languages things can be much clearer.

For example, Latin participles inflect just like adjectives: they have a number, gender, and case and agree with any parent noun (Griffin 1991: 63):

(106) Romani   urb-em   cap-t-am   incenderunt.
       Romans   city-Ac+F capture-passive-Ac+F   burned
       'The Romans burned the captured city.'
(107) Romani   urb-e   cap-t-a   gaudebant.
       Romans   city-Ab+F capture-passive-Ab+F   celebrated
       'With the city captured, the Romans celebrated.'

In (106), the inflections of both the noun and the dependent participle show them to be accusative feminine singular, in contrast with (107), where they are both inflected as ablative feminine singular. Moreover, the morpho-phonology of participles is typical of adjectives:

- Passive participles (e.g. *captus*, with the nominative masculine singular suffix {us}) inflect like 'first and second declension' adjectives such as *bonus*, 'good'.
- Future participles (e.g. *capturus*, 'about to capture') are also like *bonus*.
- Present participles (e.g. *capiens*, 'capturing') are like third declension adjectives such as *ingens*, 'huge'.

What is very clear is that these words are adjectives in terms of their inflectional morphology, in contrast with finite verbs which inflect for tense, person, and so on. On the other hand, they are also full verbs in terms of their own dependencies because their valency is always exactly the same as that of the corresponding finite verbs (with obvious caveats about passives); moreover, the categories Passive, Present, and Future apply to finite inflections of verbs, so they are verbal.

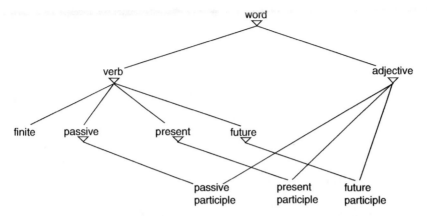

FIGURE 3.33.   Latin participles are verbs and adjectives

The traditional Latin grammarians were clearly right to see a participle as a mixture of a verb and an adjective. A WG analysis is sketched in Figure 3.33, where I assume that the 'declension' differences will be handled as classes of forms, not of words (see s. 2.3 for a general justification of this assumption).

In Latin, participles are non-finite so they lack the typical verbal inflections for person and number. This is assured in Figure 3.33 by keeping the participles separate from Finite, but there are some languages where this separation is not found. For example, in the Cushitic language Beja a finite verb, complete with its normal tense, person, gender, and number inflections, may be used as an adjective (i.e. as the head of a subject-relative clause) by adding the normal adjectival agreements for number, gender, and case (Hudson 1974). Thus in (108), the suffix {b} marks *laga:b* as accusative, masculine.

(108)   Laga-:b   tam-i-a
        Calf-Ac   eat-past-he
        'He ate the calf.'

In (109), the same suffix is added to the ordinary past tense of the verb to make it agree with the head noun, *tak* (which, unlike *laga:b*, has no accusative marking because it ends in a consonant). In this example, the word *tamia:b* is both a finite verb and an adjective at the same time.

(109)   Tak   akra-:b   laga-:b   tam-i-a-:b̲   rih-ani
        man   strong-Ac calf-Ac   eat-past-he-Ac see-I
        'I see the strong man who ate the calf.'

In conclusion, there seems very little doubt that mixed categories are real.

3.7 Unrealized Words and Ellipsis

Until the late 1990s I was convinced that syntactic theory could stick firmly to the surface, with abstract relations (dependencies) linking thoroughly concrete words. It seemed clear that some words had no independent meaning, but I could see no reason to assume words that had no pronunciation. All the cases where transformational grammar had postulated deletions, traces, or unpronounced elements such as PRO and *pro* seemed to call for analyses in which the elements concerned were part of the semantics but did not figure at all in the syntax. Although it never seems to have been spelled out explicitly, the avoidance of abstract words was implicit in WG. So, for example, I assumed that an imperative verb (as in *Eat your vegetables!*) simply had no (syntactic) subject, although of course it had a semantic structure showing that the addressee was the agent. Similarly, the pronoun THIS could be used either with a dependent common noun (as in *I prefer this cup*) or without one (as in *I prefer this*), and if no noun was pronounced, none was part of the syntax even when one was clearly understood from the context. The understood meaning was located where it belonged, in the semantic structure. In short, all ellipsis involved a mismatch between semantics and syntax—i.e. a semantic element which corresponded to absolutely nothing in the syntax.

This position had the attraction of parsimony, in contrast with the situation in transformational syntax where new 'empty categories' seemed to be welcomed with open arms as a sign of sophistication. These empty categories, like the earlier deletions, seemed to rest on very flimsy evidence which too often ignored the possibility of semantic solutions (such as the WG treatment of imperatives). However as the WG analyses became more complex, doubts started to arise about the feasibility of handling all ellipsis in the semantics. For example, consider the syntactic and semantic structure of sentence (110).

(110)   You keep talking.

The crucial fact about this sentence is that *keep* shares its subject with *talking*, and more generally that *keep* always shares its subject with its 'sharer' complement. This works well when *keep* has a subject; for example, it guarantees that (in this example) the addressee is also the talker. But what happens if *keep* has no subject, as in (111)?

(111)   Keep talking!

How does this affect the interpretation of *talking*? The fact is, of course, that it has no effect—the talker is still linked to the subject of *keep*, even though this is merely understood. But this linkage does not seem to follow from any general principle because the linking rule only seems to apply to cases where both verbs have a subject; in cases where neither has one, we might have expected it simply to be suspended.

A similar problem arises with more complicated structures like (112):

(112)   What do you think the others will bring?

This is an example of extraction, where *what* is extracted, via *do*, *think*, and *will*, from *bring*. This extraction relation allows it to act as the object of *bring*, and it is only this dependency which integrates it into the sentence's semantic structure. (See Hudson 1990: 354–403 for a detailed discussion of extraction.) This analysis works smoothly, but ellipsis is a serious problem, as pointed out by Rosta (p.c.). The last verb depends on an auxiliary verb, so it may be omitted giving (113):

(113)   I know what you're going to bring to the party, but what do you think the others will?

In this case there is no *bring*, so *what* cannot be passed as extract-ee beyond *will*. This has two consequences, both negative:

- *What* cannot be integrated into the semantics because it cannot be treated as 'bring-ee'.
- The sentence will count as ungrammatical because of the relation between *what* and *will*. When word A (*what*) is extract-ee of word B (*will*), there are just two possible configurations, but *what* does not fit either of them. One possibility is that A has some other dependency relation to B (e.g. object), but *will* does not allow such dependents; the other is recursion, in which A is extract-ee of a later dependent of B—but *will* has no later dependent.

In contrast, there would be no problem at all if we recognized *bring* as part of the syntactic structure even when elided.

The relevant characteristic of problems like these is that their solution does not, and cannot, lie in the semantics. Even if we assume that some pragmatic process can enrich the semantic structure by adding the meaning of *bring* to (113), there is no way to link *what* to this meaning without using the syntax of extraction. The same conclusion seems to emerge from a different kind of example, illustrated in (114) as uttered by someone holding a pair of trousers (or bathroom scales):

(114)   Whose are these?

Why plural? Obviously because the nouns *trousers* and *scales* happen to be plural. But if (as I believe) this plurality is purely syntactic and not represented in the semantics, then we cannot explain the plurality of *these* as a choice forced by its 'plural' referent. The only explanation must lie in the syntax, which means that in some sense the syntax must contain the word *trousers* (or *scales*) even though it is not pronounced. Moreover, since the same choice applies to ordinary personal pronouns it is at least tempting to assume that they too are agreeing with an inaudible dependent noun—for example, *they* would be syntactically *they [trousers]*. Similar arguments apply, but even more strongly, in languages where the choice of pronoun reflects the grammatical gender of the understood noun rather than the sex of its referent—e.g. in formal written German, where sentences like (115) are found (Durrell 1996: 13):

(115) Dem   Mädchen   hat   es   sehr   gefreut, dass
       The   girl (neuter) has   it   very   pleased that
       es   seine   Grossmutter   wiedersehen   konnte.
       it   its   grandmother   see.again   could
       'The girl was very pleased that she could see her grandmother again.'

Once again it is important to link the choice of the neuter pronoun *es* to the neuter noun *Mädchen*, and the easiest way to do this is to assume that the pronoun agrees with an inaudible copy of the noun which depends on it.

Yet another piece of evidence in favour of covert words came (surprisingly, perhaps) from sociolinguistics. Addressee pronouns are often sensitive to the social relation between the speaker and the addressee; so for example in French a speaker chooses between TU and VOUS, both meaning 'you' and used to a single addressee, according to fine judgements about their perceived power and solidarity relations to the person addressed (Hudson 1996: 122–32). Once again, agreement is what makes this fact relevant. In languages such as French which have such pronoun contrasts and which have subject-verb agreement, the verb has different forms for *tu* and *vous*; for example, *tu viens* and *vous venez* both mean 'you come', and can both be addressed to a single addressee. So long as the pronoun is overt, we can let it determine the verb's inflections in a mechanical way; but what if it is covert, as in an imperative verb? Here too we have exactly the same choice between V*iens!* and *Venez!*, but if there is no subject, how can we explain the sociolinguistic conditions on this choice? One option, of course, would be to treat the verb and pronoun choices as separate, so both *tu* and verb forms such as *viens* would be chosen when addressing a person who is a close intimate, and so on. But if the pronoun and verb are chosen separately, we might expect some flexibility of combination—e.g. *tu venez* in cases where the addressee is on the borderline between intimate and distant. This situation does arise with names, where the choice between (say) *Jean* and *Monsieur Leblanc* ('Mr White') can be made, to some extent, independently of that between *tu* and *vous*. And yet mismatched combinations like *tu venez* and *vous viens* are absolutely impossible, suggesting that the sociolinguistic choice is actually made just once, for the pronoun, and the verb form follows from this in a mechanical way. But if the choice between *viens* and *venez* is based on the choice of pronoun, the same must also be true in imperatives, so they too must have a subject pronoun, albeit a covert one.

If this conclusion is correct, then we can probably generalize it to all subject-agreement forms in languages where overt subjects are optional; so for example, Latin *venio*, 'I come', agrees with an understood *ego*, 'I', while *venimus*, 'we come', agrees with *nos*, 'we'. Once again this means that the semantics affects the choice of pronoun directly, and only affects the verb forms indirectly via the mechanical process of agreement. This may imply a more complicated model of processing, but it simplifies the grammar by avoiding semantic links in the verb which duplicate those for pronouns. In Latin these agreement properties would include person, number, and (in some sentences) gender—for example, *captus est*, 'he has been captured', contrasts with *capta est*, 'she has been captured'. The more complex the agreement patterns, the stronger the evidence for covert subjects.

These uncertainties about understood elements came to a critical point when I started to look at case agreement in predicatives, which is found in languages such as Icelandic and Ancient Greek where adjectives and nouns have overt case inflections, and predicative adjectives agree with the subject of their clause. The possibilities are illustrated clearly in the following Icelandic examples (Andrews 1982: 445):

(116) a Hún$_N$ er   vinsæl$_N$.
          she   is   popular
       b þeir   segja   hana$_A$ (vera)   vinsæla$_A$.
          they   say   her   (be)   popular
          'They say she is popular.'
       c Hún$_N$ er   sögð$_N$ (vera)   vinsæl$_N$.
          she   is   said   (be)   popular
          'She is said to be popular.'
       d þeir   telja   hana$_A$ (vera)   sagða$_A$ (vera)   vinsæla$_A$.
          they   believe   her   (be)   said   (be)   popular
          'They believe her to be said to be popular.'

e   Hún$_N$ er   talin$_N$ (vera) sögð$_N$ (vera) vinsæl$_N$.
    she   is   believed (be)   said (be)   popular
    'She is believed to be said to be popular.'

In all these examples, the predicative adjective 'popular' has the same case
(N = nominative or A = accusative) as the pronoun meaning 'she' or 'her';
and the only reasonable explanation for this agreement must be that the two
words are bound by a grammatical agreement rule. In the clear cases such as
(a), this agreement ties the adjective to the subject of its clause, so again the
only reasonable assumption is that the same is true in all the examples. But if
that is so, the pronoun must be the subject of the lower clause even when it is
also the object of the higher one. Similar patterns are found in other languages
where predicatives show case-agreement (Hudson 2003*a*).

The relevant question for us is what happens to the predicative's case when
the clause has no overt subject, and when it does not share the higher clause's
subject or object as it does in (116). In Icelandic, the predicative is always
nominative:

(117) Að   vera   kennari$_N$/ *kennara$_A$ er   mikilvægt
       to   be   teacher   is   important
       'It is important to be a teacher.'

In the case of verbs like 'request' or 'order', however, the lower clause's
predicative may either agree with the higher clause's object (which may be
accusative or dative), or it may be nominative:

(118) a   Hún bað hann$_A$ að vera góðan$_A$/ góður$_N$.
           'She requested him to be good.'
       b   Hún skipaði honum$_D$ að vera góðum$_D$/ góður$_N$.
           'She ordered him to be good.'

The best explanation for this alternation is that the lower clause has two
possible structures: either it has an overt subject, which is the same as the
higher clause's object, or it has no overt subject, but it does have a covert
nominative subject (like the infinitival clause in (117)). Given these assumption, the case of the predicative is predictable from the case of the subject,
whether overt or covert.

It is helpful to contrast this pattern with the one in Ancient Greek, where
the predicates of apparently subject-less clauses are accusative rather than
nominative (Lecarme 1978: 105):

(119) a   sumphérei   autois$_D$ phílous$_A$ einai.
           is-useful   to-them   friends   be
           'It is useful to them to be friends.'

b exarkesei   soi$_D$ túrannon$_A$ genésthai.
   will-suffice   to-you   king   become
   'It will be enough for you to become king.'

c dei   philánthrōpon$_A$ einai.
   is-necessary   philanthropic   be

The easiest explanation for the difference between Icelandic and Greek is that the subject of a non-finite clause has a different default case—nominative in Icelandic and accusative in Greek—but that in both languages a covert subject has just the same effect as an overt one. Interestingly, Greek shows the same alternation as Icelandic between agreement with a higher noun and agreement with a covert subject:

(120) a prépei   soi$_D$ einai   prothúmō$_D$/ prothúmon$_A$.
          befits   you   be   zealous
          'It befits you to be zealous.'

      b éxestin   umin$_D$ genesthai   eudaimosin$_D$/ eudaimonas$_A$.
         is allowed   you   be   happy
         'You are allowed to be happy.'

In short, a non-finite clause must have a subject that can carry case; and in the absence of an overt one (such as a structure-shared one), there must be a covert one.

This conclusion is crucial for the question of covert elements in syntax because case is a purely syntactic notion which (presumably) has no reflex in semantics. Even if 'quirky' number and gender in examples like English *scales* and German *Mädchen* (with neuter gender but the meaning 'girl') can be explained semantically, this kind of explanation is definitely not possible for case agreement. The nominative predicatives in Icelandic and accusative in Ancient Greek demand a purely syntactic explanation, and the only explanation that is at all convincing is that these non-finite clauses do in fact have a syntactic subject which is sufficiently real to have a real case. The evidence is actually even more convincing than this brief survey suggests (Hudson 2003*a*; Creider and Hudson 2006), and it is very hard to avoid the conclusion that at least subjects of non-finite verbs may be inaudible. The conclusion is certainly uncomfortable for those like me who cling to the idea of a completely 'surface' syntactic structure; but it is almost equally uncomfortable for those who claim that covert subjects of non-finite clauses cannot carry ordinary cases (Chomsky 1995*b*: 109).

Let us assume, then, that covert words are possible. What exactly does this mean in terms of WG theory? Having answered this question, I shall ask what limits there are on the occurrence of such words, and what implications these limits have for a theory of how we process them.

Covert words have just the same syntactic and semantic characteristics that we expect in overt words; and indeed, it is these characteristics, especially the syntactic ones, that provide the clearest evidence that covert words exist. For example, the agreement data reviewed above showed that (depending on the language concerned) covert subjects may have:

- syntactic case (e.g. in Icelandic and Ancient Greek)
- person, number and gender (e.g. in Latin)
- sociolinguistic properties of power and solidarity (e.g. in French).

Apart from covert subjects, I also reviewed evidence from agreement with the more or less arbitrary grammatical number or gender of covert complement nouns; this evidence is compelling in examples like *these* for *these scales*, and rather speculatively I suggested in the earlier discussion of example (114) that the same analysis might extend even to the choice of *they*, where the complement noun is always covert. The obvious conclusion is that covert words are ordinary words like *I, tu*, and *scales*, with the ordinary syntax and semantics of these words (Creider and Hudson 2006). (To judge by Chomsky 1995*b*: 43, Chomsky agrees.) The only difference between them and their ordinary counterpart is that they are inaudible. This is very different from analyses in terms of the covert pronouns PRO and *pro*, unique words which combine the very special properties of completely free reference (including the speaker and addressee—something not found in any overt pronoun) and zero pronunciation—a remarkable and unexplained coincidence.

If covert words are words without either pronunciation or spelling, then (in the WG architecture) they are words without a realization (more precisely, they have no 'formation'), so I shall refer to them as 'unrealized' words. WG already provides a mechanism for accommodating such words. First, we already have the relation 'realization' which links a word to a form; and secondly, we have the 'quantity' relation which I introduced in section 1.3. As I explained there, an entity may have (or inherit) a quantity which shows how many instances of it are expected among the observed tokens; for example, the quantity for a bird's beak is 1 while that for its legs is 2. Like other properties, quantity is inherited by default, so exceptional birds without beaks or with four legs could be accommodated. Similarly, a word's realization is by default a form whose quantity is 1, but exceptionally this quantity may be 0. This is why a word may be unrealized. The structure in Figure 3.34 is the WG analysis of the simple imperative *Hurry!*, contrasting the realized verb with its unrealized subject. It shows that a default word has 1 form as its

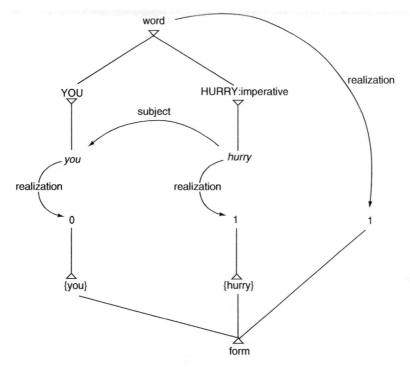

FIGURE 3.34.   *Hurry!* has an unrealized subject

realization, but that the realization of *you* (i.e. of the particular token of you found in this sentence) has the quantity 0. On the other hand, the diagram also shows that the form would have been (an example of) {you}.

This mechanism seems to distinguish satisfactorily between realized and unrealized words. Notice that there is no need to assume that unrealized words are stored as such, and (contrary to the old PRO and *pro*) there is certainly no need for words which are always unrealized (with all the learnability problems that such words would raise). Every word has the potential for being unrealized, if the grammar requires this. So we come (as promised earlier) to the question of how the grammar controls realization, and what limits there are on unrealized words.

All the examples discussed earlier share a common characteristic: the unrealized word is a dependent of a word which allows it to be unrealized. In these cases it is easy to see that the parent word controls realization in the same way that it controls any other property of its dependents. For example, an imperative verb requires its subject to have no realization in just the same way that KICK_bucket (in the idiomatic KICK THE BUCKET) requires its dependent

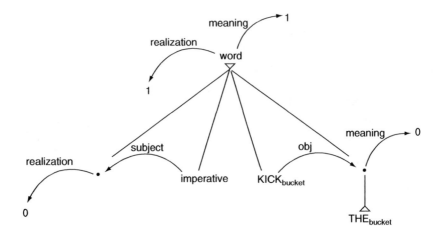

FIGURE 3.35.   Unrealized subjects are like meaningless prepositions

the to have no independent meaning. These two parts of the grammar are shown in Figure 3.35 for comparison. Unrealized words like this are easy to accommodate in a grammar because their presence is utterly predictable (even if the identity of the missing word has to be supplied contextually). For the same reason, they are easy for a listener or reader to handle because their presence can be predicted as soon as the parent word has been processed; so there is no question of having to postulate an indefinite number of empty categories in every utterance just in case they are needed.

It is true that not all ellipsis involves dependents of specific words or word-types, but in every case the overt words indicate the presence of the unrealized words though the identity of these words varies with the context. For example, take answers to questions like (121):

(121)   Speaker 1: Who did you see?
        Speaker 2: John.

Given the apparatus for ellipsis in WG, it seems reasonable to suggest that the answer *John* is in fact a syntactically complete sentence: *I saw John,* in which the two words which repeat words in the question are unrealized. The same is possible for corrections like (122):

(122)   Speaker 1:   Bill has bought a car.
        Speaker 2:   No, a van.

In this case, it seems likely that both speakers mentally build a structure for the correction which includes an unrealized copy of each word in the first utterance except the corrected part. Given the apparatus of default inheritance, this should be a very simple mental operation in which the overt replacement isa the word that it replaces; for example, if *John* in (121) isa *who*, then it will inherit all the latter's properties except those which it overrides (such as its meaning and form). The inherited properties include its syntactic and semantic links to the rest of the sentence, so the result will be a copy of the question in which *who* and its effects (such as the question semantics) are replaced by those of *John*.

Some grammatical constructions allow us to leave unrealized those words which can easily be recovered from the situation. The following examples illustrate some constructions which permit this. (I discuss several of them in some detail in Hudson 1990: 416–21.) The bracketed words are unrealized.

(123)   Jane left the party before Bill [left it].
(124)   I seem to think about you more than you [seem to think about] me.
(125)   Bill donated his books to the college and Belinda [donated] her art collection [to the college].
(126)   I know what you're going to bring to the party, but what do you think the others will [bring to the party]?

Notice that the last example is the same as (113), which illustrated one of the problems of the earlier analyses without unrealized words.

The details of these analyses remain to be worked out, but unrealized words seem to open up some promising avenues of research which are not available if we insist that every syntactic word must be realized. Needless to say, one major benefit of this analysis is to greatly simplify the job of mapping syntactic structures to semantic structures—for example, of mapping *before Bill* in (123) to the same meaning as *before Bill left it*.

3.8 A Summary of Syntactic Categories

This chapter has discussed most of the standard topics in syntax:

- Dependencies
- Word order
- Selection
- Constructions
- Agreement
- Features
- Adjuncts and valents
- Mixed categories
- Ellipsis

The one major gap in the discussion is coordination, where I have very little to add to the analysis that I offered in 1990 (Hudson 1990: 404–21).

My general theme has been the same as in the chapter on morphology: that language structure is very similar to the structure found in the other parts of our cognitive network. But of course syntax has a particular subject-matter— how words combine in sentences in such a way as to express complex meanings—so it does use some entities and relations which are not found elsewhere; but the list is very short. Here is a summary of the main categories that I have introduced in this chapter (to which we should add a few more which are needed for coordination).

- Entities
  - Word-classes
  - Inflections
  - Lexemes
  - Feature-values
- Relations
  - Dependent, and sub-types such as:
    - Subject
    - Object
    - Pre-dependent
    - Extractee
- Proxy
  - Parent
  - Feature, and its sub-types such as number

These specifically syntactic categories interact with others which are found elsewhere, such as Landmark; and all of them fit comfortably into the general ontology and logic of cognitive categories.

4

Gerunds

4.1 Introduction

This chapter is adapted from Hudson 2003*b*, where I offer a WG account of English gerunds[1] such as *having* in (127).

(127) (We were talking about) John <u>having</u> a sabbatical.

What makes gerunds interesting and challenging is that they combine the internal characteristics of a clause with the external characteristics of a noun phrase. Previous analyses have tried to recognize the mixed character of gerunds by assigning them two separate nodes, one verbal and the other nominal. However dependency analyses such as WG syntax allow only one node per word, so they do not allow analyses of this kind. Two-node analyses would be strong evidence against dependency analysis so it is important to be sure whether they are needed. This chapter presents an analysis similar to the one proposed by Malouf in which the verbal and nominal classifications are combined on a **single** node which inherits both verbal and nominal characteristics (Malouf 2000); but unlike Malouf's analysis it does not assume phrase structure. Like his, it exploits the logic of multiple default inheritance which allows a single node to inherit from two supercategories—in this case from both Verb and Noun. As Malouf points out, multiple inheritance works because English grammar is organized in such a way that the characteristics of these categories are orthogonal. In short, a gerund is both a verb and a noun, as in traditional analyses. Simple stipulations are needed to allow for 'possessive' subjects (e.g. *about John's having a sabbatical*) and a number of very specific constructions

---

[1] Terminology varies from author to author. What I am calling simply 'gerunds' are often called 'verbal gerunds', in contrast with 'nominal gerunds' which I shall call nominalizations. Some authors (e.g. Bresnan 2001: 287) use an adjective 'gerundive' (e.g. 'gerundive VP') for patterns that involve verbal gerunds. The term 'gerund' is used quite differently in Romance linguistics, where it refers to verb forms which I would call 'present participles'. The term derives from Latin, where the form *gerundum* was in fact the gerund of the verb *gerere*, 'to do', so my usage is in line with that of traditional Latin grammars (Griffin 1991: 82).

peculiar to gerunds: *no* in prohibitions or existentials (e.g. *No playing loud music! There's no mistaking that voice*), and a very few constructions which demand a gerund rather than a noun phrase (e.g. *It's no use ...*, *They prevented us from ...*).

4.2 The Challenge of English Gerunds

Gerunds, such as the word *having* in (127), repeated as (128), are one of the most troublesome areas of English grammar:

(128)   We were talking about John having a sabbatical.

The trouble with words like *having* in this example is that they are half-verb and half-noun, which makes them a serious challenge for any theory of grammatical structure. The facts are well known and uncontentious, but there is a great deal of disagreement about precisely, or even approximately, how to accommodate gerunds. The history of modern linguistics is littered with attempts to do this (Malouf 2000). Meanwhile, and more or less independently of this debate about gerunds in present-day English, there has been a great deal of discussion of how they developed since Old English (which had no gerunds).[2] We shall see later that the historical development is important in evaluating any theory of modern gerunds, because the same theory must also be able to accommodate the range of intermediate forms that are found in earlier stages of English.

We can easily summarize the main facts, as illustrated by *having* in the above example. It must be a verb, in fact an example of the ordinary verb HAVE, because it has a bare subject and a bare direct object and it can be modified by *not* or an adverb:

(129)   We were talking about John not having a sabbatical.
(130)   We were talking about John soon having a sabbatical.

These are characteristics which not only distinguish verbs from nouns but also distinguish them, at least in combination, from other word classes. On the other hand, it must also be a noun because the phrase that it heads is used as the object of a preposition (*about*), and could be used in any other position where plain noun phrases are possible:

(131)   John having a sabbatical upset Bill.

---

[2] The following is an incomplete and no doubt unrepresentative sample: Rusteberg 1874; Poutsma 1923; Langenhove 1925; Wik 1973; Tajima 1985; Donner 1986; Jack 1988; Houston 1989; Wurff 1993; Fanego 1996*b*; Fanego 1996*a*; Wurff 1997. Denison gives a convenient summary (Denison 1993: 403–4).

(132) Did John having a sabbatical upset Bill?
(133) They discussed John having a sabbatical.
(134) John not having a sabbatical and Mary's failure to get study-leave meant that we weren't short-staffed after all.

The word *having* must be a noun if these positions are indeed reserved for noun phrases and if noun phrases must be headed by nouns.

In addition to these main facts, however, there are three others which complicate the picture. The first is the well-known fact that the gerund's subject may be a 'possessive'—i.e. a possessive pronoun or a noun phrase with suffixed _'s:

(135) We were talking about John's/his having a sabbatical.

What is not always recognized is that this pattern is not a straightforward alternative to the bare subject. According to Quirk et al., the possessive is preferred in some syntactic contexts (when the gerund itself is in subject position and its subject is a personal pronoun) and dispreferred in others (Quirk, Greenbaum, Leech, and Svartvik 1985: 1064, 1194); thus *my* is preferred to *me* in example (136) below, whereas *his* and *your* in the other examples are described as 'awkward or stilted' in comparison with *him* and *you*:

(136) My/me forgetting her name was embarrassing.
(137) I dislike him/his driving my car.
(138) We look forward to you/your becoming our neighbour.

Similarly, Biber and colleagues refer to a prescriptive tradition in favour of the possessive form (Biber, Johansson, Leech, Conrad, and Finegan 1999: 750). On the other hand, in American English possessives are (apparently) much more normal, and bare subjects may even be rejected (suggesting a somewhat more archaic grammar, as we shall see s. 4.7). If this is true, it may explain why discussions of gerunds by American linguists have tended to take the possessive subject as the normal pattern (as witness the name 'POSS-ING' which was widely used for the gerund pattern in the 1970s).

The second fact has been much less widely acknowledged, but it deserves to be taken seriously. Even in present-day English we find some patterns in which a gerund is used with an ordinary determiner, especially *no* or *any* (Quirk, Greenbaum, Leech, and Svartvik 1985: 1066; Jorgensen 1981). This happens in two constructions. One construction consists of *no* and a gerund clause used as a main-clause prohibition:

(139) No playing loud music!
(140) No eating sweets in lectures!

The other construction is a clause whose subject is *there*, whose verb is a form of BE, and whose delayed subject is *no* or *any* followed by a gerund clause:[3]

(141)   There's no mistaking that voice.
(142)   There was no lighting fireworks that day.
(143)   There isn't any telling what they will do.
(144)   There must be no standing beyond the yellow line.
(145)   There was no turning the other cheek.
(146)   There's no pleasing some people.
(147)   There's no denying it.

It is true that these constructions are restricted in terms of what is possible outside the gerund clause; for example, in both patterns the negative is mandatory. However there is also no denying that they are fully productive as far as the gerund clause is concerned, so they cannot simply be listed as archaic relics of an earlier stage of the language (comparable with *come what may* or *if you please*). They have the classic characteristics of the idiosyncratic but productive constructions discussed in 3.3—non-canonical syntax and semantics combined with productivity. A complete account of present-day gerunds cannot ignore them.

A third detail which should be borne in mind is the existence of constructions in which only a gerund phrase, and no other kind of noun phrase, may be used (Malouf 1998: 34, quoting Quirk, Greenbaum, Leech, and Svartvik 1985: 1231). On the one hand we have constructions where the gerund phrase is extraposed (examples from Quirk et al.):

(148)   It's/There's no use telling him anything.
(149)   There's no point telling him anything.
(150)   It's scarcely worth(while) you/your going home.
(151)   It's pointless buying so much food.

In none of these examples is it possible to replace the gerund phrase by an ordinary noun phrase:

(152)   *It's no use a big fuss.
(153)   *There's no point anything else.
(154)   *It's scarcely worthwhile a lot of work.
(155)   *It's pointless purchase of so much food.

On the other hand we also have at least one verb, PREVENT, which allows only a gerund phrase after its complement preposition.

---

[3] The last two examples were provided by David Denison and the Collins Cobuild English Dictionary; the remaining examples are from Quirk et al. (Quirk, Greenbaum, Leech and Svartvik 1985: 1066).

(156)   They prevented us from finishing it/*its completion.

In short, these are all cases where some construction selects specifically for gerund phrases, so it is important that these should be distinguishable from other noun phrases.

These facts about possessive subjects, *no/any* and gerund selection are important because they confuse the simple view of the relationship between the nominal and verbal characteristics of gerunds. If we think of a gerund in terms of the phrase that it heads, the following generalization is almost true:

(157)   A phrase headed by a gerund is:
   a   *an ordinary clause as far as its internal structure is concerned, but*
   b   *an ordinary noun phrase (or DP) in terms of its external*
        distribution.

Thus the gerund's nominal properties are all properties that it contracts as a dependent while its verbal ones are those that it has by virtue of being the head. This description comes very close to being true, but it is falsified by examples like *his driving my car* and *no mistaking that voice*, both of which look as though they start with a determiner—part of the internal structure of noun phrases, not clauses. Similarly, the description has trouble with con-structions like *prevent from*, which show that the external distribution of a gerund phrase is not totally identical to that of ordinary noun phrases.

On the other hand it would be wrong to take these exceptions too seriously. After all, it is almost true that gerund phrases are verbal inside but nominal outside, so we must not abandon this generalization just because of the exceptions just noted. What is needed, therefore, is an analysis which solves two problems:

- Problem A. How to reconcile the nominal and verbal features found in straightforward examples, where verbal features control internal struc-ture and nominal features control external distribution.
- Problem B1. How to reconcile the fact that possessive subjects and *no/any* are determiners with the fact that they can introduce a gerund phrase.
- Problem B2. How to reconcile the fact that PREVENT *from* does not allow noun phrases with the fact that it does allow gerund phrases, and similarly for the extraposed examples in (148) to (151).

Problem A will turn out not to be a problem at all, thanks to the way that English is organized. I shall argue for the simplest possible analysis, in which gerunds themselves are indeed both verbs and nouns; and I shall show that the characteristics of verbs and nouns never conflict, because nominal features always control external distribution but verbal features never do, whereas the reverse is true of internal structure. We shall also see that it is crucial to assign gerunds to specific subclasses of both noun and verb in order to get the desired results. Given the right classification, nothing more needs to be said about straightforward gerunds.

Problem B is the problem of how to accommodate exceptional cases, and since by definition exceptions must be stipulated, we must look for a solution which stipulates these; but the simpler the stipulations are, the better.

4.3 Previous Analyses

One of the great attractions of English gerunds for theoretical grammar is that the facts are both clear and challenging, so they serve as a good test-bed for grammatical theories. What kind of theoretical 'machinery' does their mixture of noun and verb characteristics call for? Most previous analyses have taken it for granted that no node in a sentence structure can be classified as both a noun and a verb[4]—an assumption encouraged by the widely accepted analysis of word-classes in terms of the features N and V. As I commented in 3.6, since nouns and verbs carry opposite values for both these features it is logically impossible for 'verb' and 'noun' to combine; and the combination [+N,+V] is normally assumed to define the class of adjectives. As Malouf points out (1998: 90), this is contrary to the Western grammatical tradition which has always recognized 'mixed' categories such as participles. The analysis which I shall offer below is very much more traditional in this respect than any other recent one except Malouf's.

If one node cannot carry two conflicting classifications, the obvious solution is to assume two separate nodes, one for the nominal classification and the other for the verbal one. Moreover, the natural way to show that the nominal classification controls external distribution while the verbal classification controls internal structure is to make the verbal node subordinate to the nominal node: a verb phrase inside a noun phrase. This has the further attraction of providing a position for a possessive subject, in the 'determiner' position within the higher noun phrase. Most theoretically motivated analyses assume some kind of 'two-node' analysis in which the grammar generates a sentence structure with two nodes for the gerund, one of which can be classified as nominal and the other as verbal. In his survey of the various analyses that have been offered within the generative tradition,

---

[4] Apart from Malouf's analysis, I know of only two in which the similarities to both clauses and noun phrases are shown on a single node: Hudson 1976a: 37–43 and Wurff 1993.

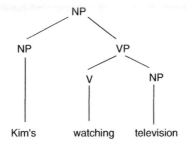

FIGURE 4.1. A typical two-node structure for a gerund

Malouf observes (1998: 87) that they all assign gerund phrases some variation of the structure shown in Figure 4.1, where VP is contained within NP.

Is this much machinery really needed? The question is crucial for theories in which multiple phrasal nodes are not available. If a theory (such as WG) simply does not permit two-node analyses, then either it is falsified by gerunds, or two-node analyses are not necessary. WG excludes phrases in principle from the descriptive apparatus, so it excludes, as a matter of principle, most of the analyses that have been suggested to date. The following list summarizes the main contenders:

- The NP is exocentric and consists of a VP (Chomsky 1970; Jackendoff 1977; Hudson 1976*a*).
- The NP's head is {ing} and a transformation or cliticization lowers the nominal -*ing* onto the verb (Baker 1985; Hudson 1990: 316–26).
- An abstract category which is classified either as D or N and selects either IP or VP is combined with a rule which affixes this null suffix to a verb that already has the {ing} suffix (Abney 1987; Yoon 1996).
- A weakened Head Feature Convention allows the mother phrase and its head to have different values for N and V (Pullum 1991).
- The NP and VP nodes have 'dual' lexical categories $<X|Y>$, where X and Y determine external and internal properties respectively (Lapointe 1993).
- One word projects (as head) to two different phrasal nodes—to an NP node and to a VP node within the NP—with the higher node unordered with respect to the lower one (Wescoat 1994).
- A single c-structure N (the gerund) maps to an N and a V position in f-structure (Bresnan 1997).
- Lexical rules convert a VP into an NP (Kaiser 1997; 1999).

This survey (which is based in part on Malouf's) is interesting as evidence not only for the ingenuity of linguists but also for the weakness of current theories. Malouf also finds more or less serious empirical problems in all the proposed analyses, but regardless of their merits they all presuppose the two-node approach to analysis.

The aim of this chapter is to show that gerunds can be accounted for extremely easily without assuming two nodes. All we need to assume is that the gerund itself is a single word which is simultaneously both a noun and a verb. So long as we distinguish gerunds from other kinds of nouns and verbs (as explained in ss. 4.5 and 4.6), all the general facts will follow naturally and without any further assumptions. The exceptional facts (e.g. the possibility of possessive subjects) will then be very easy to stipulate. If such a simple analysis is possible with a single-node analysis, the extra theoretical apparatus provided by phrase structure is not just redundant, but may be getting in the way of a simpler analysis.

4.4 Noun Classes and Noun Phrases

If gerunds are nouns, their analysis has to mesh with a more general analysis of nouns and noun phrases. Traditionally there are two main subclasses of Noun: Common noun and Proper noun. These are used as the head of phrases which have the same distribution and somewhat similar internal structures, though there are enough differences in the internal structures to justify a distinction. For example, the rules for combining determiners with common and proper nouns are rather different, and adjectives are rather hard to use as modifiers of proper nouns.

However, since noun phrases are defined by their distribution, they must also include phrases headed by pronouns, and so pronouns must also be nouns (Huddleston 1988: 85; Hudson 1990: 268; Pollard and Sag 1994: 249). We thus recognize (at least) three subclasses of noun:

- Common noun: *boys, people, mud*
- Proper noun: *Sam, Wednesday, London*
- Pronoun: *them, what, someone, his*

All these words can be used as the head of a phrase with the same range of possible functions, that is, as subject, object, complement, and so on. In a dependency analysis, the distribution of the whole phrase is (and must be) that of its head, so a noun phrase is simply a noun plus any dependents that it may have. The phrase itself however has no theoretical status since it is totally redundant given the word-classes and dependencies. A phrase-structure analysis expresses the same insight but in a rather more complicated way, because it distinguishes the phrase node from the head node. The main point is that in either kind of analysis the underlined examples below are all nouns, and it is this classification that explains why they all have the same overall distributional possibilities.

(158)   I heard <u>boys</u>.
(159)   I heard <u>Sam</u>.
(160)   I heard <u>them</u>.

How do determiners fit into this picture? This question is important for gerunds because (as we saw in s. 4.2), these can combine with certain determiners, most obviously possessives. There are good reasons for taking a determiner as the head of its phrase (though, as I mentioned in s. 3.2, there are also good reasons for the converse analysis); for example, in *this book*, the head must be *this* rather than *book*, because *book* is optional but the determiner is not:

(161)   I have read this book.
(162)   I have read this.
(163)   *I have read book.

The evidence for the head-hood of the determiner explains the popularity of the DP analysis (Abney 1987). WG has also generally treated the determiner as head in a determiner-noun pair (Hudson 1981*b*; 1984: 90–2; 1990: 268–70; 2000*c*; 2004*a*), so this is the structure that we shall assume for gerunds too. Figure 4.2 shows the dependency structure for a representative noun phrase.

If a determiner is the head of its phrase, how can we show the similarity of distribution between this phrase and one headed by a noun? If the former is a DP and the latter an NP, they belong to different basic classes in spite of their similarities. The solution adopted in Chomskyan analyses is to treat them all as DPs, with a zero determiner in those that seem to lack one, but the zero determiner raises a number of problems which have not yet been resolved (see Hudson 2000*c*). In contrast, WG offers a much simpler analysis in which they are all NPs. The only controversial elements in this analysis are two assumptions, namely that pronouns are nouns (as already suggested), and that determiners are pronouns.

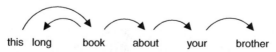

this   long   book   about   your   brother

FIGURE 4.2. Dependencies in a typical noun phase

The similarities between determiners and pronouns are well known (Greenbaum 1996: 163), and indeed it is commonly assumed that pronouns are determiners (Postal 1966). WG accepts this relationship but reverses it by treating determiners as 'transitive' pronouns. For example, the 'pronoun' THIS and the 'determiner' THIS are different uses of one and the same word, one with and one without an overt complement noun, exactly comparable to the two uses of EAT with and without an object. (As explained in s. 3.7, the complement may also be unrealized, so a bare pronoun such as *this* allows two syntactic analyses, one with an unrealized complement and the other without any complement at all.) Under this analysis, therefore, the word-class Determiner disappears, since the possibility of a complement noun is handled by means of valency, not via the apparatus of word-classes.

To summarize the WG treatment of noun phrases that I have outlined so far:

- There are different subclasses of noun including Common, Proper, and Pronoun.
- Where determiners are present, they are the head of the phrase and the common noun is their complement.
- Determiners are pronouns that have a complement common noun.

This analysis succeeds in unifying all the following examples by treating them all as headed by a noun; this analysis avoids the need to invoke either a phrasal category (whether 'noun phrase' or DP) or the fiction of a zero determiner:

(164)   I read <u>Shakespeare</u> [Proper noun].
(165)   I read <u>books</u> [Common noun].
(166)   I read <u>those</u> [Pronoun] books.
(167)   I read <u>those/them</u> [Pronoun].

In each case the head of the phrase is underlined and classified, to show that it is a subtype of noun. This classification of the head allows all four patterns to be subsumed under a single generalization about the distribution of nouns. For example, if we allow the object of a verb such as READ to be a noun, we thereby allow any phrase whose head isa noun, regardless of its subclass.

I have emphasized so far the similarities among the different subclasses of Noun, but what about their differences, and especially their syntactic differences? A common noun such as *books* clearly heads noun phrases with very different structures from those headed by, say, the pronoun *me*. These differences will play a crucial role in the argument of the next section so I shall survey them here and offer a WG analysis. The crucial question is what structural patterns, if any, are available to all noun phrases regardless of head type. Since the internal structure of a noun phrase consists of the head noun plus its dependents, the question can be reworded as: what kinds of dependents are possible for all kinds of head noun. I shall suggest that in fact there are **no** such dependents.

The case can be made easily with *me*, which does not seem to allow any dependents at all unless we include dependents that are in fact irrelevant. Let us consider some possible counter-examples:

(168)   Poor me! I've got to work over the weekend.

A few adjectives (including *poor*) can combine with personal pronouns or proper nouns (compare *Poor John!*), but the result is not a dependent-head combination as in (169):

(169)   I found a poor little cat lying in the road.

It is not obvious how examples like (168) should be analysed, but they are clearly not noun phrases because they cannot be used as such.

(170)   *They've given poor me too much work.

Examples like (170) seem at best marginal, which suggests that the head of *Poor me!* is not the pronoun but the adjective. In other words, it is a clause rather than a noun phrase.

Another candidate worth considering contains a restrictive relative clause:

(171)   I who stand before you can vouch for it.

Such examples are possible, but extremely limited in terms of both style and syntax. They are inconceivable in everyday conversation, in clear contrast with ordinary common-noun + restrictive relative clause combinations. Moreover they are even worse in object position, where *me* would normally replace *I*:

(172)   ???You must believe me who stands/stand before you.

My judgement is that this example is ungrammatical, and remains unacceptable however we manipulate the context. Similarly Quirk, Greenbaum, Leech, and Svartvik 1985: 352 note that although restrictive relative clauses can modify *he* and *she* in highly formal style, they are absolutely impossible for *they* and *it*.

The next candidate for a pronoun with a dependent combines the pronoun with a name:

(173)   I John Smith do take thee, Mary Brown, to be my lawfully wedded wife.

The stylistic restrictions are obvious, but again *me John Smith* seems even worse.

(174)   ???To me John Smith that appears unjust.

Here too the possibility of modifying *me* turns out to be vanishingly small.

Two much more plausible candidates remain, but these turn out to be irrelevant to the comparison with common nouns. The first is an 'emphatic' reflexive pronoun:

(175)   I myself rather like it.

This is stylistically unrestricted with *I*, and although it is harder to match with *me*, this does seem to be possible, especially when *me* is subject of a non-finite verb:

(176)   For me myself to enjoy the food I cook is unusual.

Emphatic reflexive pronouns can modify other kinds of noun as well:

(177)   John himself is quite mild.
(178)   The picture itself isn't too bad.
(179)   Hard work itself doesn't worry me.

However they may even be able to modify non-nouns:

(180)   ?To work hard itself doesn't worry me.

This being so it is hardly surprising that they combine fairly easily with a gerund:

(181)   ?Working hard itself doesn't worry me.

Lastly we must consider non-restrictive relative clauses. These seem to combine quite easily with *me*:

(182)   She lost her temper with me, who really didn't deserve it.

More generally, non-restrictive relative clauses can modify virtually any other kind of noun, so we might conclude that they, at least, are available for any kind of noun phrase, regardless of its head type. This may well be true, but non-restrictive relative clauses can in fact modify virtually any kind of word, including adjectives, prepositions, and verbs (i.e. in phrase-structure terms, they can modify APs, PPs, and clauses):

(183)   He was really naughty, which he never used to be when he was little.
(184)   He was behind the coal-shed, which is his favourite play-spot.

(185)   He wasn't at all naughty, which surprised us.

Not surprisingly, therefore, they can also modify gerunds:

(186)   Working hard, which never did anyone any harm, is part of the job.

In short, the only modifiers that are possible with *me* are emphatic reflexives and non-restrictive relative clauses, which are possible with a wide range of words which goes beyond nouns.

In contrast with *me*, a common noun such as *books* allows a wide range of both pre-modifiers and post-modifiers: adjectives, nouns, prepositions, and clauses:

(187)   big dusty boring library books about linguistics which I have to
        return tomorrow.

None of these modifiers is possible with *me*, so we have at least two nouns, *books* and *me*, whose possible dependents show no overlap apart from the two much more general types of modifier mentioned above. There are of course many other kinds of noun, and in particular many different subclasses of pronoun (including the determiners), each of which allows a distinct range of modifiers. It would be pointless however to pursue these differences further, now that we have established the main point: different kinds of head noun allow different modifiers, and no modifiers are common to all nouns.

It could be objected that these differences are simply the result of semantic and pragmatic differences. After all, since *me* uniquely and unambiguously refers to the speaker, there seems to be little point in modifying it, so why might we ever want to add, say, a relative clause or an adjective? In contrast, *book* identifies a general category which it is useful to be able to make more precise by means of modifiers, so it is hardly surprising that modifiers are possible. However, although it is true that meaning ultimately explains a lot of syntax, the relation between syntax and meaning is no simpler in noun phrases than in other areas of grammar. There are a number of reasons for believing that at least some of these differences are in fact syntactic.

For example, modifiers can be descriptive, as in famous examples such as *the industrious Chinese*, where *industrious* applies to all Chinese and not just to a subset. This being so, we might expect descriptive modifiers to be possible with any nouns, including those that have unique referents; and indeed we find that some are possible with proper names:

(188)   Poor John got fired yesterday.

With personal pronouns they would be just as easy to interpret, but as we have seen they are not possible; so the explanation must be a specific syntactic restriction.

A second reason for interpreting differences as syntactic rather than purely semantic is that the range of possible modifiers has varied over time. For example, at one time restrictive relative clauses were possible with *they* or even *me*:

(189)   All they that take the sword shall perish with the sword. (King James Version; Matthew 26: 52)

(190)   ... but to attack me who am really so innocent—and who never say an ill natured thing of anybody (1777 Sheridan, *The School for Scandal* IV. iii. 411. 29, in Denison 1998)

This is no longer possible in Modern English, where *those* has replaced *they* in this construction. Similarly, it was once easier than nowadays for a relative *which* to have a complement noun of its own:

(191)   Lady Lufton ... had sent up a note addressed to Miss Lucy Robarts, which note was in Fanny's hands when Lucy stepped out of the pony-carriage. (1860–1 Trollope, Framley 35. 335, in Denison 1998)

Such variation clearly involves a change of syntax without any change of semantics, so it cannot be explained semantically.

It should also be pointed out that at least some variation in the range of possible dependents cannot be semantically motivated because synonymous dependents contrast syntactically. For example, as dependents the synonyms *other* and *else* are in complementary distribution. The default *other* is replaced by *else* just in case it modifies an indefinite pronoun such as *who* or *someone*; moreover the alternation also involves a change of word order, giving *who else* or *someone else* in place of the expected *other who* or *other someone. The compound pronouns such as *someone* also illustrate another (apparently) arbitrary syntactic restriction compared with common nouns. Although they can be modified by an adjective, this adjective:

- must follow the pronoun: *someone difficult*;
- cannot be iterated in the way that most modifiers can, so we cannot match *a tall strong person* by *someone tall strong*;
- cannot be another noun. Thus although we can say *travel things* or *meeting place* we do not find *something travel* or *somewhere meeting*.

In short, syntax allows different types of head noun to take different types of dependent, so the phrases that they head have different possible structures;

and this structural difference is so great that there is no single structural pattern which is common to all head nouns.

4.5 Gerunds as Nouns

The proposed analysis takes gerunds as examples of both nouns and verbs, so the present section will consider the consequences of analysing them as nouns, leaving the verb half of the analysis till the next section. The crucial point for the present section is the subclassification of nouns discussed in the previous section. This will be the basis for explaining why gerund phrases are nominal externally but not internally. This part of the analysis is virtually the same as the one in Malouf 1998: 154, except that it is expressed in terms of word-word dependencies rather than in terms of phrase structure.

If gerunds are nouns, how do they fit into the three-way contrast among proper, common, and pronoun? The obvious answer is that though they are nouns, they do not belong to any of these three subclasses of noun, so we must add 'Gerund' as a fourth subclass. This gives the hierarchy shown in Figure 4.3 where the line of question marks stands for a relationship that will be made more precise in the next section.

This classification immediately explains why a gerund heads a phrase whose distribution is that of a noun phrase: its distribution is like that of a noun because it is a noun—more technically, because Gerund isa Noun. However it also allows gerunds to be distinguished from other kinds of noun in those contexts where other kinds of noun are not allowed. In section 4.2 we noticed

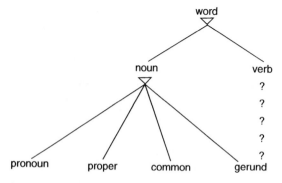

FIGURE 4.3. Gerunds are nouns.

two such contexts. One was in examples such as those that follow, where a gerund is used in a context that excludes other kinds of noun phrase:

(192)   It's/There's no use *telling him anything/*a big fuss.
(193)   There's no point *telling him anything/*anything else.
(194)   It's scarcely worthwhile *you/your going home/* a lot of work.
(195)   It's pointless *buying so much food/*purchase of food.

The other was after at least one verb, PREVENT, which only allows a gerund phrase after its complement preposition:

(196)   They prevented us from *finishing it/*its completion.

The possibility of distinguishing gerunds from other kinds of noun allows us to prevent over-generation in these areas by permitting only gerunds in these contexts. (The details of the rules concerned are irrelevant, the main point being that they can apply to 'Gerund' rather than more generally to 'Noun'.) The analysis seems to give us just the right combination of specificity and generality in defining the contexts in which gerunds may act as dependents.

However, the noun classification also introduces a new problem: if gerunds are nouns, why do gerund phrases not have the internal structure of noun phrases? As we know, the fact is that gerund phrases have the internal structure of clauses, as witness all the evidence for their being verbs: their use with direct objects and predicative complements, with non-possessive subjects, with adverbs rather than adjectives, and with *not*, plus the fact that a gerund may itself be an auxiliary verb. The gerund phrase (italicized) in the following sentence illustrates all these well-known facts:

(197)   I object to *him not yet having been given an appointment.*

This gerund phrase clearly has nothing at all in common with ordinary noun phrases such as *the idea of chocolate* or *his irrational anxiety.*

However, this problem disappears as soon as we notice that there is **nothing** which has 'the internal structure of a noun phrase'. As we saw in the previous section, the only thing that all noun-headed phrases have in common is their external distribution—the fact that they can all be used freely as subject, object, complement of a preposition, and so on. Beyond this, the phrase's structure depends on whether its head is a pronoun (i.e. pronoun/determiner), a common noun or a proper noun.

This being so, the grammar of nouns (as such) says nothing at all about their dependents, so there are no 'dependent facts' to be inherited by gerunds. This is why this section started by saying that the subclassification of nouns is the key to the analysis. If nouns had all been of one type, all taking the same range of dependents, these facts would have been stored at the level of 'noun' and would therefore have been inherited by gerunds. Given the logic of multiple default inheritance, the result would have been a clash with the structures inherited from 'verb', a clash which could have been solved only by stipulating a winner. As it is, however, the classification of gerunds as nouns is almost entirely 'free' as far as the phrase's internal structure is concerned, because there is no need for special rules or apparatus to resolve conflicts between nominal and verbal features. The exception is the very limited possibility of a determiner (possessive subjects and *no/any*), which will be discussed in section 4.7.

The outcome of this section, therefore, is that the classification of gerunds as nouns has important consequences for how they are themselves used as dependents, but none at all for their own dependents—in other words, gerund phrases have the external distribution of noun phrases, but not their internal structure. In the next section we shall see how the converse is true of their classification as verbs.

4.6 Gerunds as Verbs

As nouns, gerunds contrast with common nouns, proper nouns, and pro-nouns, all of which are word-classes—that is, classes of lexemes. The same is not true of their relationship to verbs, where gerunds differ from other verbs in their inflections. Any verb which can be non-finite (i.e. any verb other than a modal and a handful of full verbs such as BEWARE) can be a gerund, but gerunds are distinguished by their inflectional suffix -*ing*. As explained in section 2.2, inflections and lexemes are different kinds of subdivisions of Word, and any inflected lexeme inherits from both an inflection and a lexeme; but exceptionally, the inflection Gerund isa Noun as well as Verb (just as Participle isa both Adjective and Verb—see s. 3.6). Figure 4.4 completes Figure 4.3 in which the link from Gerund to Verb was left unspecified.

In terms of lexemes, of course, a gerund is an instance of whatever lexeme provides its base—*having* is an instance of HAVE, *walking* is an instance of WALK, and so on—which means that gerunds are basically verbs being used as nouns, rather than nouns being used as verbs. It is the verb lexeme that determines its meaning and its possible dependents as well as its stem. The fact that the lexeme is a verb has implications for the kinds of modifier that are possible—in particular, a verb may be modified by an adverb but not by an adjective, which is why the same is true of gerunds. All that the noun classifi-cation contributes is the possibility of being used as a dependent where a noun is required. The explanation, then, for why gerund phrases have the internal structure of clauses is that they are clauses (i.e. phrases headed by a verb).

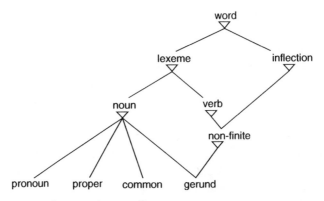

FIGURE 4.4. Gerunds are verbs as well as nouns

This part of the analysis is somewhat different from Malouf (1998), where gerunds are not verbs at all, but a subclass of 'relational', a category which includes adjectives as well as verbs. It is true that, as he observes, adjectives are similar to verbs in allowing adverbs as modifiers (e.g. *sufficiently thick*), but the same is true of prepositions (e.g. *exactly above the house*). The correct generalization seems to be that adverbs may modify any kind of word except nouns. Modifying adverbs therefore do not in themselves justify Malouf's category of relationals. Moreover, there are at least two characteristics that distinguish both gerunds and verbs from adjectives. One is that when an adjective is modified by an adverb, the adverb has to come first, whereas most adverbs can stand either before or after a verb or a gerund:

(198)   a sufficiently thick layer
(199)   * a thick sufficiently layer
(200)   Often making mistakes is normal.
(201)   Making mistakes often is normal.

The other difference between gerunds and adjectives is that although a few adjectives combine with *not*, as in *not insignificant* or *not many*, the possibilities are extremely limited and the best generalization is that adjectives typically do not combine with non-contrastive *not*:

(202)   *a not angry man.
(203)   *He seems not angry.

This use of *not* is distinct from contrastive *not . . . but*, which combines freely with most word-classes:

(204)   He seems not angry but worried.
(205)   He built not a house but a mansion.

Free combination with non-contrastive *not* is possible only for two word-classes: non-finite verbs and gerunds:

(206) He tends to not do anything.
(207) Not doing anything is unacceptable.

The evidence therefore points to a classification in which gerunds are grouped with verbs to the exclusion of adjectives—in other words, they are verbs rather than 'relationals'. This simple conclusion is confirmed, of course, by the fact that they are formed morphologically in exactly the same way as present participles; so, since they are inflected verbs then *a fortiori* they are verbs. In contrast, Malouf's analysis involves a rule to change the lexical class of a verb into that for a gerund—either a lexical rule which takes a verb and turns it into a gerund (Malouf 1998: 90) or an inflectional class which overrides the classification as a verb (ibid. 163). No such rule is needed in the present analysis because gerunds are simply verbs.

But if gerunds really are verbs, why don't their phrases have the external distribution of a verb phrase? This is similar to the question in the previous section about why gerund phrases do not have the internal structure of noun phrases, and the answer is also similar: because there is **nothing** that has the external distribution of a verb phrase. The fact is that there are no rules (or principles) which permit some position to be occupied by 'a verb phrase'; every rule that allows a verb phrase also requires the head verb to have some particular inflection—tensed, participle, infinitive, or whatever. In dependency terminology, a verb's inflection is sensitive to whether or not it depends on another verb; for example, a verb must be finite if it is independent (i.e. the root of the whole sentence), it must be an infinitive if it is the complement of *will*, and so on. Just like the case inflections of a noun, each inflection of a verb is available for a different range of syntactic positions, and each such position is limited to a specific range of inflections. Consequently, none of these positions will be available to gerunds unless gerunds are specifically named as possible; and (most important of all), no distributional facts at all are available for inheritance from the general category Verb.

The conclusion to which the last two sections have led us is that the grammar of gerunds is very simple indeed. They are inflected by the addition of the same {ing} suffix as present participles, but they are not present participles: they constitute a unique inflectional class, Gerund. This word-class isa both Noun (where it contrasts with Proper, Common, and Pronoun) and Non-finite (which isa Verb). Having said this, all the main facts about gerunds follow automatically, without any stipulations or special provisions at all: seen as heads, they are ordinary non-finite verbs, but seen as dependents they are ordinary nouns.

This simplicity is possible because of one very general difference between verbs and nouns. What all verbs have in common is their valency—the range of dependents that they permit—and not their functions as dependents, which vary according to the verb's inflectional class. In contrast, nouns have no comparable inflectional distinction because English has no case (Hudson 1995) so all nouns share the same range of possible functions as dependents— the possibility of being used as subjects, objects, and so on; but different subclasses of noun have no common valency. Because of this difference, the general characteristics of nouns and verbs are in fact orthogonal, so they can both be inherited without conflict.

4.7 The Debris of History: Possessives and *No/Any*

The simplicity of gerunds in present-day English lies at the end of many centuries of gradual evolution whose beginnings in Old English were entirely different. In Old English there were no gerunds, but there were nominaliza-tions ('verbal nouns') comparable to modern nouns like *nominalization, arrival,* and *reading,* as in (208):

(208)   Fast reading of linguistics articles is difficult.

In Old English the regular verbal noun ended in either {ing} or {ung}. The following example is from Denison 1993: 387.

(209)   ac   gyrstandæg   ic wæs   on huntunge
        but   yesterday   I was   at hunting
        'But yesterday I was hunting.'

We shall consider the historical development of gerunds in section 4.8, but the aim of the present section is to correct the impression of perfection and simplicity which the previous two sections may have left. Gerunds developed out of a purely nominal pattern, and this history is still visible in the peculiarities of modern gerunds which were described in section 4.1.

The most obviously nominal relic is the possibility of possessive subjects, as in *John's knowing the answer.* As was mentioned in section 4.1, this strikes British speakers as rather forced and formal, though it seems to be more acceptable to Americans. In Britain the bare 'accusative' subject is more normal, as in (210) below, and the only possibility in (211):

(210)   John knowing the answer surprised us.

(211)   Our visit was spoilt by there being no one at home.

Non-finite verbs have overt subjects in other constructions:

(212)   With <u>the weather</u> turning cold, we had to stay inside.
(213)   He rushed into the room, <u>his shirt</u> hanging out.
(214)   What would be nice would be for <u>the sun</u> to come out now.

Consequently we might expect the same to be true of gerunds, so the bare subject in (210) is the form to be expected. The dependency structure for this example is as shown in Figure 4.5. If the gerund's subject had been a personal pronoun, it would have had the 'non-subject' form (*him knowing the answer*, not **he knowing the answer*), but this is as expected since 'subject' forms are used only with tensed verbs.

Where the gerund's subject is possessive it is less clear what the structure is. On the one hand, it could be argued that the structure is the same as when a possessive is used as a determiner in a noun phrase—that is, with the possessive as head. This has the advantage of revealing the similarity between these gerunds and ordinary noun phrases, and gives structures like that in Figure 4.6, where the possessive is the head of the whole noun phrase *John's knowing the answer* or *John's knowledge*. As usual in WG analyses, I assume that *'s* is a clitic rather than an inflection, and more specifically I assume that it is a determiner called POSS, and therefore a pronoun. Consequently, *John's* is syntactically two words, *John* and POSS; to include the possessive pronouns in this analysis, I also assume that possessive pronouns are syntactically complex fused words (as argued in s. 2.8) so that *my* is syntactically *me* + POSS and so on.

It can be seen that the structure for the gerund also shows a direct Subject link from *knowing* to *John*, in addition to its link to POSS. This extra link treats *John* as a raised subject so the analysis relates the possessive subject both to ordinary determiners and also to ordinary subjects using theoretical machinery which is already in use for other constructions.

On the other hand, one of the main reasons for treating determiners as the head of the noun phrase is the possibility of ellipsis. This argument applies successfully to ordinary possessive determiners such as *Bill's* in (215):

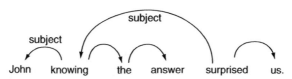

FIGURE 4.5. A gerund with bare subject

(215) John's success in the exam was surprising, and Bill's [ ] was even more so.

But gerunds are different, because ellipsis of the gerund is not possible (Malouf 1998: 51, following Abney 1987: 245):

(216) *John's passing the exam was surprising, and Bill's [ ] was even more so.

One way to explain this would be to reject the analysis just outlined, and to assume instead that the possessive is merely the gerund's subject, with just the same structural status as the bare subject in Figure 4.5. This would certainly predict that the possessive cannot occur without the gerund, but it would also throw out the baby with the bathwater by losing the comparison with ordinary noun phrases. Moreover, we shall see later that the same ban on ellipsis applies to the other gerund-taking determiner, *no*, which could not realistically be taken as the gerund's subject—see examples (222) and (224). In any case it would be very hard to explain the presence of POSS if the possessor NP was merely the subject; this would require an extra stipulation, and the structure would be totally unmotivated. In contrast, the structure suggested in Figure 4.6 does motivate POSS in relation to its use in ordinary noun phrases.

On balance, then, the structure in Figure 4.6 seems preferable to one in which the possessive is merely the gerund's subject. The preferred analysis requires two stipulations: first, that the other dependent of POSS (e.g. *John* in *John's*) doubles up as the gerund's subject—a very common syntactic pattern, similar to the one found with auxiliary verbs; and second, that when the complement is a gerund it is obligatory. Such arbitrary variations in optionality are common (Hudson, Rosta, Holmes, and Gisborne 1996); for example, the complement of *every* is obligatory whereas that of *each* is optional, and *try* does allow its infinitival complement to be elided whereas *attempt* does not.

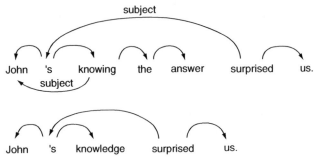

FIGURE 4.6. A gerund with 'possessive' subject

Informally, the rules for ordinary possessives are as follows:

- A pronoun's complement is a common noun.
- A pronoun's complement is optional.
- POSS is a pronoun and has a complement.

These rules allow ordinary POSS and allow its (optional) complement to be elided as in (215). What we can call 'POSS$_{gerund}$' is a special case which combines four properties:

(217) a POSS$_{gerund}$ isa POSS.
       b The complement of POSS$_{gerund}$ isa Gerund.
       c The pre-dependent of POSS$_{gerund}$ is the subject of its complement.
       d The complement of POSS$_{gerund}$ is obligatory.

None of these rules is typologically unusual, complex, or hard to learn. In diachronic terms, it is easy to see how possessive subjects formed a necessary stage in the development of modern gerunds from ordinary nominalizations, whose 'subjects' must be possessives rather than bare noun phrases. It is in this sense that I describe possessive subjects as 'the debris of history'.

Another item of debris is the determiner NO/ANY which I discussed in section 4.1, using examples that included the following:

(218) No playing loud music!
(219) There's no mistaking that voice.
(220) There isn't any telling what they will do.

These can be analysed along the same lines as the gerunds with possessive subjects. The determiner can be treated in the usual way, as the head of its phrase, but its gerund complement is unusual in being obligatory (i.e. not subject to ellipsis). This can be seen from the following examples, where the gerund is contrasted with a common noun:

(221) A: No noise, please!   B: What, none at all?
(222) A: No being noisy, please!   B: *What, none at all?
(223) A: There's no possibility of mistaking that   B: No, none at all!
       voice!
(224) A: There's no mistaking that voice!   B: *No, none at all!

In this construction there does not appear to be any alternative to a stipulation about optionality.

The semantics of these constructions is challenging, but not relevant here. The syntax is reasonably straightforward, since the pronouns *no* and *any* exceptionally allow an obligatory gerund as complement. The only uncertainty is why the gerund cannot have a subject:

(225)   a   No *(any boys) playing football here, please, but girls can play if
            they want.
        b   There's no (*a linguist) accounting for this sentence.

Informally speaking, overt subjects seem to conflict with the subject specifi-
cations that are already imposed by these constructions—for example, *No
smoking!* applies specifically to 'you'. For the time being however we must
settle for a stipulation about the gerund's subject, but there are ample
precedents for such construction-based stipulations—see for example the
analysis of *just because X does not mean that Y* in Holmes and Hudson 2006.

Once again it is obvious why these uses of NO/ANY with a gerund exist in
current English, given the origin of gerunds in ordinary common nouns and
the fact that these are also possible, with similar meanings, after NO/ANY:

(226)   a   No noise, please!
        b   There's no doubt about his intentions.
(227)   There isn't any way of telling his intentions.

But however understandable their origins may be, the fact remains that these
patterns, like the possessive subjects, are exceptional and special uses of
gerunds which cannot be explained as simply as was possible with ordinary
gerunds.

It could be objected that this analysis of the 'debris of history' fails to
explain why these particular patterns survived but others did not. In particular, why do we still combine gerunds with a handful of determiners (POSS, NO,
ANY), but not with adjectives? If we can say *my watching TV regularly,* why
can't we say **my regular watching TV*? An easy answer suggests itself: the
survivors are all single lexical items—just three specific determiners. In each
case gerunds were mentioned in a stipulation about the determiner's complement, which is a very ordinary instance of valency detail. In contrast, if
modifying adjectives had survived, the exception would have involved a whole
word-class rather than a single lexical item. The exceptional rule would have
allowed any adjective as a pre-adjunct of any gerund. As we shall now see,
English did pass through a phase where this was possible, but we can see the
modern system as a major simplification.

4.8 The Route from Old English

It is important to evaluate any analysis of current English in relation to a
much broader context. Does it explain the origins of current English in earlier
forms of English?

The diachronic question arises because the development has been very gradual, so that slightly different grammars have had to coexist over long periods. This means that it should be possible to trace a route back from current English to a much older stage via a series of grammars with only minimal differences between adjacent stages. An analysis of current English must therefore generalize, with only minor changes, to the intermediate grammars that are known to have existed in the past. The following discussion rests heavily on data from Wurff (1993; 1997), and as in his more recent account, I shall show that the changes involved a gradual evolution of fine details rather than a major reorganization of the grammar; however Wurff assumes a structural analysis which is quite different from the one proposed here. Unfortunately the early history of gerunds is very complex, unclear, and hotly disputed—not least because the suffixes used for nominalizations ({ing} and {ung} in Old English) merged in Middle English with those of the participle (formerly {ende}), to give the Modern English situation where the difference between {ing} (derived from OE {ing} and {ung}) and {in} (from {ende}) is grammatically irrelevant (both are ambiguous between participle and gerund) but socially important (Denison 1993: 387; Malouf 1998: 116; Labov 1989).

The relatively 'pure' system of current English stands at the end of a long period of gradual evolution (which Wurff dates as starting in the eleventh century), during which gerunds shed their nominal 'internal' characteristics—that is to say, the characteristics expected within a noun phrase. As we have seen, even today they still have two such characteristics—possessive subjects and occurrence after NO/ANY—but until as recently as the end of the nineteenth century they could also occur with *the* and with adjectives. In the following examples from Wurff 1993, I have underlined the relevant words:

(228) Between rheumatism and <u>constant</u> handling the rod and gun ... (1853)
(229) <u>The</u> managing an argument handsomely being so nice a Point, ... (1711)
(230) <u>The</u> writing the verbs at length on this slate, will be a very useful exercise (1829)
(231) <u>The due</u> placing them adapts the rhyme to it. (1684)

Malouf (1998: 75) quotes similar examples:

(232) <u>The untrewe</u> forgyng and contryvyng certayne testamentys and last wyll [15th century]
(233) My <u>wicked</u> leaving my father's house [17th century]
(234) <u>The</u> being weighted down by the stale and dismal oppression of the rememberance [19th century]

Denison (p.c.) has provided other examples which are worth repeating because of their relatively recent dates:

(235)   The copying them has been and still is my occupation; ... and I am trying to get the printing done also while I am finishing the copying. (1873)

(236)   At least I can't fix on any tangible object or aim in life which seems so desirable as the having got it finally over—and the remaining *in perpetuo* without desire or aim or consciousness whatsoever. (1890)

(237)   The days had been very full: the psychiatrist, the obstacle courses, the throwing herself from the hold of a slowly chugging plane. (1998)

(The last example is from Sebastian Faulks, *Charlotte Gray* (Vintage Press): 111.) All these examples strike me as extremely odd, but usage is clearly divided.

Conversely, during this long period of evolution, nominalizations sometimes had a verbal characteristic—modification by adverbs—which Malouf claims to be generally impossible (1998: 121). Again the examples are from Wurff 1993:

(238)   The *quickly* doing of it, is the grace. (1610)

(239)   He finds that bearing of it *patiently* is the best way. (1664)

(240)   ... the shutting of the gates *regularly* at ten o'clock ... (1818)

Indeed, Wurff 1997 even gives an example where an adverb is used with a derived nominalization:

(241)   ... but on an examination more *strictly* by the justices of the peace, and at the Lord Mayor's request, it was found there were twenty more. (1722)

The question, then, is what these examples tell us about the grammar.

One important fact is that 'mixed' gerunds of the kinds illustrated here were not at all common. In a collection of 400 clear gerunds or nominalizations from the eighteenth and nineteenth centuries that Wurff studied (1997), only 8 percent showed mixed characteristics by the most generous definition of this category. All the rest were either consistently verbal (82%) or consistently nominal (11%). These figures suggest that the mixed patterns may have been archaic and perhaps even impossible for most writers.

Another observation is that only two areas of grammar are involved: the use of *the*, and the choice between adverbs and adjectives. The first is easily accommodated as yet another determiner which allows a gerund complement, in addition to the possessives and NO/ANY that still do; in other words, the range of determiners which allow such complements has gradually reduced over time. This is hardly surprising given the origins of gerunds.

The change in the use of adverbs and adjectives also led to a simplification of the grammar, as suggested above, but it seems that there was a period when the choice was less rigidly determined than in current English. Example (241) above shows that adverbs could at least sometimes modify ordinary nouns in eighteenth-century English, and according to Wurff (1997), adverbs such as TELKENS, 'continually', can modify nominalizations in modern Dutch (reflecting a general flexibility in the choice between adjective and adverb compared with English):

(242) door het telkens   breken   van je   beloften
       by   the continually   breaking of   your   promises
       'Because of the continual breaking of your promises'

(243) het telkens   geven van geld   aan hem
       the continually   giving of   money   to   him
       'The continual giving of money to him'

It is worth pointing out that there is at least some flexibility even in current standard English; some adverbs may modify some nouns, and the choice between adverb and adjective is optional in some verb-modifier collocations (Swan 1995: 16–19).

(244) The weather <u>recently</u> in London has been appalling.
(245) I held it <u>tight/tightly</u>.
(246) You guessed <u>wrong/wrongly</u>.

However the fact remains that the examples quoted earlier, in which adverbs modified nouns and adjectives modified gerunds, would all be rejected in present-day English.

Clearly what has changed is that both adverbs and adjectives are more tightly restricted now than they were in earlier periods. On the one hand, adverbs are (in general) not allowed to modify nouns, and on the other adjectives are (in general) only allowed to modify common nouns (and compound pronouns like *someone*), with some latitude for proper nouns and (of course) not at all for gerunds. Without more facts it is hard to know exactly what the restrictions in earlier periods were, but one possibility is that adjectives could modify all kinds of noun, including gerunds, while the restriction on adverbs was semantic rather than syntactic (e.g. QUICKLY can modify any word which refers to an event that has a speed). Whatever the facts and the correct analysis, it seems clear that the relevant changes in the grammar can be accounted for by changes to the rules for adjectives and adverbs, and without any change to the analysis of gerunds.

4.9 Conclusion

The main conclusion is that English gerunds are indeed just what the traditional grammarians said: single words which are both verbs and nouns. Once this has been said, nothing more is needed in order to generate ordinary gerunds, though special provisions are needed for possessive subjects and NO/ANY. In particular there is no need to assume separate verbal and nominal nodes in order to prevent verbal and nominal characteristics from conflicting, because English is organized in such a way that these characteristics are always orthogonal: nominal features are exclusively concerned with relations external to the gerund phrase, and verbal features with its internal patterns.

It is also worth pointing out that this analysis has important consequences for syntactic theory that go beyond the treatment of gerunds. The analysis supports two general conclusions, both of which are central tenets of WG:

- Phrase structure may be less important than it is often considered to be. Even gerunds, which seem at first sight to call out for multiple phrasal nodes, can be analysed very satisfactorily in terms of dependency structures with no more than one node per word.
- Word-class features (e.g. [+N]) may be less satisfactory for classification than atomic word-class names (e.g. Noun); in particular, it would be wrong to use [+N,+V] for adjectives because a feature analysis would need this particular combination for gerunds.

In short, this detailed study of the details of English gerunds has complemented and supported the arguments put forward in the previous chapters.

5

Meaning: Semantics and Sociolinguistics

5.1 Meaning

What do semantics and sociolinguistics have in common? Very little, to judge by traditional approaches to the two subjects. Semantic studies of quantifiers, anaphora, and even lexical semantics seem to be located in a different intellectual world from sociolinguistic studies of accents and dialects, politeness forms, and the like. However I think this separation misses an important point which has been made strongly by functional and cognitive linguists, and perhaps especially by Halliday (Halliday 1978). Both semantics and sociolinguistics study 'meaning'—the property of a word which explains how we use the word in particular social situations. For example, the word *cookie* means 'biscuit' but it also carries the 'social meaning' of being an American; and *attempt* not only means 'try' but also signals a formal social situation. The two kinds of meaning are often merged, for example in the slogan 'one word, one meaning' which is said to guide children's learning of word meaning—in other words, 'Speakers take every difference in form to mark a difference in meaning' (Clark 1993: 64). This hypothesis is sustainable only so long as 'meaning' includes social meaning; otherwise it is too easily refuted by obvious synonyms (e.g. *bike* and *bicycle*, *loo* and *toilet*). In short, words may relate to characteristics of all sorts of things outside language with which they are correlated and which include not only the entities that they refer to, but also the speaker and other elements of the situation in which they are uttered. For an infant, words like *hullo* and *yogurt* offer the same intellectual challenge: what do adults 'mean' by them?

On the other hand, I do not accept the conclusion that the different kinds of meaning should all be lumped together into a single analytical category. Indeed, one of the best arguments for considering them together is that this allows us to consider their differences and to find ways to separate them in our analyses. For example, Halliday distinguished at least four different kinds of meaning: experiential, interpersonal, logical, and textual (Halliday 1977).

WG provides a framework not only for making such distinctions but also for expressing them formally in terms of relations. For instance, COOKIE is related in quite different ways to the meanings 'biscuit' and 'American'. The former defines its possible referents, whereas the latter defines its possible speakers. This difference is obvious and beyond dispute; for example, saying *I ate a cookie* is a way of asserting that I ate a biscuit, and we may assume that the speaker is an American, but certainly not that I ate an American.

Given this difference, therefore, we can distinguish at least two broad classes of 'meaning':

- **Referential meaning**, related to the word's **referent**—what the word refers to, roughly the same as Halliday's experiential meaning.
- **Social meaning**, related to the utterance situation—the speaker and addressee, the time and place and the social event, Halliday's interpersonal meaning.

Provided we can distinguish a word's referent from its speaker, we can accommodate both kinds of meaning without losing the important difference between them. Surprisingly few theories of language structure even try to accommodate social meaning in this way; apart from WG, the only theories I know of are HPSG (Pollard and Sag 1994: 27) and Systemic Functional Grammar (Halliday 1985).

In WG, both kinds of meaning are entirely mental—concepts of people and things which may or may not exist in the outside world. Take my familiar given name, for example: DICK. In my mind, its referent is my concept of myself, the node in my mental network which stands for me; but in your mind it is (of course) a different node, carrying different properties which include at least the property of having written this book. I do exist outside your mind and mine, but the word DICK only relates to the real me via these mental constructs in our minds. The same is true of the name's social meaning, which is less formal than my 'official' name, PROFESSOR HUDSON. Knowledge of English includes the knowledge that we use a name such as DICK when referring to an intimate—in other words, that the speaker and the referent of DICK are intimates. But once again 'the speaker' is a mental construct, my concept of the speaker, and the relation is entirely in the mind. As we all know, our mental representation of any situation may be objectively wrong: you can wrongly think I am called John and you can wrongly think I am an intimate. But that is a completely different issue from how we interpret words. The two kinds of meaning are shown diagrammatically in Figure 5.1, with a very tentative analysis of intimacy in terms of a set of intimates. Strangely, perhaps,

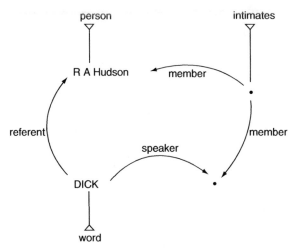

FIGURE 5.1.   The referential and social meaning of the name DICK

the most controversial part of this diagram is the relation called 'Speaker', which I shall explain and justify in the next section.

In this chapter I shall be discussing referential and social meaning, but for the record I should note that there are other kinds of meaning that I shall ignore for lack of anything constructive to say. In particular, I am thinking of 'emotive meaning' (Meidner 1994), the feelings that words express and evoke. The words concerned range over a wide variety:

- Grammatically unintegrated interjections such as OUCH and HURRAY.
- Grammatically integrated but non-referential modifiers like BLOODY (as in: *I missed the bloody bus*, where the feeling attaches to the whole situation described rather than to the bus).
- Referential words which carry emotional 'connotations' as part of the definition of their referent, e.g. TERRORIST, FREEDOM-FIGHTER.
- Words that refer directly to emotions, such as HAPPY, SNUG, FAIR, and FUN.

These feelings qualify as 'meanings' because the feelings concerned are cor-related with the words and the linkage is conventional and learned. Moreover, feelings clearly overlap strongly with both referential and social meanings, so a complete account of meaning must include them. However, this area of language is very difficult to model without a better understanding than at least I have of how emotions relate to the cognitive network, so with regret I can do no more than flag emotive meaning as an important area for research.

5.2 Language, Ontology, Signals and Symbols

WG has always made claims about how language structure fits into our general classification of the world. This classification is our personal 'ontology', and in WG it consists of the Isa hierarchy of entities that structures all our knowledge. Given the central role of words in WG, the question about the ontology of language simplifies to: What is a word? (More technically and clumsily: What does Word isa?) The WG answer has always been that, in spite of written language, a word is a kind of action (Hudson 1984: 241; 1990: 63–66, 76), so the word CAT (for example) is the action of saying the sounds [kat] while referring to a cat. In contrast, most theories of language structure assume the structuralist view that words are *sui generis*, different from everything else. The WG view has a number of important consequences which are especially important for the theory of meaning. I shall briefly review the earlier WG view of these consequences, and then suggest a slightly more sophisticated ontology for language.

One consequence of seeing words as a kind of action is that utterance properties are available in the permanent language network. If a stored word isa Action, then an uttered word (which is also an action) has a very simple relation to a word-type (i.e. a word stored in our language): the token isa the type. I explained in (s. 1.7) how we process tokens by linking them to the type which provides the best fit, and how the Isa link allows the token to inherit the properties of the type. One rather surprising result of this kind of processing is that tokens form a constantly changing 'fringe' on the edge of the language network; and a positive outcome is that learning is easily explained as the conversion of a temporary token into a permanent type (see (s. 1.8)). Conversely, if types are simply tokens which have been preserved from the usual oblivion, then they can maintain some of the situational details which we associate with action tokens—who did it to whom, when, where, and why. In short, the type may be associated with a particular actor and recipient (i.e. in the case of a word, with a particular speaker and addressee) as well as with a time and a place. These situational parameters which attach to words are an important consequence of learning language from usage, since any fact about an item of usage may be sufficiently salient to be remembered. On the other hand, most of our stored knowledge about situations is quite general—that COOKIE is used by Americans, that we say GOOD EVENING as a greeting in the evening, that we only use GEE-GEE when talking to children, and so on. This generality is the result of the usual inductive process which adds a new supercategory to bring together a range of (stored) specific cases.

In short, the parameters which are so important in sociolinguistics are ordinary properties of words, with just the same status as their word-class, valency, realization, and meaning. For some words we can remember who used them, which means that we can induce generalizations about the speaker such as the one in Figure 5.1 above. This is why the relation Speaker is available in a WG network.

Another consequence of the action-based view of words is that deictic semantics becomes very easy to accommodate, in contrast with the conventional view where it is a severe challenge. For example, the referent of the word ME is its speaker, and the time of a past-tense verb is before its time (a relation which, incidentally, is an example of the Landmark relations discussed in s. 3.2). The relevant structures for these two kinds of words are shown in Figure 5.2.

What I have presented so far is much the same as in 1990, but I think a somewhat more sophisticated analysis is possible now, partly because of the new level of form (s. 2.3) and partly because of recent work on the lexical semantics of causative constructions (Holmes 2005). Instead of classifying words simply as communicative actions, we can unpack their 'force dynamics' (Talmy 1988) in terms of actions, results, and purposes (intended results). Having done this, we can then apply the analysis to the cross-level relations of Realization and Referent.

I start with events (though these in turn probably isa Situation, which I ignore here). The most general verb for events is HAPPEN (as in *What*

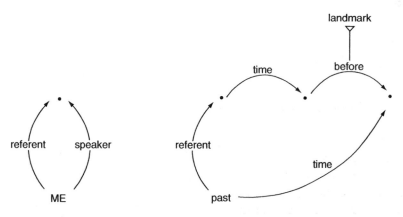

FIGURE 5.2.   The deictic meanings of ME and past tense

happened was that ...), and I assume that Event is in fact the sense of this verb so I shall replace Event by the name **Happening**, and likewise for other verb senses below. One subclass of Happening is **Doing** (i.e. action), in which there is a 'do-er' who controls the event and does it for some purpose (i.e. in order to produce some other situation); so a rainstorm is not a doing (unless one believes in weather gods), whereas a murder is. As usual in prototype semantics, there are borderline cases such as accidental killing. The prototypical action verb, DO, distinguishes these cases as expected:

(247)   !What it did was it rained.
(248)   ?What he did was he accidentally killed his own child.
(249)   What he did was he murdered his rival.

The act of saying a word is a clear case of doing, but it is less clear what this means for the word itself. This will become clearer shortly.

Another important subclass of happening is **Making**, the sense of the resultative verb MAKE: the first event makes the result happen. (I prefer to invoke the verb MAKE rather than CAUSE, as in Jackendoff 1990, because it is a much more commonplace word.) The event itself is some event which may or may not be controlled and intentional, but it results in some other situation; for example, rain can make plants grow. One particular kind of happening is **Achieving**, doing something that makes something else happen; this isa both Doing and Making as shown in Figure 5.3. Achieving inherits an actor and a purpose from Doing and a result from Making; and by stipulation the purpose and the result are the same—in other words, the result is intended

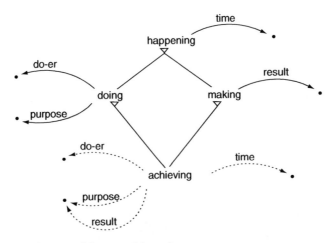

FIGURE 5.3.   The top of the event hierarchy

and is the reason for doing the action. The dotted arcs are relations that are inherited rather than stipulated, though the convergence of result and purpose is stipulated.

The very general categories distinguished so far provide the ontological background for an analysis of communication, which brings us nearer to language. As far as communication is concerned, my proposal is that it has two stages or parts: **signalling**, and a **symbol**. Signalling is an achievement—an action which achieves the effect of producing a symbol. Signalling 'makes' the symbol; for example, when I wave to someone, I do something with my hand (signalling) which makes or constitutes a symbol. In a sense, this signalling action and the symbol are the same thing, but there are good reasons for distinguishing them:

- There are plenty of precedents for seeing the symbol as a 'representational redescription' (Karmiloff-Smith 1992) of the signalling at a higher level of abstraction (in much the same way that we can 'redescribe' a lump of rock as a weapon or a hammer by considering its function).
- It is possible to make the 'same' symbol in an infinite variety of slightly different ways, involving different amounts and kinds of movement. Seen as a symbol, the gestures are equivalent, though as movements they are different.
- Both the signalling and the symbol are purposeful, but their purposes are different. The purpose of signalling is simply to create the signal; but the purpose of the signal is to influence another person's mind. Success in one does not guarantee success in the other: I can succeed in signalling by producing the intended signal (e.g. a gesture), without achieving the intended effect of the symbol.

In a nutshell, the signal is the concrete manifestation whereas the symbol is its meaning. It is the symbol rather than the signal that will concern us from now on.

The symbol's purpose is to influence the mind of some specific person (or group), so it has an **addressee**—a crucial notion as far as social meaning is concerned, of course. In relation to the addressee, the purpose is that they should 'think' something—that is to say that in network terms they should focus activation on a particular set of nodes. As Pinker puts it, 'we can shape events in each other's brains with exquisite precision.... Simply by making noises with our mouths, we can reliably cause precise new combinations of ideas to arise in each other's minds' (Pinker 1994: 15). These 'new combinations of ideas' are newly added nodes which activate, and inherit from, existing nodes; and together they constitute 'a thought'. Almost by definition, this thought must already be what the communicator is thinking, but the aim of the communication is that the addressee should think it too. This shared thought is the signal's **meaning**, so we now have a suitably cognitive and social explanation for this rather problematic notion. One of the attractions of this definition is that it embraces social as well as referential meaning, because both are thoughts that we intend to share with the addressee's mind; so in terms of gesturing, it applies as much to a farewell wave (social) or a secret handshake (social) as to pointing (referential). The analysis is summarized in Figure 5.4.

Turning now to **words** and their place in general ontology, we already have the main components of the theory. A word, in the WG sense, is a symbol, complete with a meaning, but it is linked to the signal which makes it—that is in WG terms, which, **realizes** it. As I explained in section 2.3, the relation between either words and forms or between forms and sounds is Realization, so I can now set this term in a broader context. A form is a signal and the corresponding word is a symbol that it realizes (i.e. 'makes' or constitutes); so, for example, the form { {re}+{do} } realizes the word REDO. And the same applies, *mutatis mutandis*, for sounds and forms; so [ri] realizes the form {re}. In both cases, the relation between the two units is Karmiloff-Smith's representational redescription, so redescription is just the converse of realization: units at the higher level are a redescription of those at the next level down, and conversely the latter realize the former. In contrast, a meaning is not a redescription of a word; for example, it would be nonsense to suggest that John Smith (the person) is a redescription of the name JOHN or SMITH. The word is the crucial meeting point between meaning (upwards) and realization (downwards), as can be seen in Figure 5.5. This figure is labelled

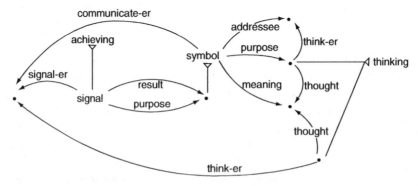

FIGURE 5.4. Communicating: signals make symbols which share thoughts

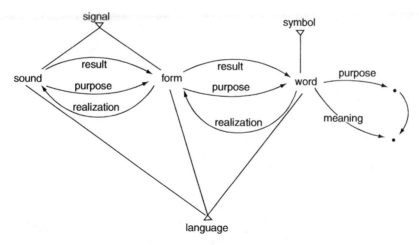

FIGURE 5.5.　The architecture of language

'The architecture of language' because it summarizes the links and mediating units that WG postulates between sounds and meanings.

5.3 Evolution and Meaning

I should like to relate these ideas about the architecture of language to two general questions that I first raised in section 1.8: how do children learn to communicate in language, and why can't other primates do the same?

One recent suggestion is that the crucial difference between children and other primates lies in the ability to use recursion in syntax (Hauser, Chomsky, and Fitch 2002), and in particular the ability to use centre-embedded recursion. I find this explanation unsatisfactory for several reasons:

- As Chomsky himself pointed out long ago, even humans have a very limited capacity for centre-embedding, and the limitations are best explained in terms of memory limitations. If so, the same kind of explanation is possible for whatever differences are found between humans and primates.
- It turns out that starlings can recognize centre-embedded patterns, so they must be able to process them (Gentner, Fenn, Margoliash, and Nusbaum 2006).
- In any case, centre embedding is beside the point because non-humans struggle even with learning words, let alone syntax of any kind, whether with or without centre embedding. Hum\an infants have a vocabulary of several thousand words by the age of 5, but even under the most favourable conditions, other primates do not manage more than a few hundred items (Williams, Savage-Rumbaugh, and Rumbaugh 1994) in many more years.

The real question, therefore, is why only humans can learn vocabulary; or as a child once asked, why don't other animals have even simple languages (Deacon 1997: 12)? Like Deacon, I believe the answer is that we can learn symbols, but other animals cannot. Why this should be I can only guess at, but I believe it may be possible to build a plausible theory on the basis of a combination of old and new ideas, including the analysis of symbols in (s. 5.2). Let us consider what mental abilities are needed in order to learn how symbols work—in other words, to induce the structure of Figure 5.4. It would be unrealistic to expect learners to go straight to this complete structure in all its detail and subtlety; for example, although I think the distinction between signals and symbols is conceptually important for understanding adults, it does not seem essential to an elementary learner.

I believe that the crucial element in this development is the Meaning link, because it is what explains the 'vocabulary spurt' found in humans but not in chimpanzees (Jackendoff 2002: 241) which 'may be due to the discovery that things have names, leading to a passion for attaching labels' (Aitchison 1994: 172). The discovery that things have names is the induction of the Meaning relation between signals and 'things' (i.e. entity concepts). Before this discovery, every meaning is learned from scratch as a correlation between an utterance and some other concept, for example, between hearing the sound [kat] and thinking about a cat. This is the ordinary Hebbian learning which I discussed in (s. 1.8), and which presupposes enough stored exemplars to justify the generalization. Learning this way is a slow business, and my impression is that this is how all non-humans manage to learn some language, via hundreds or thousands of trials. In contrast, the discovery of Meaning allows a word to be learned from a single example. If every word has a meaning, then there is no need to wait for a correlation to emerge. Instead, the learner can actively look for a meaning either by guessing or by asking. And conversely, if the learner has applied the Meaning link (wrongly, as it happens) to the default entity, then the learner can actively look for the 'name' of everything in sight.

The crucial question, then, is what mental abilities are needed in order to learn the Meaning link, and which of these seem to be missing in non-humans. If we can answer this question, we may be on the way to understanding why we are the only language-users in the animal kingdom. To make the discussion more concrete, we start with an incident in which Mummy says the word *bed* while clearly looking at a bed and also paying attention to the child. (I build in the latter feature of the situation on the assumption that children are more likely to learn from utterances that are addressed to them than to other people.) The child has a concept for the bed, and knows enough

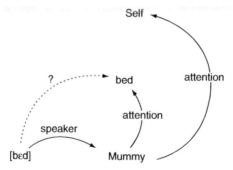

FIGURE 5.6. A child or chimp remembers Mummy using the word *bed*

phonology to store the word as [bɛd]. What the child makes of this incident is shown by the solid lines in Figure 5.6, where Attention is the relation between a person and some object to which they are paying attention. The dotted arrow is the Hebbian relation which emerges as a correlation based on numerous similar incidents, all stored in the same way. We might call this 'bed-meaning', because it is unrelated to other lexical items. This is the stage that chimpanzees can achieve.

One crucial leap is the induction of Meaning from all the individual lexical meanings which produces the general schema in Figure 5.7. In this network, the specific word and meaning have been replaced by Form and the node M, and the new Meaning relation replaces the lexeme-specific links. Each of these general categories is linked by Isa to the specific lexical items from which it has been induced. However, this is only part of the story because it does not yet explain why children should become excited by their discovery that adults tend to be paying attention to the same thing each time they say a particular word.

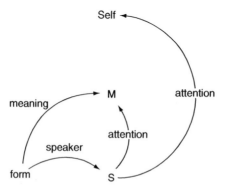

FIGURE 5.7. A child induces the Meaning relation

This in itself may be interesting, but it is not the same thing as discovering that words are for communicating. After all, if the child already knows what the adult is paying attention to, hearing the expected word conveys no new information. The Meaning relation only becomes emotionally meaningful when it is combined with other properties as in Figure 5.8. In this analysis, saying a form is a way of coordinating the attention of the speaker and the addressee; and since the speaker could be the child, it offers the child a way to control other people's minds. For example, if the child says *bed* to Mummy (where 'to' invokes the Addressee relation), then Mummy's attention as well as the child's will be on the bed (even if it is out of sight).

Our question, then, is what mental abilities the leap to this structure requires, and which of them humans do not share with other animals. The following list is meant to be suggestive rather than exhaustive:

- Complexity and abstractness: the ability to handle complex and abstract relations by recognizing their existence and then generalizing them across incidents.
- Mind-reading: the ability to read other people's minds sufficiently to know what they are paying attention to.
- Formal induction: the ability to induce general relations such as Meaning, Speaker, and Addressee from specific cases.

I shall discuss these suggestions in turn.

1. *Complexity and Abstractness*

The relations in Figure 5.8 are complex and abstract in the sense that each is defined in terms of other relations rather than in terms of concrete observables. This makes them good candidates for processing in our large prefrontal

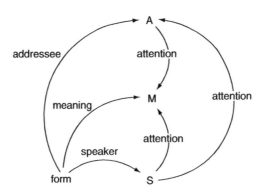

FIGURE 5.8.   The child learns why Meaning is important

cortex, which gives great capacity for processing abstract relations that are far removed from sensory input and parasitic on complex network relationships (Deacon 1997: 266). As Deacon observes, similar abstraction is needed for the complex social relations found even in primitive human societies (ibid. 388). The sheer complexity of these relations is important because they presage the complexities of the language network. Moreover, these complex social structures are important because they are abstract and not merely a matter of observing physical characteristics; for example, some of the most important parameters in human societies are built around abstractions such as friendship and interest, and on verbal agreements for institutions such as marriage (ibid. 400).

However, complexity and abstraction are not sufficient in themselves to explain language. Even baboons have complex social structures and treat each other differently according to what they know about kinship relations and abstract status (Seyfarth, Cheney, and Bergman 2005), and although the cognitive structures that our primate ancestors developed for manipulating relations no doubt helped in evolving complex language systems, something else was needed in addition.

2. Mind-Reading

Other people's minds can be read at different depths, from identifying their focus of attention to empathizing and sharing their goals. Even primates are aware of what others are paying attention to, so if this is the critical parameter it must involve a deeper kind of mind-reading such as understanding another person's motivation for speaking. According to Tomasello, 'human beings built directly on the uniquely primate cognitive adaptation for understanding external relational categories, they just added a small but important twist in terms of mediating forces such as causes and intentions. Moreover, ... human causal understanding ... evolved first in the social domain to comprehend others as intentional agents' (Tomasello 1999: 23). However, more recent research has shown that young chimpanzees can also understand motives, though they do it less well (Warneken and Tomasello 2006), so this cannot be the reason why we have so much language and they have so little (and in nature, none at all). In any case, the analysis in Figure 5.8 says nothing about speaker intentions, so it should be accessible without this depth of understanding.

3. Formal Induction

If the relation Meaning has to be induced from lexeme-specific correlations, then this process could be the hurdle that only humans can manage. The difference between Meaning and the individual lexeme meanings on which it is based is neither its abstractness nor complexity, but rather its generality. It brings together a great many specific relations by means of Isa links, so it presupposes the ability to organize relations hierarchically—in short, precisely the logical property that might have justified calling language networks 'second-order networks' (s. 1.2). Maybe other animals cannot cope with classified relations, or can only handle very flat hierarchies; if so, then the same limitations should emerge from their social structures. The research remains to be done.

What I have suggested, then, is that the distinctive characteristic of the human brain is its ability to classify relations in an extended inheritance hierarchy. If so, then this would explain why only humans can induce the Meaning relation which is so crucial for the rapid growth of vocabulary that distinguishes human infants from other animals. The stage of development shown in Figure 5.8 is still some way from the full mature system of Figure 5.4, with its deeper understanding of purposes and results, but language development is already well under way.

5.4 Referents, Definiteness, Binding, Negation, and Tense

Having defined the relation 'meaning', we can explore the well-established contrast between the two kinds of referential meaning: sense and referent. For example, in the sentence *The cookie broke*, the referent of the word *cookie* is the particular biscuit that it picks out and its sense is the general category Biscuit (i.e. the same as the sense of BISCUIT). It also has a 'social' meaning (that the speaker is an American), to which we shall return later (and which we shall find to be surprisingly hard to separate from sense).

The **referent** is a new node which the hearer introduces on hearing the word. This new node captures the idea that a word is 'about' something, which may be a person, a thing, an event or an idea. It may also be either something new (as in indefinite phrases such as *a book*) or an existing concept (e.g. *the book*), but these differences can be handled by binding the referent node to the pre-existing one; and of course it will certainly have to be related to other nodes through pragmatic enrichment and integration. The word's referent is intimately related to its **sense** because its sense limits the kinds of thing it can take as a referent; for example, the word COOKIE can (in principle) only refer to biscuits. The basic principle behind these restrictions is that the referent must isa the sense; so the referent of COOKIE isa biscuit. The basic relations between Meaning, Sense, and Referent are shown in Figure 5.9.

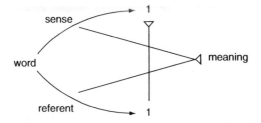

FIGURE 5. 9.   meaning = sense or referent

However, there is of course a great deal of flexibility at this point thanks to metonymy (whereby *the cookie* might be used to refer to a customer in a fast-food restaurant who has ordered a biscuit) and metaphor (as in *Mary's a real cookie*, meaning she's nice). In such cases the 'logical' Isa relation seems to be replaced by a more globally motivated one which relies strongly on spreading activation. Take the famous fast-food example where a waitress wants to refer to a customer who has ordered a ham sandwich. In this situation we can be sure that two nodes are highly active: the one for the customer and the one for the ham-sandwich order. If she can activate the 'ham-sandwich' node in her hearer's mind, and the hearer also knows that one customer has ordered a ham sandwich, then the activation will surely spread to the relevant 'customer' node. Similarly, if cookies are linked to some kind of 'positive-feeling' node, then this will receive activation from the Cookie node and will be active at the same time as the node for Mary, thereby associating Mary with the same node. In short, at least some meaning extensions work by associating an 'evoked' idea with the target referent. These ideas are rather obvious and certainly not original, but a network theory allows them to be developed and modelled with some precision.

To return to the relation between senses and referents, as I argued in Hudson 1990: 125–34, this relation runs right through the vocabulary (and the syntactic constructions), applying in principle to every word-class, and not just to nouns; for example, most word-classes can act as antecedent for a personal pronoun such as *it*, which is only possible if they have a referent. In particular, verbs also have referents, typically a particular situation; for example, 'It snowed last night' refers to a particular event of snowing which took place last night. This is equivalent, in phrase-structure terms, to the claim that a clause or sentence refers to a situation (Jackendoff 2002: 326), and contrasts with Frege's view that a sentence refers to a truth-value. Just like a noun, a verb has a sense (modified by its various dependents) and a referent which isa this sense, as we shall see in the following analysis of sentence (250).

(250)   The man made a cake.

This simple example illustrates not only the sense/referent contrast applied to verbs, but also several other important areas of semantic structure such as definiteness and tense. For the sake of simplicity, I shall not only ignore all other kinds of structure but also present the semantic structure in two stages. The first stage includes the sense/referent analysis of the nouns (including the determiners), and is shown in Figure 5.10. All the nodes displayed here are semantic except the italicized word-tokens. These word-tokens inherit their senses directly from their respective word-types, but then the processing elaborates the structure, not only by adding referents but also by taking account of the modifying effect of dependents. This is illustrated here by the node labelled 'M-making-C' (short for 'The man making a cake'—i.e. the situation-type described by the verb in combination with its subject and object).

Definiteness comes from the determiners, which relate directly to the noun's referent. In 1990 I interpreted definiteness in terms of the addressee's knowledge (Hudson 1990: 293–302), with definite referents already known to the addressee and indefinites new to the addressee. This may be an accurate analysis, but a much neater way to explain the difference is now available thanks to the binding mechanism introduced in 1.7: definite referents are bound. This is not only much easier to show in the analysis, but it also explains why the addressee is expected to know the referent already. This binding is shown by the double arrow which means 'directed identity' linking one obligatory node to another, and is only 'potential' in this diagram because the object of the binding (the antecedent) is not available in this sentence. It must be available in the interlocutors' minds, so, at least in principle, we could complete the binding if we had a network analysis of the relevant parts of either the speaker's or the hearer's mind. However, the same mechanism

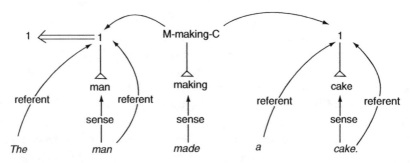

FIGURE 5.10.   The meaning of *The man made a cake*, Part 1

applies well to definite pronouns such as reflexives whose antecedent is in the same sentence, as in (251) and (252).

(251) She hurt herself.
(252) <u>She</u> has a book full of pictures of <u>herself</u>.

The basic pattern for reflexive pronouns is the one in (251), with the reflexive and its antecedent both depending, as object and subject respectively, on the same verb. This pattern is shown on the left side of Figure 5.11 as one possible 'definition' of the relation between a pronoun and its antecedent. The pattern in (252) is an equally simple triangle of relations, but much more general in its application because one of the relations is simply 'dependent' (instead of the more specific 'subject'), while the other is 'subordinate', a transitive extension of 'dependent' to include not only dependents, but also their dependents and so on recursively. This analysis of reflexive binding is again similar in spirit to the one in Hudson 1990: 297–8, but benefits from the directed identity relation.

Returning to our example (250) (The man made a cake), we can complete its semantic structure by finishing the semantics of the verb *made*. Referents are crucial here too because of their role in handling both negation and tense. The meaning of *made* is shown in Figure 5.12, which shows that the verb (i.e. in effect the whole sentence) refers to a particular example (possibly the only example) of that particular man making a cake. This referent is labelled 'E' (for Event) in the diagram, and has the 'quantity'(#) 1; in other words, the event actually happened. Had it not, the quantity would have been labelled zero, and the words would have included *not*. As far as tense is concerned, the

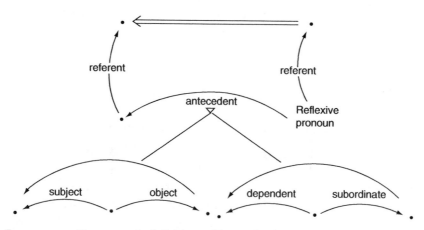

FIGURE 5. 11.   Two syntactic definitions of 'antecedent'

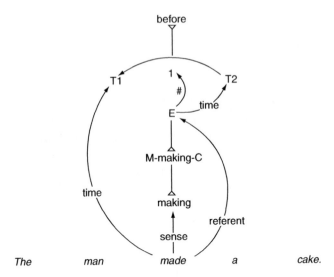

FIGURE 5.12.   The meaning of *The man made a cake*, Part 2

analysis is much the same as in 1990 (Hudson 1990: 222), with the utterance-time (T1) serving as the landmark for the event-time T2 (s. 5.2). The main advance here is that these two times are related by precisely the same relation (before or after) as we used in (s. 3.2) for word order.

5.5 Plurals, Quantifiers, and Sets

One of the main challenges for a word-based theory of language is compositional semantics, the semantics of phrases and sentences. After all, we might expect such a theory to be able to cope well with lexical semantics, but when it comes to the effects of syntax, surely we must invoke phrase structure? We already have evidence against this assumption in at least two of the earlier analyses:

- The meaning of *The man made a cake* is the meaning of its verb as modified by the verb's dependents.
- The reflexive pronoun in *She hurt herself* is bound by the verb's subject.

In both cases the relevant semantic structures are mapped onto the syntactic structure without the use of phrases. However, such examples are rather elementary so I shall consider in this section the somewhat more ambitious area of quantification. As before, the main features of the analysis are already foreshadowed in earlier work (Hudson 1990: 139–46) but recent developments have improved the details.

We start with simple plural noun phrases such as *the books*. The difference between singular and plural nouns is that plurals refer to a set. This set is defined intensionally by the relation Member, which links the set to an example of the noun's sense; for example, *books* refers to a set whose member isa Book—i.e. a set of books. Another property that a set has is Size, measured in terms of the number of members, and this property is rather obviously provided by a numeral; so *three books* refers to a set of books with three members (and *the three books* is the same except that the set is bound). Consider the meaning of (253):

(253)   Two researchers wrote three articles.

The structures for *two researchers* and *three articles* in Figure 5.13 are typical. Notice that each set is now associated with two different numbers:

- a quantity, zero or 1, which shows (as usual) whether the set exists or not.
- a size, usually greater than 1, which shows how many members it has.

The figure also shows that each of these two sets has a 'joint' relation to the verb in which it is the entire set that functions (in this case) as writer or write-ee. In this interpretation, then, the complex of events involved in producing the papers is construed as a single act of writing which involves two researchers working jointly on three papers.

Another way to construe this sentence, however, is 'distributive'. In this interpretation, the sentence refers to a set of events, each of which involves one researcher and one article. The semantic structure of this sentence is very similar to the previous one, the main differences being that the writer and

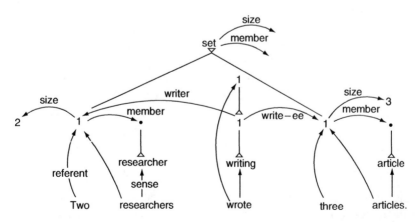

FIGURE 5.13.   The joint reading of *Two researchers wrote three articles*.

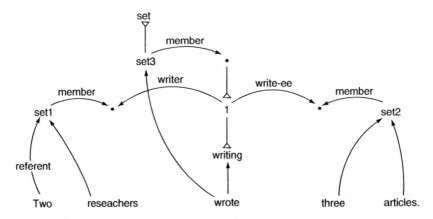

FIGURE 5.14.   The distributive interpretation of *Two researchers wrote three articles*

write-ee are set-members rather than entire sets, and that the verb's referent is itself a set, each of whose members is one of these acts of writing of one paper by one author. The structure is shown (with irrelevant details from the previous figure omitted) in Figure 5.14. To understand this diagram it is important to bear in mind that every node stands for 'the typical X', so (as explained in 1.5) it receives a universal interpretation when inherited. This general principle applies even to the dot nodes which stand for set-members, so they mean 'every member' rather than 'some member'. Consequently, the writer of the event-type described ranges over all the members of Set1 (the two researchers), the write-ee ranges over all of Set2 (the three articles), and every member of Set3 (the events referred to by this sentence) is an instance of one person writing one article. The size of Set3 is clearly related to those of Set1 and Set2, and we can calculate it by multiplying 2×3; however I am not suggesting that this is possible in general because we can understand a sentence such as *Fifty-three researchers wrote twenty-seven articles* without having any idea of the total number of events. Instead, I suggest that we leave the size of Set3 unspecified.

One attraction of analysing plural nouns in terms of sets is to bring out the similarities between them and other syntactically distinct constructions. On the one hand, they are similar to clauses, which (as we have just seen) also have set-reference. For example, consider the meaning of (254).

(254)   He confirmed that two researchers wrote three articles.

Imagine a research manager checking the publication claims of the research staff against some database of publications; and assume that the facts are as shown in the distributive interpretation of the embedded sentence, *two researchers wrote three articles*, in Figure 5.14. In that case, the set of writing-events may project up to determine the number of confirming-events, just as if it had been a noun phrase. This follows automatically from the present set-based analysis.

The other important comparison for plural nouns is with coordinated phrases such as (255):

(255)   Dr Green and Dr Brown wrote three articles.

This offers exactly the same range of interpretations as (253), ranging from writing three joint articles to 'distributive' writing of six single-authored articles. Moreover, in both the plural and the coordinated examples, the purely joint and purely distributive interpretations are simply the two extremes, and at least two mixed interpretations are possible, with either the researchers or the articles taken jointly.

These examples lay the foundations for analysing other kinds of quantifier such as *every* in *Every researcher wrote an article* (where the second noun phrase has been simplified). In this case, *every researcher* still refers to a set of researchers and each member of this set is still involved individually in an act of article writing, just as in Figure 5.14; so this part of the semantic structure is the same in both sentences. What is different about *every* is the mapping between syntax and semantics: in brief, the determiner and common noun exchange roles, as can be seen clearly in Figure 5.15. Here it is the common noun that refers to a set (exceptionally, of course, for a singular noun), while

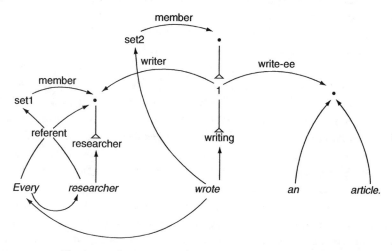

FIGURE 5.15.   The semantic structure of *Every researcher wrote an article*

the determiner refers to the individual set-member. The syntactic dependencies are included beneath the words to remind us that it is the determiner, not the common noun, that is the head of the noun phrase, so the head of the phrase refers to a single member (and a present-tense verb would have had singular agreement). This generalizes as before to all the members of the set, so the sentence is forced to have a distributive reading.

These examples are intended simply to show that the WG apparatus is suitable for at least some quantifiers and to point the way to future research.

5.6 Semantic Relations and Recycling

One of the main areas of disagreement in semantics concerns semantic relations: how many different semantic relations need to be distinguished, what are they, and how should they be distinguished in a formal theory? This is part of a more general debate about the 'vocabulary' of semantic analysis which is polarized between versions of rationalism (all concepts are innate) and empiricism (all concepts are learned). My own view is that most (but not all) concepts are learned, which puts me near the opposite end of the spectrum from those who think that all concepts are innate (Fodor 1983; Wierzbicka 1996). In such a fundamental and long-running debate there is no point in looking for knock-down arguments, but it is important at least to explain one's position clearly and to show how one can handle a few crucial cases.

My rejection of innate concepts is linked to the basic principle that the entire content of a network is held by the links between nodes (s. 1.2). The nodes in a network are not little boxes full of information held in some other format; rather, nodes are nothing but the points where links meet. In a slogan, 'It's network all the way down'. All the content of a concept—the properties which distinguish cats from dogs, for example—is held in terms of network links. Nor is there any distinction in a network between links which somehow define a concept and those which merely describe it (i.e. between 'analytic' and 'synthetic' knowledge): from this point of view, all links have the same status. In this view, then, it would be meaningless to say that some concept is innate but that it has no innate links to other concepts; how would we distinguish this concept from every other concept in the network? The only way in which a specific concept, with a specific content, might be innate is for all its links also to be put in place genetically. But this means that every single concept must be innate, because every concept is defined by its relations to other concepts. For example, if Cat is innate and links to Fur, then Fur must also be innate, and so on until the entire network is innate. Given the evident fact that different people know different things, this conclusion is absurd. In short, we have to choose between a network model of knowledge and the idea that all (or even many) concepts are innate; we cannot have both. Personally, I find the evidence for networks (especially the evidence from spreading activation) so overwhelming that the choice is easy.

However, a network also offers a plausible model for learning in which new concepts are based on existing ones. As I explained in section 1.8, we can add new nodes and links to our networks either by preserving tokens or by inductive generalization based on correlated properties. The point here is that once a concept is created, it is then available for defining further concepts—we can, and do, 'recycle' it. For example, a child might learn the concept 'bicycle' by direct observation—after all, bicycles have a very learnable set of physical and functional properties which correlate helpfully. But once this concept is learned, it can later be recycled as the sense of the word BICYCLE, as the 'whole' referred to in the definition of frames, pedals, and so on, and as the vehicle used in cycling or riding. (There is a rather detailed WG account of this particular conceptual area: Hudson and Holmes 2000.)

The idea that concepts are recycled may seem obvious, but it conflicts directly with the attractive and popular idea that all of meaning can and should be defined in terms of a small universal vocabulary (Wierzbicka 1996). For example, an analysis of the concept Bicycle needs to refer repeatedly to the pedals: its parts include the pedals, the pedals fit through the bottom bracket of the frame, the rider pushes the pedals. But Pedal is not part of the universal vocabulary, so it is not available. The only solution is a complex analysis of pedals which does use only this vocabulary, but this entire structure would have to be rebuilt every time we wanted to refer to the pedals in relation to Bicycle (not to mention the sense of the word PEDAL). I simply cannot believe that this is how our minds work. Moreover, I believe there is some empirical evidence against it. If concepts really are recycled as I am suggesting, then all the details and complexities in the definition of one concept should apply to the concepts that are based on it. This seems to be true in at least some cases. To take a simple example, I assume that the concept Grandmother refers to the more basic concept Mother, which is notoriously complicated; but all the uncertainties about birth mothers, nurture mothers, foster mothers, and so on reappear in the concept Grandmother. This is as expected if Mother is recycled in Grandmother, but unexpected if Grandmother is in some way defined without reference to Mother.

The principle of recycling is also important in the WG analysis of semantic relations because it provides a way out of the impasse into which most discussions of semantic relations lead. On the one hand they offer a limited (and often tiny) universal vocabulary of relations for use in mapping semantic relations onto syntactic ones, especially onto subjects and objects. If this is taken as the sole purpose of semantic relations, only a very small number of semantic relations is needed such as argument structure (Williams 1984), proto-agent or proto-patient (Dowty 1991), or 'deep cases' (Fillmore 1968). However, mapping onto subjects and objects is a very limited goal for a theory of semantic relations; the other properties that can be taken into account include syntactic behaviour such as diathetic alternation (Levin 1993) or indeed the relations among word meanings themselves—for example, the similarities and differences between states, actions, and so on.

A number of analytical systems have been proposed which claim to explain syntactic mappings on the basis of some kind of meaning-based analysis. Each such system focuses on a particular kind of meaning relation, but claims to be able to extend this focus to cover at least most kinds of meaning:

- localist analyses based on relations in space (Gruber 1965; Anderson 1977; Jackendoff 1990).
- force-dynamic analyses based on causal interactions (Talmy 1988; Croft 1998).
- analyses based on a prior classification of events or states (Halliday 1970; Dik 1991).

The more seriously we take the analysis of word meanings themselves, the more relations seem to be needed. Each of these approaches reveals important similarities and differences which a complete analysis should no doubt incorporate, but it is easy to find substantial gaps in any existing system of semantic relations, especially if we look beyond verbs to other word-classes. The most obvious gaps are in the meanings of relation nouns, such as kinship terms, and those of prepositions.

The impasse, therefore, is how to cover the entire vocabulary exhaustively in terms of a very limited system of relational categories. The WG solution is to find a limited range of elementary categories, but to allow them to be recycled in defining other categories. For verb meanings, each of the elementary categories is defined as part of the meaning of an ordinary verb such as DO or BE where it has a simple mapping to syntax, but this mapping can change in more complex verb meanings. For example, suppose we take Being, Getting, and Doing (the ordinary basic senses of the verbs BE, GET, and DO) as basic. Each of these has a single subject argument, which we can label 'er' (for be-er or do-er), though all that these arguments have in common is that of being mapped to the subject. We can then recycle these categories as shown in Figure 5.16.

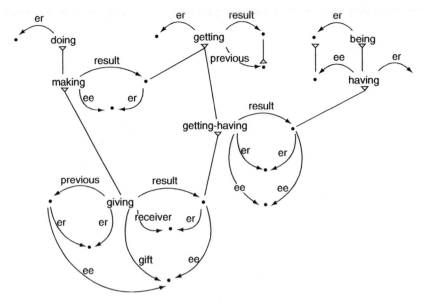

FIGURE 5.16.   From Doing, Getting, and Being to Giving

Starting in the top right corner of this diagram, the analysis works as follows:

- As has often been noted, Having is like Being except that it has an extra argument. In English, the extra argument of Having is its 'er', so the possession must have a different role which we can call 'ee' (the argument expressed by the object).
- Getting involves a change from a previous state to a later one (as in 'It got colder'); the Isa link between the states indicates their similarity, but allows for deviation.
- Getting-having is a kind of Getting in which the result isa Having (as in 'He got an axe from the shed'). Its er and ee arguments correspond to the er and ee arguments of both Getting and Having.
- Doing involves just an er, though it is usually combined with a syntactic object which simply makes the doing more specific; for example, *He did a dance* refers to a single action of dancing, whereas *He did the potatoes* means that he did to the potatoes whatever they needed. It also involves an input of energy and a purpose which are not shown in the diagram.
- Making is a particular kind of Doing in which there is a result, as in 'He made a cake' or 'He made it hot'.

- Giving is a particular kind of Making in which the result is a kind
  of Getting-having. It combines the er of Doing with the er and ee of
  Getting-having, so it has three arguments: an er, a receiver, and a gift.
  These are defined as indicated in terms of the recycled arguments of
  Getting-having. In other words, if A gives B to C, then A does something
  whose result is that B changes hands from A to C.

This extended example shows how new semantic relations that map easily to
syntax can be defined in terms of simpler ones. This particular analysis is
extended into the realm of commercial transactions in Hudson (2006a). The
same kind of WG analysis has been applied in detail to verbs of perception
(Gisborne 1996) and to verbs of motion, resultative constructions, and causative verbs (Holmes 2005).

5.7 Power and Solidarity

As explained in section 5.1, there is no clear dividing line between 'referential'
meaning and 'social' meaning. This is especially clear in the areas of grammar
and vocabulary which are sensitive to the social relations between the speaker
and the referent. To take a familiar example, the proper nouns *Dick, Hudson*, and
Dad (as in *Where's Dad?*) may all be used to refer to me, but their users have
very different social relations to me. These differences are not merely matters
of usage, but are built into the grammar of English via general word-classes
which we can call Given name, Family name, and Kin name. The sociolinguistic facts about English and other languages deserve a great deal more
research, but the outlines of some general principles are well established
(Hudson 1996: 122–32). The questions that arise here are remarkably similar
to those that arise with the relations of referential semantics.

The first question, however, is how to include speaker-relations in the
grammar at all. Suppose we wish the grammar to say that kin names such as
Dad are only used when the person referred to has the specified relation to the
speaker. Most theories of language structure have no place for the speaker
because the speaker is not part of the language, and language only has two
interfaces with non-language: phonetic and semantic (i.e. Chomsky's Phonetic
Form and Logical Form). In contrast, the speaker has a central part in WG
thanks to the view of words as actions outlined above (s. 5.2). The typical word is
an action, so it has an actor (the speaker), and it is also a communication so it
also has an addressee; so these two relations can be inherited by any word-token.

For most words the speaker and addressee nodes have no specific restrictions, so they just inherit the same speaker properties of the language; but the

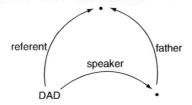

FIGURE 5.17.   The referent of DAD is the speaker's father

nodes are available for any words that are subject to special social restrictions. Social restrictions are of many different kinds; for instance, the word may only be used by a certain kind of person defined geographically (e.g. BONNY is used by people from Scotland) or socially (e.g. the personal pronoun ONE is associated in British minds with the Royal Family and its adherents). When dealing with power and solidarity relations, however, the restrictions are more complicated because they apply not to the word itself, but to its referent: in our earlier example, *Dad* is only used when its referent is the father of the speaker. This restriction is easy to incorporate in a network which includes the Speaker relation as shown in Figure 5.17.

The next question is the balance between genetics and learning in social relations, and in particular in the two 'dimensions' that are of particular interest to sociolinguists: power and solidarity. In this case we can be sure that genetics plays a major part because other primates also recognize these relations; as examples, baboons use different calls to each other according to their respective places in the social structure of kinship (solidarity) and dominance (power) (Seyfarth, Cheney, and Bergman 2005). On the other hand, learning is important too in spelling out the content of these relations: what makes one person more powerful than another, and what is the basis for solidarity? These questions have very different answers in different societies, but so far as I know every society has power and solidarity built into its structure.

If power and solidarity really are part of our primate mind, perhaps we can assume two innate relations which are linked in a fairly direct way to both perception and behaviour. Power is linked in a rather obvious way to the size of one and submissive behaviour by the other; and solidarity is linked to frequent encounters in early life and to trusting behaviour by both parties. This linkage must take place in cognitive structure because it depends on recognizing other people as individuals. Moreover, it must define conceptual relations between arbitrary individuals, rather than always taking oneself as one of its terms, because primates can recognize the power and solidarity relations between other con-specifics. Consequently we can be sure that we are born with primitive conceptual relations for power and solidarity (or at least with the propensity to develop these relations early in life).

What is less clear is how these relations fit into a network of the WG kind. We are accustomed to thinking of power and solidarity as parameters with different settings: power ranges over Superior, Equal, and Subordinate, and solidarity over categories such as Stranger, Acquaintance, Friend/Colleague/ Relative, and Intimate. However it is possible that the primitive innate system is much simpler than this. In terms of power, the really important category is Superior, because submission avoids bloodshed and conflict; how we treat equals or subordinates is less important. (There is no need for the superior to recognize the other as subordinate, so long as the other's behaviour is submissive, because submissive behaviour is designed to avoid provocation rather than to signal subordination as such.) If this is so, all we need in order to conceptualize these primitive power relations is the single relation Superior which divides others into superiors and the rest (who need no special behaviour). Similarly, in solidarity we only need to recognize intimates, because only these need special behaviour based on mutual trust and support. Indeed, it would be better to say that with strangers we have no relation at all than to recognize a relation 'stranger'. In short, we may be born knowing just two social relations: Superior and Intimate.

These assumptions provide the basis for a full analysis of all the subtleties of the cultural systems that we learn, with the various power and solidarity relations as subcategories of Superior and Intimate. Exactly how power and solidarity are expressed linguistically varies enormously from language to language and from culture to culture. For example, although there is a very general tendency for kin names such as *Dad* only to be applied to superior relatives, there are exceptions such as the practice in some parts of America and England for fathers to address their sons as *Son* (an exception which never seems to be extended to daughters). Just to give one simple example, then, consider the analysis in Figure 5.18 of the English word sɪʀ, which in the UK always indicates deference.

Power and solidarity relations are important for linguistic theory because they show particularly clearly how close the relation is between the linguistic parts of our conceptual system and other parts. They are primarily part of social cognition, the system of categories that we apply in general social interaction and which govern all aspects of our behaviour. However, as we have just seen, they are also built into the conditions for using words such as names, to which we could have added other important word categories such as personal pronouns (e.g. the famous T/V contrast between pronouns such

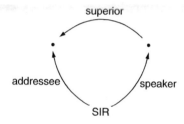

FIGURE 5.18.   We use SIR to our superiors

as the French *tu* and *vous*) and 'polite' words such as *please* and *sorry* (Brown and Levinson 1987). These cases have the added interest of involving not only the speaker but also the addressee. However, power and solidarity are recycled in other parts of the language system too. For example, they reappear in the referential meanings of verbs such as ASK and TELL (as in *He asked/told her to do it*), which imply different social relations between the interactants in the state of affairs being referred to. None of this is surprising given the important social function of language as our main tool for handling interpersonal relations.

5.8 Languages, Stereotypes, and Code-Mixing

Power and solidarity are a convenient bridge between the purely referential meanings of semantics and the purely social meanings which theoretical linguists generally leave entirely to sociolinguists. In section 5.1, I gave the example of COOKIE, which has the same referential meaning as BISCUIT but a different social meaning. No doubt there are a number of personal and historical reasons why most theoretical linguists ignore such facts, but one reason seems to be the belief that they are merely manifestations of more general differences between entire language systems, with COOKIE belonging to the system called American English and BISCUIT to British English. If this is so, then there is no need for this choice to be mentioned as part of any one language system any more than the system of English needs to recognize that another alternative is French. In other words, a grammar defines a single language system and has nothing to say about how it relates to other language systems.

This argument suffers from serious weaknesses if our grammars are meant to be models of some kind of psychological reality. One weakness is the assumption that language theories already accommodate our knowledge of large-scale language systems. One of the categories which is strikingly absent from most theories of language is 'language X' (where X ranges over English, French, and so on). The fact is that a large percentage of the world's population must be fluent in at least two languages, and in the mind of a bilingual speaker the languages are always distinguished (and often have names). (It is true that many bilingual communities engage in code-mixing in mid-sentence but this is not evidence for a 'mixed code' in the sense of a single language system which merges the two languages without distinction; if this had been so, speakers would be unable to use one language without the other, but in fact any bilingual speaker can use one language at a time when speaking to monolingual speakers.) Any general theory of linguistic competence must go beyond the idealization to monolingualism ('Linguistic theory is concerned primarily with an ideal speaker-listener, in a completely homogeneous speech-community, ...' Chomsky 1965: 3), but this presupposes an ability to assign words, sounds and meanings to a particular language.

Unlike most other theories, WG does allow a single grammar to include words from more than one language and to assign words to the relevant language (Hudson 1990: 67). The simplest way to do this is to recognize Language as a relation between a word and a language; so the language of BONJOUR is French while that of CIAO is Italian. 'Metalinguistic' knowledge such as this is, in fact, part of our knowledge of language and in a network model it would in any case be hard to separate formally from other kinds of knowledge. The Language relation applies to all degrees of multilingualism. At one extreme are isolated words which exhaust what we know of some language L, so these words are directly related to L, but at the other extreme we might know language L in full. In this case, we not only know all the words of L, but we also know a lot of general properties concerning the pronunciation, morphology, and so on of words in L which distinguish them from the words in any other languages we may know. These generalizations are carried by the general category L-word (a sub-type of Word, e.g. English-word or French-word), and each word of L isa L-word. In this situation, the Language relation links L-word to the language L, so it can be inherited by all the individual words. These two extreme types of multilingualism are illustrated in Figure 5.19, representing someone who knows that CIAO is Italian (without knowing any other Italian words) but who also speaks Spanish and English fluently. In between the two cases, of course, are many different possibilities which I cannot explore further here, including knowledge of etymology (where one knows the historical origin of a current word).

The idea of clearly individuated 'languages' is, of course, seriously prob- lematic when we consider the objective world of so-called languages such as

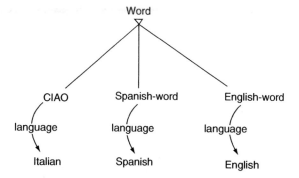

FIGURE 5.19.   A single Italian word known by a Spanish-English bilingual

Swedish and Norwegian which are mutually intelligible and so-called dialects such as Mandarin and Cantonese which are mutually unintelligible (in speech), not to mention the logical problem of dialect continuums such as the one which links the French of Calais to the Italian of Sicily via a chain of mutually intelligible neighbouring dialects (Hudson 1996: ch. 2). However, the reality of an individual speaker covers only that person's limited experience and is a lot simpler, so it can often be modelled in terms of separate 'languages' where the distinction between languages and dialects does not arise.

Languages are helpful social constructs which allow us to link a very large number of linguistic items (words, sounds, and so on) to a complex social structure. For example, the language we call 'English' allows us to link tens of thousands of linguistic items to hundreds of millions of individual speakers via generalizations such as: 'People in the UK mostly speak English.' The reality of these mental links emerges very clearly from work on language stereotypes, the personal properties that we associate with the speakers of a language. The social-psychological attitude studies of the 1970s showed beyond reasonable doubt that the language a person speaks affects the judgements a listener makes about such things as their intelligence, trustworthiness, and toughness (Giles and Powesland 1975; Hudson 1996: 206–20). The stereotypes and prejudices revealed by these studies do not, of course, belong to languages as such, but to social types—types of people—whose characteristics include speaking the language concerned; but by association the languages too may develop a reputation for refinement, ugliness, or whatever. The complex of concepts in this area thus includes the following:

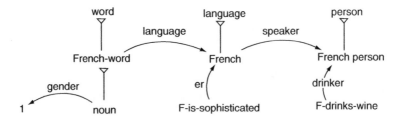

FIGURE 5. 20.   Properties of French words, the French language and French people

- Language-words (e.g. French word), which have default properties that define their possible pronunciation, morphology, and so on.
- Social types (e.g. French person), whose default properties include all the stereotypes and prejudices that are included in our attitudes to the people concerned.
- Languages (e.g. French), which are linked by Language to language-words and by Speaker to social types, and which (by association) evoke attitudes and judgements.

Figure 5.20 shows a hypothetical mind in which French nouns have a gender, French is a sophisticated language, and French people drink wine.

This model of the relation between languages and society is relevant to code-switching in a multilingual community, where it can explain at least two well-known phenomena: situational switching and sentence-internal code-mixing. Situational code-switching arises in a community where the different languages are associated with different 'domains', situation-types such as Home, School, and Work. As expected in the WG model, each domain is defined by a combination of properties which combine by default but which, in reality, allow exceptions; for example, Home and School are usually distinct, but the teacher could produce an exceptional and potentially problematic overlap by being the mother of one of the pupils. This kind of association between a language and a type of social situation is shown

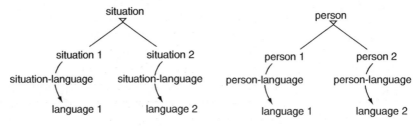

FIGURE 5.21.   Languages linked to situations and person-types in a bilingual mind

schematically on the left of Figure 5.21, where Situation-language is the relation between a situation (which I assume is an abstract kind of 'place') and the language it demands (not to be confused with the Language relation between a word and the language it belongs to). If we assume that people are constantly monitoring the changing social situation, then it follows from this structure that a change from Situation 1 to Situation 2 will trigger a switch from Language 1 to Language 2.

The right side of Figure 5.21 represents the other common social linkage in a bilingual community, in which different languages are associated with different kinds of people (represented in the diagram as 'person 1' and 'person 2', which are social types rather than individuals). This division is often found in the bilingual intersection of two otherwise monolingual communities, so the associated social types are the typical monolingual speakers of the languages concerned; for example, a Greek-English bilingual in London might associate Greek and English with Greek and English stereotypes. Almost by definition this situation entails that bilingual members of this intersection of the two communities have allegiances divided between the communities concerned, with some degree of allegiance to both; so a Greek-English Londoner feels partly Greek and partly English. The automatic consequence is sentence-internal code-mixing between Greek and English, producing fascinating syntactic configurations which seem generally to satisfy the grammars of both languages. This is not just a happy coincidence, but the result of choices well below the level of consciousness: 'in cases of systematic linguistic differences between contact languages, competent bilinguals seek out the closest possible match between the two linguistic systems and use categorical equivalence ... to facilitate switching' (Eppler 2004).

An important question that arises from the research on code-mixing is how speakers represent themselves conceptually, and in particular how they can represent themselves as members, to different degrees, of different communities. Let us call the node which represents the person whose mind we are modelling 'Ego' (which means 'I' in Latin but is commonly used in this way in anthropology). If Ego belongs to one community, then Ego isa the typical member of that community; for example, Ego isa Greek. If on the other hand Ego belongs to two communities we might think we could invoke multiple inheritance, with Isa links to both—for example, Ego isa both Greek and British. However, this would be wrong because of the unavoidable conflicts produced by the inheritable properties; if the typical Greek drinks wine while the typical Briton drinks beer, the result should be a conflict like the one which blocks *amn't (s. 1.4). There are two ways to avoid these conflicts. One is to posit a specific mixed type such as 'London Greek', in which all the conflicts are resolved by fiat and which is explicitly recognized as bilingual. In

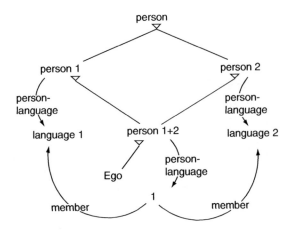

FIGURE 5.22.   A typical member of a bilingual community

this case the two languages should be equal members of a two-member set as shown in Figure 5.22.

The other solution to the problems raised by dual community membership may be more appropriate where the bilingual overlap of the communities is too small to have its own cultural identity. Here Ego has different 'guises', each of which isa Ego: in our example, Ego-the-Greek and Ego-the-Brit. Each of these guises isa one consistent social type, speaking one language, so when Ego flips from one guise to another the language changes automatically. The network in Figure 5.23 adds this Ego-representation to the previous diagram.

These models raise an important research question about the psycholinguistics of sentence-internal code-mixing: why does the language change? The theoretical literature offers a number of accounts of the patterning found in code-mixing conversations, but none of these accounts is fully satisfactory (Eppler 2004). One problem is that these discussions have focused on the units of language choice—that is to say whereabouts in the utterance the choice-points are—rather than on how the choices are made. The assumption has been that each language choice applies to large syntactic chunks such as syntactic phrases, but every theory runs into difficulties with examples of 'wild' code-mixing such as (256) (ibid.)

(256) is(t)   doch   noch [ə] mehr reason   nicht to come out!
       is   though   still one more   not
       'That's one more reason not to come out, then!'

An alternative, which is much more compatible with the dependency approach of WG, is to assume that the units for language choice are individual

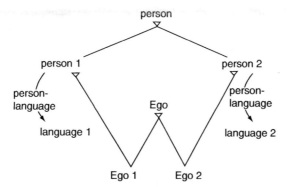

FIGURE 5.23.   Dual allegiance to two social types (and their languages)

words. If this is so, then every word is a potential switch-point so the question is not where choices are made but rather how they are made.

Suppose that each language in a bilingual speaker's mind is associated with a distinct social stereotype as shown in Figure 5.22 or Figure 5.23. It is these social stereotypes which ultimately determine the choice of language because bilinguals match their language to the social circumstances as noted earlier; the question is exactly what mechanism allows the social stereotype to influence the choice of language. In broad outline, the answer presumably involves activation spreading from the stereotypes, via the language, to the words of the language. When only one language is active, then the speech is monolingual; but to the extent that other languages are also active, their words can also be selected. The processes involved in this language-choice are exactly the same as in monolingual speech (see s. 1.7), where the speaker chooses the word which makes the 'best fit' by simply using the most active candidate.

However, code-mixing data raise a technical problem in applying this general idea. Suppose the two language nodes, L1 and L2, are both active, but L1 is more active than L2. In that case L1 should win every time, producing monolingual speech in L1; but of course the actual outcome is code-mixed speech which includes some words from L2, albeit fewer than from L1. Code-mixed speech is an example of a 'stochastic process'—a series of events of different types which alternate in a random way but with a particular probability distribution—so the general question is how to use the activity levels in a network to produce a 'stochastic' output.

One possible answer is based on the widely accepted idea that nodes only spread their activation when they 'fire', and that they only fire when they reach a critical threshold level. In this view, the activation from the language nodes is intermittent rather than constant, so the choice of language at a particular point in time depends on which of the language nodes has fired most recently. Moreover, different nodes may have different 'basic' levels of activation which they return to after firing and which determine how much more activation they need in order to reach threshold; for example, frequently used nodes are much easier to activate than rarely used nodes. Similarly, if one of the language nodes has a higher basic activation level than the other, then (given similar activation input) it will fire more frequently. This is how the theory could model the frequency-differences between languages which are often reported in the code-mixing literature. However, it is important to bear in mind that the language nodes must be able to adjust their basic activation levels dramatically to take account of the changes of circumstance mentioned above; for instance, when speaking to a monolingual speaker of L1, L2 must be switched off completely even if in other circumstances it is the dominant language.

The most general conclusion about code-mixing, it seems to me, is that we badly need a psycholinguistic model of speech processing which is sufficiently general and flexible to accommodate code-mixing as a special case. I believe that WG provides the basis for such a model, though I admit that almost all the work remains to be done.

5.9 Acts of Identity and Inherent Variability

This book ends with a celebration of quantitative dialectology (e.g. Labov 1972; Hudson 1996: ch. 5). This is actually an odd choice for a book on the theory of language structure because this work has had virtually no impact on most theories of language structure. Instead, it has produced a vast amount of well-analysed data which challenges every theory. I hope to show that at least some of these data can be accommodated comfortably in the theory of WG, and especially so in the light of the WG theory of code-mixing sketched in the previous section.

The main achievement of quantitative dialectology has been to reveal both the intimate connection between the fine details of linguistic and social structures and also the importance of probabilities. One of the basic ideas is 'inherent variability', which refers to a free choice between two alternative ways of expressing the same referential meaning such as the choice between [ɪŋ] and [ɪn] as realizations of the {ing} suffix in English (e.g. the choice between *hunting* and *huntin'*); this kind of contrast is called a sociolinguistic 'variable', with the alternative forms as its 'variants'. What emerges from the empirical research is that each of these variables is influenced in some way by social stereotypes that are important in the society concerned, so the act of choosing is an 'act of identity' whereby the speaker identifies themself with one or more stereotype. However, the identity that the speaker builds in this way is fine-tuned to an astonishing degree thanks to two further facts. On the one hand, different linguistic choices are linked to different social contrasts: the relevant variables include social class, geography, sex, age, and ethnicity, as well as complex combinations of these parameters. On the other hand, a speaker's linguistic choices on a particular linguistic variable need not be consistent within the same conversation. In short, the choices are a stochastic process just like the code-mixing that I discussed in the previous section.

To make the discussion more concrete, let us consider a very small sample of the data from one of the classic works in this tradition, Milroy (1980). Milroy's data are from speakers in three working-class areas of Belfast, whose social structures she analysed in terms of the speakers' social networks—an approach which is, of course, particularly appropriate to the theme of this book. One of the nine sociolinguistic variables that she studied was (*a*), the vowel in words such as *hat, man,* and *grass* which varies between a pure front vowel [æ] and a back diphthong [ɔə]. In her analysis every token of the variable receive a score between 1 (for [æ]) and 5 (for [ɔə]), so each speaker has an average between 1 and 5. She also gave each speaker a 'Network-strength score', calculated on the basis of the number and quality of their links to others in the neighbourhood, with one point for each of five indicators of strong local links (e.g. substantial ties of kinship or work). The scores of seven speakers for network strength and for (*a*) are given in Table 5.1; Ballymacarrett and Clonard are the areas of Belfast in which the speakers lived. The speakers shown here are all women aged between 40 and 55.

TABLE 5.1. Scores for (*a*) and network-strength of seven Belfast speakers

Location	Speaker	Network-strength score	(*a*) score
Ballymacarrett	MB	3	2.33
	BM	3	2.48
	ED	1	2.13
	MT	1	1.73
Clonard	PC	2	2.63
	LC	1	1.75
	HM	0	1.05

The data in Table 5.1 are typical for inherent variability, with every speaker showing some variation, though HM is almost consistent in her use of [æ]. This variability is part of their individual competence, so there can be no question of locating all variation somehow between internally consistent speakers. Moreover, the figures themselves deserve attention. The (*a*) score for each speaker is based on between 60 and 80 tokens, so the differences between speakers are significant and demand explanation. The explanation must, presumably, lie in the speakers' minds rather than in external circumstances, and a suitably mental explanation lies in the network-strength scores. Table 5.1 shows a very clear correlation between the two scores (the higher the network-strength score, the higher the (*a*) score) which is confirmed by a highly significant correlation for the entire corpus which, however, only applies to speakers in the 40–55 age range; younger speakers show no correlation. Again the complexity and subtlety of the links between language and social structures are typical. We can only speculate about the reason for this correlation, but it seems to indicate that speakers use the (*a*) variable to show how closely integrated they are into the local community. Even more speculatively, the 'local community' node may be directly linked to the [ɔə] node, so activation of one spreads to the other in the same way that stereotypes activate languages in code-mixing.

The example is a conveniently concrete hook for some of the main ideas that I have developed in this book. Language is a network in which activation can spread from node to node, with one node per concept. This network is easy to link to the rest of our cognitive network (such as our social network) because there are no boundaries and the two networks have just the same formal characteristics. Almost all of the network is learned from experience, so activation shows not only our current concerns but also the pattern of past experiences. And above all, it is both possible and enlightening to analyse any part of the super-network that includes language. Language really is a window on the human mind.

References

Abeillé, A. (2004). *Building and using Parsed Corpora.* Dordrecht: Kluwer.

Abney, S. (1987). *The English Noun Phrase in its Sentential Aspect.* Ph.D. MIT.

Aitchison, J. (1994). *Words in the Mind: An Introduction to the Mental Lexicon.* 2nd edition. Oxford: Blackwell.

Allerton, D. (1994). 'Valency and valency grammar', in R. Asher (ed.), *Encyclopedia of Language and Linguistics.* Oxford: Pergamon. 4878–86.

Anderson, J. (1977). *On Case Grammar: Prolegomena to a Theory of Grammatical Relations.* London: Croom Helm.

Anderson, J. R. (1983). 'A spreading activation theory of memory'. *Journal of Verbal Learning and Verbal Behavior,* 22: 261–95.

—— and Lebiere, C. (1998). *The Atomic Components of Thought.* Hillsdale, NJ: Erlbaum.

Anderson, S. (1992). *A-morphous Morphology.* Cambridge: Cambridge University Press.

—— (1996). 'How to put your clitics in their place, or why the best account of second-position phenomena may be something like the optimal one'. *Linguistic Review,* 13: 165–91.

Andrews, A. (1982). 'The representation of case in Modern Icelandic', in J. Bresnan (ed.), *The Mental Representation of Grammatical Relations.* Cambridge, Mass.: MIT Press. 427–503.

Aronoff, M. (1976). *Word Formation in Generative Grammar.* Cambridge, Mass.: MIT Press.

—— (1994). *Morphology by Itself: Stems and Inflectional Classes.* Cambridge, Mass.: MIT Press.

Baddeley, A., and Logie, R. (1999). 'Working memory: the multiple-component model', in A. Miyake and P. Shah (eds), *Models of Working Memory: Mechanisms of Active Maintenance and Executive Control.* Cambridge: Cambridge University Press. 28–61.

Baker, M. (1985). 'Syntactic affixation and English gerunds'. *Proceedings of the West Coast Conference on Formal Linguistics,* 4: 1–11.

Barabási, A.-L. (2003). *Linked: How Everything is Connected to Everything Else and What it Means for Business, Science and Everyday Life.* London: Penguin.

Barlow, M., and Kemmer, S. (2000). *Usage Based Models of Language.* Stanford, Calif.: CSLI.

Bates, E. (1998). 'Construction grammar and its implications for child language research'. *Journal of Child Language,* 25: 462–6.

Bauer, L. (2003). *Introducing Linguistic Morphology.* 2nd edition. Edinburgh: Edinburgh University Press.

Beard, R. (1994). 'Lexeme-morpheme base morphology', in R. Asher (ed.), *Encyclopedia of Language and Linguistics*. Oxford: Pergamon. 2137–40.

Berko Gleason, J. (1958). 'The child's learning of English morphology'. *Word*, 14: 150–77.

Bharati, A., Chaitanya, V., and Sangal, R. (1995). *Natural Language Processing: A Paninian Perspective*. New Delhi: Prentice-Hall of India Private Ltd.

Biber, D., Johansson, S., Leech, G., Conrad, S., and Finegan, E. (1999). *Longman Grammar of Spoken and Written English*. London: Longman.

Blake, B. (1990). *Relational Grammar*. London: Croom Helm.

Blevins, J. P. (2001). 'Paradigmatic derivation'. *Transactions of the Philological Society*, 99: 211–22.

—— (2003). 'Stems and paradigms'. *Language*, 79: 737–67.

Bloomfield, L. (1933). *Language*. New York: Holt, Rinehart and Winston.

Bock, K., and Griffin, Z. (2000). 'The persistence of structural priming: transient activation or implicit learning?' *Journal of Experimental Psychology–General*, 129: 177–92.

Bod, R. (1998). *Beyond Grammar: An Experience-Based Theory of Language*. Stanford, Calif.: CSLI.

Borer, H. (1992). 'Clitics: pronominal clitics', in W. Bright (ed.), *International Encyclopedia of Linguistics*. Oxford: Oxford University Press. 270–71.

Branigan, H. P., Pickering, M. J., Liversedge, S. P., Stewart, A. J., and Urbach, T. P. (1995). 'Syntactic priming: investigating the mental representation of language'. *Journal of Psycholinguistic Research*, 24(6): 489–506.

Bresnan, J. (1978). 'A realistic transformational grammar', in M. Halle, J. Bresnan, and G. Miller (eds), *Linguistic Theory and Psychological Reality*. Cambridge, Mass.: MIT Press. 1–59.

—— (1994). 'Locative inversion and universal grammar'. *Language*, 70: 72–131.

—— (1997). 'Mixed categories as head sharing constructions', in M. Butt and T. Holloway King (eds), *Proceedings of the LFG97 Conference*. Stanford, Calif.: CSLI Publications.

—— (2001). *Lexical-Functional Syntax*. Oxford: Blackwell.

Broadwell, G. (1999). 'Focus alignment and optimal order in Zapotec'. *Proceedings of the Chicago Linguistic Society*, 35: 15–28.

Bröker, N. (1998). 'A projection architecture for dependency grammar and how it compares to LFG', in M. Butt and T. Holloway King (eds), *Proceedings of the LFG 98 Conference*. Stanford, Calif.: CSLI.

—— (2000). 'Unordered and non-projective dependency grammars'. *Traitement Automatique des Langues*, 41: 245–72.

—— (2001). 'Formal foundations of dependency grammar', in V. Ágel (ed.), *Dependency and Valency: An International Handbook of Contemporary Research*. Berlin: Walter de Gruyter.

Brookes, A., and Hudson, R. (1982). 'Do linguists have anything to say to teachers?', in R. Carter (ed.), *Linguistics and the Teacher*. London: Routledge and Kegan Paul. 52–74.

Brooks, P., and Macwhinney, B. (2000). 'Phonological priming in children's picture naming'. *Journal of Child Language*, 27: 335–66.

Brown, D., Corbett, G., Fraser, N., Hippisley, A., and Timberlake, A. (1996). 'Russian noun stress and network morphology'. *Linguistics*, 34: 53–107.

Brown, P., and Levinson, S. (1987). *Politeness: Some Universals in Language Usage.* 2nd edition. Cambridge: Cambridge University Press.

Browne, A., and Sun, R. (2001). 'Connectionist inference models'. *Neural Networks*, 14: 1331–55.

Bybee, J. (1995). 'Regular morphology and the lexicon'. *Language and Cognitive Processes*, 10: 425–55.

—— (1998). 'The emergent lexicon'. *Proceedings of the Chicago Linguistics Society*, 34: 421–35.

—— (1999). 'Use impacts morphological representation'. *Behavioral and Brain Sciences*, 22: 1016–17.

—— and Moder, C. (1983). 'Morphological classes as natural categories'. *Language*, 59: 251–70.

Camdzic, A., and R. Hudson (2007). 'Serbo-Croat clitics and word grammar'. *Research in Language* (University of Lodz), 4.

Carroll, J., Minnen, G., and Briscoe, T. (2004). 'Parser evaluation: using a grammatical relation annotation Scheme', in A. Abeille, (ed.), *Building and Using Parsed Corpora.* Dordrecht: Kluwer.

Carstairs-McCarthy, A. (1992). *Current Morphology.* London: Routledge.

—— (1998). 'Paradigmatic structure: inflectional paradigms and morphological classes', in A. Spencer and A. Zwicky (eds), *The Handbook of Morphology.* Oxford: Blackwell. 322–34.

Carston, R. (1997). 'Relevance-theoretic pragmatics and modularity'. *UCL Working Papers in Linguistics* 9: 29–53.

Chametzky, R. (2003). 'Phrase structure', in R. Hendrick (ed.), *Minimalist Syntax.* Oxford: Blackwell. 192–235.

Chang, F., Dell, G. S., Bock, K., and Griffin, Z. (2000). 'Structural priming as implicit learning: a comparison of models of sentence production'. *Journal of Psycholinguistic Research*, 29: 217–29.

Charniak, E. (1981). 'The case-slot identity theory'. *Cognitive Science*, 5: 285–92.

Chipere, N. (2003). *Understanding Complex Sentences: Native Speaker Variation in Syntactic Competence.* London: Palgrave Macmillan.

Chomsky, N. (1957). *Syntactic Structures.* The Hague: Mouton.

—— (1965). *Aspects of the Theory of Syntax.* Cambridge, Mass.: MIT Press.

—— (1970). 'Remarks on nominalizations', in R. Jacobs and P. Rosenbaum (eds), *Readings in Transformational Grammar.* Waltham, Mass.: Ginn. 184–221.

—— (1995a). 'Categories and transformations', in N. Chomsky (ed.), *The Minimalist Program.* Cambridge, Mass.: MIT Press. 219–394.

—— (1995b). *The Minimalist Program.* Cambridge, Mass.: MIT Press.

Clark, E. (1993). *The Lexicon in Acquisition.* Cambridge: Cambridge University Press.

Collins, M. (1996). 'A new statistical parser based on bigram lexical dependencies'. *Proceedings of the Association for Computational Linguistics*, 34: 184–91.

Corbett, G., and Fraser, N. (1993). 'Network morphology: a DATR account of Russian nominal inflection'. *Journal of Linguistics*, 29: 113–42.

Covington, M. (1984). *Syntactic Theory in the High Middle Ages*. Cambridge: Cambridge University Press.

Cowan, N. (1997). *Attention and Memory: An Integrated Framework*. New York: Oxford University Press.

—— (1999). 'An Embedded-Processes Model of Working Memory', in A. Miyake and P. Shah (eds), *Models of Working Memory: Mechanisms of Active Maintenance and Executive Control*. Cambridge: Cambridge University Press. 62–101.

Creider, C. (2002). 'Swahili verbal inflection in theoretical perspective', in K. Sugayama (ed.), *Studies in Word Grammar*. Kobe: Research Institute of Foreign Studies, Kobe City University of Foreign Studies. 33–46.

—— and Hudson, R. (1999). Inflectional Morphology in Word Grammar. Lingua 107: 163–187.

—— —— (2006). 'Case agreement in Ancient Greek: implications for a theory of covert elements', in K. Sugayama and R. Hudson (eds), *Word Grammar: New Perspectives on a Theory of Language Structure*. London: Continuum. 35–53.

Crestani, F. (1997). 'Application of spreading activation techniques in information retrieval'. *Artificial Intelligence Review*, 11: 453–82.

Croft, W. (1998). 'The structure of events and the structure of language', in M. Tomasello (ed.), *The New Psychology*. London: Lawrence Erlbaum. 67–92.

—— (2001). *Radical Construction Grammar: Syntactic Theory in Typological Perspective*. Oxford: Oxford University Press.

—— and Cruse, A. (2004). *Cognitive Linguistics*. Cambridge: Cambridge University Press.

Culicover, P. (1999). *Syntactic Nuts: Hard Cases, Syntactic Theory and Language Acquisition*. Oxford: Oxford University Press.

Deacon, T. (1997). *The Symbolic Species: The Co-evolution of Language and the Human Brain*. London: Penguin.

Denison, D. (1993). *English Historical Syntax*. London: Longman.

—— (1998). 'Syntax', in Romaine, S. (ed.), *The Cambridge History of the English Language*, volume iv: *1776–1997*. Cambridge: Cambridge University Press. 92–329.

Dik, S. (1991). 'Functional Grammar', in F. Droste and J. Joseph (eds), *Linguistic Theory and Grammatical Description*. Amsterdam: Benjamins. 247–74.

Donner, M. (1986). 'The gerund in Middle English'. *English Studies*, 67: 394–400.

Dowty, D. (1991). 'Thematic proto-roles and argument selection'. *Language*, 67: 547–619.

—— (2000). 'The dual analysis of adjuncts/complements in categorial grammar'. *ZAS Papers in Linguistics* (Zentrum Für Allgemeine Sprachwissenschaft, Berlin) 17: 1–26.

Durrell, M. (1996). *Hammer's German Grammar and Usage*. 3rd edition. London: Arnold.

Ellis, N. (2002). 'Reflections on frequency effects in language processing'. *Studies in Second Language Acquisition*, 24: 297–339.

—— and Schmidt, R. (1998). 'Rules or associations in the acquisition of morphology? The frequency by regularity interaction in human and PDP learning of morphosyntax'. *Language and Cognitive Processes*, 13: 307–36.

Elman, J. (1993). 'Learning and development in neural networks—the importance of starting small'. *Cognition*, 48: 71–99.

Eppler, E. (2004). *The syntax of German-English code-switching*. Ph.D. UCL.

Ericsson, K. A., and Delaney, P. (1999). 'Long-term working memory as an alternative to capacity models of working memory in everyday skilled performance', in A. Miyake and P. Shah (eds), *Models of Working Memory: Mechanisms of Active Maintenance and Executive Control*. Cambridge: Cambridge University Press. 257–97.

—— and Kintsch, W. (1995). 'Long-term working-memory'. *Psychological Review*, 102: 211–45.

Evans, N., Brown, D., and Corbett, G. (2001). 'Dalabon pronominal prefixes and the typology of syncretism: a Network Morphology analysis', in G. Booij and J. van Marle, (eds), *Yearbook of Morphology 2000*. Dordrecht: Kluwer. 187–231.

Fanego, T. (1996a). 'The development of gerunds as objects of subject-control verbs in English (1400–1700)'. *Diachronica*, 13: 29–62.

—— (1996b). 'The gerund in early modern English: evidence from the Helsinki corpus'. *Folia Linguistica Historica* 17: 97–152.

Ferrer i Cancho, R. (2004). 'Euclidean distance between syntactically linked words'. *Physical Review E*, 70: 056135.

—— and Solé, R. (2001). 'The small world of human language'. *Proceedings of the Royal Society Series B*, 268: 2261–65.

—— —— and Köhler, R. (2004). 'Patterns in syntactic dependency networks'. *Physical Review E*, 69: 1–8.

Fillmore, C. (1968). 'The case for case', in E. Bach and R. Harms (eds), *Universals in Linguistic Theory*. New York: Holt, Rinehart and Winston. 1–90.

—— Kay, P., and O'Connor, M. (1988). 'Regularity and idiomaticity in grammatical constructions: the case of let alone'. *Language*, 64: 501–38.

Fitch, W. T., Hauser, M., and Chomsky, N. (2006). 'The evolution of the language faculty: clarifications and implications'. *Cognition*, 97: 179–210.

Fodor, J. (1983). *The Modularity of the Mind*. Cambridge, Mass.: MIT Press.

Frazier, L. (1985). 'Syntactic complexity', in D. R. Dowty, L. Karttunen, and A. M. Zwicky (eds), *Natural Language Parsing: Psychological, Computational and Theoretical Perspectives*. Cambridge: Cambridge University Press. 129–89.

Gaifman, H. (1965). 'Dependency systems and phrase-structure systems'. *Information and Control*, 8: 304–37.

Gentner, T., Fenn, K., Margoliash, D., and Nusbaum, H. (2006). 'Recursive syntactic pattern learning by songbirds'. *Nature*, 440: 1204–7.

Gibson, E. (1998). 'Linguistic complexity: locality of syntactic dependencies'. *Cognition*, 68: 1–76.

Gibson, E. (2002). 'The influence of referential processing on sentence complexity'. *Cognition*, 85: 79–112.

Giles, H., and Powesland, P. (1975). *Speech Style and Social Evaluation*. London: Academic Press.

Gisborne, N. (1996). *English Perception Verbs*. Ph.D. UCL, London.

—— (2006). 'Factoring out the subject dependency', in K. Sugayama and R. Hudson (eds), *Not Known*. London: Continuum.

Givón, T. (1998). 'The functional approach to grammar', in M. Tomasello (ed.), *The New Psychology of Language*. London: Lawrence Erlbaum. 41–66.

Goldberg, A. (1995). *Constructions: A Construction Grammar Approach to Argument Structure*. Chicago: University of Chicago Press.

Greenbaum, S. (1996). *The Oxford English Grammar*. Oxford: Oxford University Press.

Griffin, R. (1991). *Cambridge Latin Grammar*. Cambridge: Cambridge University Press.

Gruber, J. (1965). *Studies in Lexical Relations*. MIT.

Guy, G. (1994). 'The phonology of variation'. *Chicago Linguistics Society Parasession* 30: 133–49.

—— and Boyd, S. (1990). 'The development of a morphological class'. *Language Variation and Change*, 2: 1–18.

Haider, H. (1990). 'Topicalization and other puzzles of German syntax', in G. Grewendorf and W. Sternefeld (eds), *Scrambling and Barriers*. Amsterdam: Benjamins. 93–112.

Halle, M., and Marantz, A. (1993). 'Distributed morphology and the pieces of inflection', in K. Hale and S. Keyser (eds), *The View from Building 20: Essays in Linguistics in Honor of Sylvain Bromberger*. Cambridge, Mass.: MIT Press. 111–76.

Halliday, M. (1970). 'Language structure and language function', in Lyons, J. (ed.), *New Horizons in Linguistics*. Harmondsworth: Penguin. 140–65.

—— (1977). 'Text as semantic choice in social contexts', in T. Van Dijk and J. Petofi (eds), *Grammars and Descriptions (Studies in Text Theory and Text Analysis)*. New York: Walter de Gruyter. 176–225.

—— (1978). *Language as Social Semiotic*. London: Arnold.

—— (1985). *An Introduction to Functional Grammar*. London: Arnold.

—— (2002). *On Grammar*. New York: Continuum.

Harley, T. (1990). 'Environmental contamination of normal speech'. *Applied Psycholinguistics*, 11: 45–72.

—— (1995). *The Psychology of Language*. Hove: Psychology Press.

Harris, Z. (1951). *Structural Linguistics*. Chicago: University of Chicago Press.

Haspelmath, M. (2002). *Understanding Morphology*. London: Arnold.

Hauser, M., Chomsky, N., and Fitch, W. T. (2002). 'The faculty of language: what is it, who has it, and how did it evolve?' *Science*, 298: 1569–79.

Hawkins, J. A. (2001). 'Why are categories adjacent?' *Journal of Linguistics*, 37: 1–34.

Hebb, D. (1949). *The Organization of Behaviour*. New York: Wiley.

Heringer, H.-J., Strecker, B., and Wimmer, R. (1980). *Syntax: Fragen—Lösungen—Alternativen*. Munich: Wilhelm Fink Verlag.

Hiranuma, S. (1999). 'Syntactic difficulty in English and Japanese: a textual study'. *UCL Working Papers in Linguistics*, 11: 309–22.

Hirst, G. (1988). 'Resolving lexical ambiguity computationally with spreading activation and Polaroid Words', in S. Small, G. Cottrell, and M. Tanenhaus (eds), *Lexical Ambiguity Resolution: Perspectives from Psycholinguistics, Neuropsychology, and Artificial Intelligence*. San Mateo, Calif.: Morgan Kaufmann. 73–107.

Holmes, J. (2005). *Lexical Properties of English Verbs*. Ph.D. UCL, London.

—— and Hudson, R. (2006). 'Constructions in word grammar', in J.-O. Östman and M. Fried (eds), *Construction Grammar(s): Cognitive Dimensions*. Amsterdam: Benjamins.

Houston, A. (1989). 'The English gerund: syntactic change and discourse function', in R. Fasold and D. Schiffrin (eds), *Language Change and Variation*. Amsterdam: Benjamins. 173–95.

Huddleston, R. (1988). *English Grammar: An Outline*. Cambridge: Cambridge University Press.

Hudson, R. (1964). *A Grammatical Study of Beja*. Ph.D. University of London.

—— (1971). *English Complex Sentences: An Introduction to Systemic Grammar*. Amsterdam: North Holland.

—— (1973). 'An "item-and-paradigm" approach to Beja syntax and morphology'. *Foundations of Language*, 9: 504–48.

—— (1974). 'A structural sketch of Beja'. *African Language Studies*, 15: 111–42.

—— (1976a). *Arguments for a Non-transformational Grammar*. Chicago: Chicago University Press.

—— (1976b). 'Beja', in M. L. Bender (ed.), *The Non-Semitic Languages of Ethiopia*. East Lansing: African Studies Center, Michigan State University. 97–132.

—— (1981a). 'Some issues on which linguists can agree'. *Journal of Linguistics*, 17: 333–44.

—— (1981b). 'Wanna and the lexicon'. *Nottingham Linguistic Circular*, 10: 132–54.

—— (1984). *Word Grammar*. Oxford: Blackwell.

—— (1990). *English Word Grammar*. Oxford: Blackwell.

—— (1992). *Teaching Grammar: A Guide for the National Curriculum*. Oxford: Blackwell.

—— (1995). Does English really have case? *Journal of Linguistics*, 31: 75–392.

—— (1996). *Sociolinguistics*, 2nd edition. Cambridge: Cambridge University Press.

—— (1998). *English Grammar*. London: Routledge.

—— (1999). 'Subject-verb agreement in English'. *English Language and Linguistics*, 3: 173–207.

—— (2000a). '*I amn't'. *Language*, 76: 297–323.

—— (2000b). 'Discontinuity'. *Traitement Automatique des Langues*, 41: 15–56.

—— (2000c). 'Grammar without Functional Categories', in R. Borsley (ed.), *The Nature and Function of Syntactic Categories*. New York: Academic Press. 7–35.

—— (2001a). 'Clitics in Word Grammar'. *UCL Working Papers in Linguistics*, 13: 243–94.

Hudson, R. (2001*b*). 'Grammar teaching and writing skills: the research evidence'. *Syntax in the Schools*, 17: 1–6.

—— (2002). 'Richard Hudson', in K. Brown and V. Law (eds), *Linguistics in Britain: Personal Histories*. Oxford: Blackwell. 127–38.

—— (2003*a*). 'Case-agreement, PRO and structure sharing'. *Research in Language*, 1: 7–33.

—— (2003*b*). 'Gerunds without phrase structure'. *Natural Language & Linguistic Theory*, 21: 579–615.

—— (2003*c*). 'Mismatches in default inheritance', in E. Francis and L. Michaelis (eds), *Mismatch: Form-Function Incongruity and the Architecture of Grammar*. Stanford, Calif.: CSLI. 269–317.

—— (2003*d*). 'Trouble on the left periphery'. *Lingua*, 113: 607–42.

—— (2004*a*). 'Are determiners heads?' *Functions of Language*, 11: 7–43.

—— (2004*b*). 'Why education needs linguistics (and vice versa)'. *Journal of Linguistics*, 40: 105–30.

—— (2006*a*). 'Buying and selling in Word Grammar', in J. Andor and P. Pelyvás (eds), *Empirical, Cognitive-Based Studies in the Semantics-Pragmatics Interface*. Oxford: Elsevier Science.

—— (2006*b*). 'Wanna revisited'. *Language*, 82.

—— (2007*a*). 'Word Grammar', in H. Cuyckens and D. Geeraerts (eds), *Handbook of Cognitive Linguistics*. Oxford: Oxford University Press.

—— (2007*b*). 'Word Grammar, cognitive linguistics and second-language learning and teaching', in P. Robinson and N. Ellis (eds), *Handbook of Cognitive Linguistics and Second Language Acquisition*. Lawrence Erlbaum.

—— and Holmes, J. (2000). 'Re-cycling in the Encyclopedia', in B. Peeters (ed.), *The Lexicon/Encyclopedia Interface*. Amsterdam: Elsevier. 259–90.

—— Rosta, A., Holmes, J., and Gisborne, N. (1996). 'Synonyms and syntax'. *Journal of Linguistics*, 32: 439–46.

—— and Walmsley, J. (2005). 'The English Patient: English grammar and teaching in the twentieth century'. *Journal of Linguistics*, 41: 593–622.

Jack, G. (1988). 'The origins of the English gerund'. *Nowele*, 12: 15–75.

Jackendoff, R. (1977). *X-bar Syntax: A Study of Phrase Structure*. Cambridge, Mass.: MIT Press.

—— (1990). *Semantic Structures*. Cambridge, Mass.: MIT Press.

—— (1997). *The Architecture of the Language Faculty*. Cambridge, Mass.: MIT Press.

—— (2002). *Foundations of Language*. Oxford: Oxford University Press.

Jaeger, J., Lockwood, D., Kemmerer, R., Van Valin, R., Murphy, B., and Khalek, H. (1996). 'A positron emission tomographic study of regular and irregular verb morphology in English'. *Language*, 72: 451–98.

James, L., and Burke, D. (2000). 'Phonological priming effects on word retrieval and tip-of-the-tongue experiences in young and older adults'. *Journal of Experimental Psychology—Learning, Memory and Cognition*, 26: 1378–91.

Jorgensen, E. (1981). 'Gerund and to-infinitive after it-is-(of)-no-use, it-is-no-good, and it-is-useless'. *English Studies*, 62: 156–63.

Joshi, A., and Rambow, O. (2003). 'A Formalism for Dependency Grammar Based on Tree Adjoining Grammar', in S. Kahane and A. Nasr (eds), *Proceedings of the First International Conference on Meaning-Text Theory*. Paris: École Normale Supérieure.

Kaiser, L. (1997). 'CPR for Korean Type III Nominalizations', in L. Kaiser (ed.), *Yale A-Morphous Linguistics Essays*. New Haven: Yale University, Linguistics Dept. 89–99.

—— (1999). *The Morphosyntax of Clausal Nominalization Constructions*. Ph.D. Yale.

Karlsson, F. (1995). *Constraint Grammar: A Language-Independent System for Parsing Unrestricted Text*. Berlin: Mouton de Gruyter.

Karmiloff-Smith, A. (1992). *Beyond Modularity: A Developmental Perspective on Cognitive Science*. Cambridge, Mass.: MIT Press.

Kay, P. (2002). 'An informal sketch of a formal architecture for construction grammar'. *Grammars*, 5: 1–19.

—— and Fillmore, C. (1999). 'Grammatical constructions and linguistic generalizations: the what's X doing Y? construction'. *Language*, 75: 1–33.

Keenan, E. (1976). 'Towards a universal definition of "subject" ', in C. Li (ed.), *Subject and Topic*. New York: Academic Press. 303–33.

Kempson, R., and Quirk, R. (1971). 'Controlled activation of latent contrast'. *Language*, 47: 548–72.

Klein, D., and Manning, C. (2004). 'Corpus-based induction of syntactic structure: models of dependency and constituency'. *Proceedings of the Annual Meeting of the Association for Computational Linguistics* (ACL 2004) 42: 478–85.

Kreps, C. (1997). *Extraction, Movement and Dependency Theory*. Ph.D. UCL.

Kuzar, R. (1998). 'Constructions: a construction grammar approach to argument structure'. *Journal of Pragmatics*, 29: 359–62.

Labov, W. (1972). *Sociolinguistic Patterns*. Oxford: Blackwell.

—— (1989). 'The child as linguistic historian'. *Language Variation and Change*, 1: 85–97.

—— (2001). *Principles of Linguistic Change*, vol. ii: *Social Factors*. Oxford: Blackwell.

Laird, J., Newell, A., and Rosenbloom, P. (1987). 'Soar: an architecture for general intelligence'. *Artificial Intelligence*, 33: 1–64.

Lamb, S. (1966). *Outline of Stratificational Grammar*. Washington, DC: Georgetown University Press.

—— (1971). 'The crooked path of progress in cognitive linguistics', in R. J. O'Brien (ed.), *Linguistics: Developments of the Sixties—Viewpoint for the Seventies*. Washington, DC: Georgetown University Press.

—— (1998). *Pathways of the Brain: The Neurocognitive Basis of Language*. Amsterdam: Benjamins.

Langacker, R. (1998). 'Conceptualization, symbolization and grammar', in M. Tomasello (ed.), *The New Psychology of Language: Cognitive and Functional Approaches to Language Structure*. Mahwah, NJ: Erlbaum. 1–39.

—— (2000). 'A dynamic usage-based model', in M. Barlow and S. Kemmer (eds), *Usage-Based Models of Language*. Stanford, Calif.: CSLI. 1–63.

Langenhove, G. C. van (1925). *On the Origin of the Gerund in English*. Grand: van Rysselberghe & Rombaut.

Lapointe, S. (1993). 'Dual lexical categories and the syntax of mixed category phrases', in A. Kathol and M. Bernstein (eds), *Proceedings of the Eastern States Conference of Linguistics*. 199–210.

Lecarme, J. (1978). 'Aspects syntaxiques des complétives du Grec'. Ph.D. University of Montreal.

Levelt, W. J. M., Roelofs, A., and Meyer, A. S. (1999). 'A theory of lexical access in speech production'. *Behavioral and Brain Sciences*, 22: 1–45.

Levin, B. (1993). *English Verb Classes and Alternations: A Preliminary Investigation*. Chicago: University of Chicago Press.

—— and Rappaport Hovav, M. (1991). 'Wiping the slate clean: a lexical semantic exploration', in B. Levin and S. Pinker (eds), *Lexical and Conceptual Semantics*. Oxford: Blackwell. 123–51.

Lewis, R. (1996). 'Interference in short-term memory: the magical number two (or three) in sentence processing'. *Journal of Psycholinguistic Research*, 25: 93–115.

Lieberman, P. (2002). 'On the nature and evolution of the neural bases of human language'. *American Journal of Physical Anthropology Supplement: Yearbook of Physical Anthropology*, 119: 36–62.

Lin, D. (2004). 'Dependency-based evaluation of Minipar', in A. Abeillé (ed.), *Building and Using Parsed Corpora*. Dordrecht: Kluwer.

Liu, H., and R. Hudson (2006). 'Measuring dependency distance based on a Chinese treebank'. Anon.

Luger, G., and Stubblefield, W. (1993). *Artificial Intelligence: Structures and Strategies for Complex Problem Solving*. New York: Benjamin Cummings.

Macdonald, M. C., Pearlmutter, N. J., and Seidenberg, M. S. (1994). 'Lexical nature of syntactic ambiguity resolution'. *Psychological Review*, 101: 676–703.

Macwhinney, B. (1989). 'Competition and teachability', in M. Rice and R. Schiefelbusch (eds), *The Teachability of Language*. Baltimore: Brookes. 63–104.

McClelland, J., and Rumelhart, D. (1988). *Explorations in parallel distributed processing: a handbook of models, programs, and exercises*. Cambridge, Mass.: MIT Press.

McRae, K., Spivey-Knowlton, M., and Tanenhaus, M. (1998). 'Modeling the influence of thematic fit (and other constraints) in on-line sentence comprehension'. *Journal of Memory and Language*, 38: 283–312.

Malouf, R. (1998). 'Mixed categories in the hierarchical lexicon'. Ph.D. Stanford University.

—— (2000). *Mixed categories in the hierachical lexicon*. Stanford, Calif.: CSLI Publications.

Marslen-Wilson, W. (1984). 'Function and structure in spoken word recognition', in H. Bouma and D. Bouwhuis (eds), *Attention and Performance*, vol x: *Control of Language Processes*. Hillsdale, NJ: Lawrence Erlbaum.

Meara, P. (2002). 'Modelling attrition in vocabularies', in A. Hauksdóttir, B. Arn-björnsdóttir, M. Gardharsdóttir, and S. Þorvaldsdóttir (eds), *Forskning i Nordiske Sprog Som Andet- Og Fremmedsprog*. Reykjavík: Háskóli Islands. 153–75.

Meidner, O. M. (1994). 'Emotive meaning', in R. Asher (ed.), *Encyclopedia of Language and Linguistics*. Oxford: Pergamon. 1111.

Mel'cuk, I. (1997). *Vers une linguistique sens-texte*. Paris: Collège de France: Chaire Internationale.

Michaelis, L., and Lambrecht, K. (1996). 'Toward a construction-based theory of language function: the case of nominal extraposition'. *Language*, 72: 215–47.

Miller, G. (1956). 'The magical number seven plus or minus two: some limits on our capacity for processing information'. *Psychological Review*, 63: 81–97.

Milroy, L. (1980). *Language and Social Networks*. Oxford: Blackwell.

Miyake, A., and Shah, P. (1999). 'Toward unified theories of working memory: emerging general consensus, unresolved theoretical issues and future research directions', in A. Miyake and P. Shah (eds), *Models of Working Memory: Mechanisms of Active Maintenance and Executive Control*. Cambridge: Cambridge University Press. 442–81.

Mollá, D., Schneider, G., Schwitter, R., and Hess, M. (2000). 'Answer extraction using a dependency grammar in Extrans'. *Traitement Automatique des Langues*, 41: 145–78.

Ninio, A. (1994). 'Predicting the order of acquisition of three-word constructions by the complexity of their dependency structure'. *First Language*, 14: 119–52.

—— (1996). 'A proposal for the adoption of dependency grammar as the framework for the study of language acquisition', in G. Ben Shakhar and A. Lieblich (eds), *Volume in Honor of Shlomo Kugelmass*. Jerusalem: Magnes. 85–103.

—— (1998). 'Acquiring a dependency grammar: the first three stages in the acquisition of multiword combinations in Hebrew-speaking children', in G. Makiello-Jarza, J. Kaiser, and M. Smolczynska (eds), *Language Acquisition and Developmental Psychology*. Cracow: Universitas.

Nivre, J. (2004). 'Incrementality in deterministic dependency parsing'. Anon.

—— Hall, J., and Nilsson, J. (2004). 'Memory-based dependency parsing' in H. T. Ng and E. Riloff (eds), *Proceedings of the Eighth Conference on Computational Natural Language Learning (CoNLL), May 6–7, 2004*. Boston, Mass.: 49–56.

Owens, J. (1988). *The Foundations of Grammar: An Introduction to Mediaeval Arabic Grammatical Theory*. Amsterdam: Benjamins.

Pake, J. (1998). *The Marker Hypothesis: A Constructivist Theory of Language Acquisition*. Ph.D. Edinburgh.

Percival, K. (1990). 'Reflections on the history of dependency notions in linguistics'. *Historiographia Linguistica*, 17: 29–47.

Pickering, M., and Barry, G. (1991). 'Sentence processing without empty categories'. *Language and Cognitive Processes*, 6: 259.

Pinker, S. (1994). *The Language Instinct*. London: Penguin.

—— (1998). 'Words and rules'. *Lingua*, 106: 219–42.

Pollard, C., and Sag, I. (1994). *Head-Driven Phrase Structure Grammar.* Chicago: Chicago University Press.

Postal, P. (1966). 'On so-called "pronouns" in English'. *Monographs on Languages and Linguistics,* 19: 177–206.

Poutsma, H. (1923). *The Infinitive, the Gerund and the Participles of the English Verb.* Groningen: P. Noordhoff.

Pullum, G. (1991). 'English nominal gerund phrases as noun phrases with verb-phrase heads'. *Linguistics,* 29: 763–99.

Quillian, M. R. (1968). 'Semantic memory', in M. Minsky (ed.), *Semantic Information Processing.* Cambridge, Mass.: MIT Press.

—— and Collins, A. M. (1969). 'Retrieval time from semantic memory'. *Journal of Verbal Learning and Verbal Behavior,* 8: 240–7.

Quirk, R., Greenbaum, S., Leech, G., and Svartvik, J. (1985). *A Comprehensive Grammar of the English Language.* London: Longman.

Rambow, O., and Joshi, A. (1994). 'A formal look at dependency grammars and phrase-structure grammars, with special consideration of word-order phenomena', in L. Waner, (ed.), *Current Issues in Meaning-Text Theory.* London: Pinter.

Reisberg, D. (1997). *Cognition: Exploring the Science of the Mind.* New York: Norton.

Richards, N. (2004). 'Against bans on lowering'. *Linguistic Inquiry,* 35: 453–64.

Robins, R. H. (2001). 'In Defence of WP' (Reprinted from TPHS, 1959). *Transactions of the Philological Society,* 99: 114–44.

Robinson, J. (1970). 'Dependency structure and transformational rules'. *Language,* 46: 259–85.

Robinson, P. (1986). 'Constituency or dependency in the units of language acquisition? An approach to describing the learner's analysis of formulae'. *Linguisticae Investigationes,* 10: 417–37.

Roelofs, A. (1997). 'The WEAVER model of word-form encoding in speech production'. *Cognition,* 64: 249–84.

Roland, D. (2001). *Verb sense and verb subcategorization probabilities.* Ph.D. University of Colorado.

Rosch, E. (1976). 'Classification of real-world objects: origins and representations in cognition' in S. Ehrlich, and E. Tulving (eds), *La Mémoire sémantique.* Paris: Bulletin de Psychologie. Reprinted in P. Johnson-Laird and P. C. Wason (eds) (1977) *Thinking: Readings in Cognitive Science.* Cambridge: Cambridge University Press. 212–22.

Rosta, A. (1997). *English Syntax and Word Grammar Theory.* Ph.D. UCL, London.

—— (2005). 'Structural and distributional heads', in K. Sugayama and R. Hudson (eds), *Word Grammar: New Perspectives on a Theory of Language Structure.* London: Continuum. 171–203.

—— (2006). 'Structural and distributional heads', in K. Sugayama and R. Hudson (eds), *Word Grammar: New Perspectives on a Theory of Language Structure.* London: Continuum.

Rumelhart, D., and McClelland, J. (1986). 'On learning the past tenses of English verbs', in J. McClelland and D. Rumelhart (eds), *Parallel Distributed Processing: Explorations in the Microstructure of Cognition*, vol. ii: *Psychological and Biological Models*. Cambridge, Mass.: MIT Press.

Rushton, J. N. (2004). 'Natural language parsing using simple neural networks', in Anon., *Proceedings of the 2003 International Conference on Artificial Intelligence*.

Rusteberg, F. G. A. (1874). *Historical Development of the Gerund in the English Language*. Göttingen: Druck der Dieterichischen Univ-Buchdruckerei.

Sadock, J. (1991). *Autolexical Syntax: A Theory of Parallel Grammatical Representations*. Chicago: University of Chicago Press.

Sag, I. (1997). 'English relative clause constructions'. *Journal of Linguistics*, 33: 431–83.

Sapir, E. (1921). *Language*. New York: Harcourt, Brace and World.

Saussure, F. de (1959). *Course in General Linguistics* (trans. by W. Baskin; French edition 1916). Lausanne: Payot.

Seyfarth, R., Cheney, D., and Bergman, T. (2005). 'Primate social cognition and the origins of language'. *Trends in Cognitive Sciences*, 9: 264–66.

Sgall, P., Hajicova, E., and Panevova, J. (1986). *The Meaning of the Sentence in its Semantic and Pragmatic Aspects*. Prague: Academia.

Shieber, S. (1986). *An Introduction to Unification-based Approaches to Grammar*. Stanford, Calif.: CSLI Publications.

Siewierska, A. (1991). *Functional Grammar*. London: Routledge.

Smith, N. V. (1999). *Chomsky: Ideas and Ideals*. Cambridge: Cambridge University Press.

Solé, R. (2005). 'Syntax for free?' *Nature*, 434: 289.

Somers, H. (1984). 'On the validity of the complement-adjunct distinction in valency grammar'. *Linguistics*, 22: 507–31.

Sperber, D., and Wilson, D. (1995). *Relevance: Communication and Cognition*. Oxford: Blackwell.

Sproat, R. (1988). 'Bracketing paradoxes, cliticization and other topics: the mapping between syntactic and phonological structure', in M. Everaert, A. Evers, R. Huybregts, and M. Trommelen (eds), *Morphology and Modularity: in Honour of Henk Schultink*. Dordrecht: Foris. 339–60.

Steedman, M. (2000). *The Syntactic Process*. London: MIT Press.

Stump, G. (1993). 'On rules of referral'. *Language*, 69: 449–79.

Sturt, P., Pickering, M., Scheepers, C., and Crocker, M. (2001). 'The preservation of structure in language comprehension: is reanalysis the last resort?' *Journal of Memory and Language*, 45: 283–301.

Sutcliffe, R., Koch, H.-D., and McElligott, A. (1996). *Industrial Parsing of Software Manuals*. Amsterdam: Rodopi.

Swan, M. (1995). *Practical English Usage*. Oxford: Oxford University Press.

Tajima, M. (1985). *The Syntactic Development of the Gerund in Middle English*. Tokyo: Nanun-do.

Talmy, L. (1988). 'Force dynamics in language and cognition'. *Cognitive Science*, 12: 49–100.

Tesnière, L. (1959). *Éléments de syntaxe structurale*. Paris: Klincksieck.

Tomasello, M. (1998). 'Constructions: a construction grammar approach to argument structure'. *Journal of Child Language*, 25: 431–42.

—— (1999). *The Cultural Origins of Human Cognition*. London: Harvard University Press.

—— (2000). 'The item-based nature of children's early syntactic development'. *Trends in Cognitive Sciences*, 4: 156–63.

—— (2003). *Constructing a Language: A Usage-Based Theory of Language Acquisition*. Harvard University Press.

Touretzky, D. (1986). *The Mathematics of Inheritance Systems*. Los Altos, Calif.: Morgan Kaufmann.

Tzanidaki, D. (1996). *The Syntax and Pragmatics of Subject and Object Position in Modern Greek*. Ph.D. UCL.

—— (1998). 'Clause structure and word order in Modern Greek', in B. Joseph, G. Horrocks, and I. Philippaki-Warburton (eds), *Themes in Greek Linguistics 2*. Amsterdam: Benjamins. 229–54.

Van Langendonck, W. (1987). 'Word Grammar and child grammar'. *Belgian Journal of Linguistics*, 2: 109–32.

Van Valin, R. (1993). *Advances in Role and Reference Grammar*. Amsterdam: Benjamins.

Vosse, T., and Kempen, G. (2000). 'Syntactic structure assembly in human parsing: a computational model based on competitive inhibition and a lexicalist grammar'. *Cognition*, 75: 105–43.

Warneken, F., and Tomasello, M. (2006). 'Altruistic helping in human infants and young chimpanzees'. *Science*, 311: 1301–3.

Wells, R. (1947). 'Immediate constituents'. *Language*, 23: 81–117.

Wescoat, M. (1994). 'Phrase structure, lexical sharing, partial ordering and the English gerund'. *Proceedings of the Berkeley Linguistics Society*, 20: 587–98.

Wierzbicka, A. (1996). *Semantics: Primes and Universals*. Oxford: Oxford University Press.

Wik, B. (1973). *English Nominalizations in -ing: Synchronic and Diachronic Aspects*. Uppsala: Almqvist & Wiksell.

Williams, E. (1984). 'Grammatical relations'. *Linguistic Inquiry*, 15: 639–74.

Williams, S., Savage-Rumbaugh, S., and Rumbaugh, D. M. (1994). 'Apes and language', in R. Asher (ed.), *Encyclopedia of Language and Linguistics*. Oxford: Pergamon. 139–46.

Winograd, T. (1976). 'Towards a procedural understanding of semantics'. *Revue Internationale de Philosophie*, 30: 260–303.

Wurff, W. v. d. (1993). 'Gerunds and their objects in the Modern English period', in J. v. Marle (ed.), *Historical Linguistics 1991*. Amsterdam: Benjamins. 363–75.

Wurff, W. van den (1997). 'Gerunds in the Modern English period: structure and change'. *History of English*, 3: 163–96.

Yoon, J. (1996). 'Nominal gerund phrases in English as phrasal zero derivations'. *Linguistics*, 34: 329–56.

Zwicky, A. (1977). *On clitics*. Bloomington, Ind.: Indiana University Linguistics Club.

—— (1992a). 'Clitics: an overview', in W. Bright (ed.), *International Encyclopedia of Linguistics*. Oxford: Oxford University Press. 269–70.

—— (1992b). 'Morphology: morphology and syntax', in W. Bright (ed.), *International Encyclopedia of Linguistics*. Oxford: Oxford University Press. 10–12.

Index

Abeillé 123
Abney 189, 191, 204
abstractness 222–3
achieving 216
act of identity 247–8
action 214–19, 236
activation—*see* spreading activation
active network 43
ACT-R 42
addressee 174, 214, 217–18, 220, 222
adjacency principle 140
adjective 200, 208–9
adjunct 162–5
adverb 208–9
affix 74
after—*see* before 132–3
age 248
agent-noun 64
agreement 69–71, 109–10, 144,
    157–60, 174–7
Aitchison 220
allegiance 243–5
Allerton 164
allomorphy 79, 115
amn't 12, 28, 63, 243
a-morphous morphology 68
analogy 81
analytic knowledge 232
anaphora 227
anchor 109
and operator 34
Anderson xi, 42, 68, 74, 104, 234
Andrews 175–6
antecedent 227
Arabic 75, 98, 117
architecture of language 217–18
argument 12, 16–17, 31–2

argument structure 234
Aronoff 67, 74, 81
arrow 119
artificial intelligence viii, 10, 24, 32–3, 62
associative network, association 10, 43, 61
attention 221–2
attitude 241
attribute 71

Babbage 62
baboon 223, 237
Baddeley vii
Baker 189
Barabasí 9, 123
Barry 125
base 64, 79, 81
basic level of activation 246
basic relation—*see* primitive relation
basic-level category 56
Bates 151
Bauer 38, 73, 94
Beard 74
before (and after) 132–3
behaviour 237
Beja 92, 97, 107–11, 171
Belfast 247–8
Berko Gleason 77
best-fit principle 25, 44, 48, 55, 245
Bharati 117
Biber 185
bilingualism 240–6
binary morphological structure 97
binding 31, 34, 43–4, 46–50, 225–7, 229
Blake 120
Blevins 67, 81, 84
blocking—*see* default inheritance
Bloomfield 118

Bock 38
Bod 3, 53
Borer 104
Borsley 126
bound token 46
Boyd 58
Bresnan xi, 15, 60, 66, 75, 120, 167, 183, 189
Broadwell 147
Bröker 118, 130
Brooks 38
Brown 63, 86, 239
Browne 21
Burke 38
Bybee xi, 9, 22, 41, 42, 53, 76

Camdzic 63, 114
Cantonese 241
Carroll 123
Carstairs-McCarthy 76, 84
Carston 6
case, case agreement 75–7, 201–2
categorial grammar 122
categorization—*see* classification
c-command 122
centre embedding 219
Chaitanya 117
Chametzky 120, 121
Chang 38
change 184, 202–10
Charniak 15
child language 128–30
CHILDES database 128
chimpanzee 220–1
Chinese 126
Chinese 241
Chipere 8
Chomsky vii, xi, 2, 60, 74, 117, 119, 121,
    144, 151, 169, 177, 178, 189, 219, 236,
    240
Clark 211
classification 10–18, 24, 42–3, 46, 50, 156, 157
classified relation—*see* relation type
clause 113–14, 183, 187, 199

clitic, cliticization 65, 77, 104–15, 150,
    189, 203
co-dependent 134–5
code-switching 242–6
cognition, cognitive structure x, 4–8, 10,
    135, 159, 223, 237
cognitive grammar 2, 53, 132
cognitive linguistics vii, 2, 3, 151
cognitive psychology—*see* psychology
Collins 50, 57, 121, 128
common noun 190, 192
common-sense reasoning ix, 22
communicating,
    communication 217–19, 236
competence vii–ix, xi, 7, 248
competition 51
complement 105–6, 162–5
complexity 222–3
compositional semantics 228–32
compounding 93–6
computational linguistics 3, 123
computer modelling 62
computing power 16
concatenative morphology 96–7
concept 12–14, 20–1, 39–40, 56, 212
conceptual network—*see* network
conjugation 76
connection 117
connectionism 5, 9, 10, 63
consistently-mixed language 161–2
constant 21
constituent structure 96
construction 152–8, 160–7, 184–6, 206
construction grammar 2, 154, 157, 166
context 39–40, 42, 55
contrast-set 157
convergent dependency 160
coordination 34, 139–40, 182, 231
Corbett 9, 63, 86
core viii–ix
corpus 123–5, 128–30
correlation 156, 220, 233
covert subject, covert word 172–82

Covington 117
Cowan 8
Creider 63, 74, 177, 178
Crestani 42
Crocker 41
Croft 9, 151, 234
Cruse 9
c-structure 189
Culicover 9
cumulative expression 92

daughter dependency grammar xi
Deacon xi, 18, 220, 223
declarative analysis 42, 68, 96–100, 102
declension 76, 170–1
deep case 234
default 69–70, 162–3, 242
default inheritance viii–x, 21–31, 43–4,
    50–2, 55, 66–7, 160, 180–1
default logic 61
default order 133
default property 68
defining concept 232
definiteness 47, 224–6
deictic meaning, deixis 55, 89–90, 215
Delaney 8
deletion 98
Denison 184, 186, 196, 207–8
dependency distance 124–129, 161
dependency type 160–7
dependency, dependency analysis,
    dependency structure 51–2, 57, 80,
    118–30, 132, 151, 156, 183; *see*
    convergent dependency
derivational morphology 64–8, 82, 87–93
determiner 128, 145–6, 158, 187, 190–2,
    203, 208–9
diachrony—*see* change
dialect, dialect continuum 241
dialectology—*see* quantitative
    dialectology
diathesis 234
Dik 234

discontinuous pattern 131
distance—*see* dependency distance,
    topological distance
distributed network—*see*
    connectionism
distribution 190, 198–9, 201
distributive interpretation 229–31
ditransitive 154–6
doing, do-er 216
domain 242
dominance 237
Donner 184
Dowty 164, 234
DP 187, 191
Dutch 209
dvandva compounds 94

education xi
ee 235
ellipsis 150, 172–82, 203–5
Ellis 22, 53
Elman 57, 128
elsewhere condition ix
emotion, emotive meaning 213
empiricism 232
empty category,
    empty node 40–1, 172
endocentricity, exocentricity 118, 187
enrichment 45, 46, 50–2, 224
entity 12–14
entrenchment 53
Eppler 57, 126, 243, 244
er 234–5
Ericsson 8, 42
er-variant 64
etymology 77, 240
evaluation 59–62
Evans 86
event, event type 215–16, 234
evocation 225
exception—*see* default
existential quantification 33–4
extra dependency 146

extraction, extractee 128, 131, 147–50, 160–1, 167, 173
extraposition 130

Fanego 184
feature 29, 70, 157–60, 169, 188
Ferrer i Cancho 8, 123, 128
fif—*see* fully inflected form
Fillmore xi, 151, 156, 234
finite, finiteness 199–201
firing 245–6
first 79
Fitch 219
Fodor 6, 232
force dynamics 215
force-dynamic analysis 234
form 64, 72–81, 150, 171, 215, 221
formality 211–12
formation 79
fps—*see* full phonological structure
Fraser 9, 63
Frazier 125
free word order 133–4
Frege 225
French 99, 100–2, 105, 111–12, 152–3, 174, 241
frequency viii, 20, 53, 246
front-shifting 142; *see* extraction
f-structure 189
full ordering 133
full phonological structure 79, 98
fully inflected form 65, 79, 104
function—*see* grammatical function
function word 68, 105
functional explanation x, 116, 148
functional grammar 120
functional-generative description 122
fused words 77, 100–4, 112, 203

Gaelic 101
Gaifman 120
gender 174–5
generalization ix, 10–11, 21, 33
generation, generative grammar xi, 66, 163

genetics—*see* innate concepts
Gentner 219
German 97, 101, 126, 143–4, 174, 177
gerund 60, 88, 92, 183–210
gesturing, gesture 218
Gibson 125, 126
Giles 241
Gisborne 167, 204, 236
Givón 9
Goldberg 2, 9, 151–2, 154, 165
grammatical function 119
grammatical metaphor 165
grammatical relation—*see* grammatical function
grammaticization 104
graph theory 123–4
graphology—*see* writing
Greek, Ancient Greek 101, 117, 175–7
Greenbaum 192
Griffin 38
Gruber 234
guise 244
Guy 58, 77

Haider 143, 144
Halle 74
Halliday xi, 1, 2, 29, 120, 165, 211, 213, 234
happening 216
Harley 37–8
Harris 118
hasa, has 19
Haspelmath 84, 88
Hauser 219
Hawkins 126
head feature convention 189
head, head word 118–9, 190, 232
head-initial, head-final language 161
Hebb, Hebbian learning 58, 220–1
Hebrew 128
Helsinki constraint grammar 123
Heringer 124
hierarchical modularity 9
Hiranuma 126

Hirst 42
Holmes 156–7, 165, 167, 204, 215, 232, 236
host 105–6, 109–11
host-form 107–15
host-word 114
Houston 184
HPSG 66, 120, 122, 212
Huddleston xi, 190
hyphenation 95

Icelandic 175–7
ideational meaning 213
identity, directed identity 12, 47, 226
idiom 94, 166
if operator 36
I-language 2
immediate-constituent analysis 118
imperative 172, 175, 178–9
incorporation 115
individual 1–2, 30
induction 4, 22, 53, 57–8, 129, 152, 214–15, 223–4
inflected clitic 108
inflection 65, 68–72, 87–8, 169–70, 199
inflection class 76
inflectional morphology 64–8, 82, 87–93
information encapsulation 6
inherent variability 77–8, 246–8
inheritance 11–12, 21–4, 135–6, 156, 163
inheritance hierarchy ix, 50, 69, 83, 87, 129, 213–19
inheritance network 11, 30
innate concepts, innate language 3–4, 152, 232–3, 237
interdependence 142
interdigitation 92, 98
intermediate base 81
interpersonal meaning 213, 239
intimacy 212
intimate 238
intonation 78
inversion 133
irregular morphology 51, 63

isa hierarchy—*see* inheritance hierarchy
isa relation 10–18, 21–31, 214, 224–5
Italian 82, 100, 241

Jack 184
Jackendoff xi, 8, 21, 24, 39, 41, 42, 53, 74, 118, 132, 189, 216, 220, 225, 234
Jaeger 51
James 38
Japanese 133
joint interpretation 229–31
Jorgensen 185
Joshi 122

Kaiser 189
Karlsson 123
Karmiloff-Smith 217–8
Kay 151, 156
Keenan 59
Kempen 42
Kempson 75
kinship 234, 237–8
Kintsch 8, 42
Klein 123
Köhler 123, 128
Kreps 122
Kuzar 152

labels 18–19, 33
Labov xi, 2, 207, 246
Laird 42
Lakoff xi
Lamb viii, xi, 2, 9, 18, 41, 60
Lambrecht 152
landmark 132–51, 147–50, 215
landmark transitivity 135, 139–41
Langacker xi, 2, 9, 53, 74, 132
Langenhove 184
language, language system x, 5, 239–46
Lapointe 189
last 79
Latin 71–2, 82, 92, 118, 169–70, 175

learning 2–4, 15, 30, 52–9, 128, 152–3, 160, 214, 220–4, 232–3
Lebiere 42
Lecarme 176
level of analysis xi, 7, 72–81, 215
Levelt 39, 62, 74, 77
Levin xi, 165, 234
Levinson xi, 239
lexeme 56, 64, 68–72, 87–8
lexeme class 68, 88, 92, 169, 192–9, 206, 210, 225
lexical item—*see* lexeme
lexical rule 189, 201
lexical semantics 32–3, 89, 215
lexically specific
    construction 129–30
lexico-grammar viii
lexicon viii, 2–3
LFG 66, 120
Lieberman 7
Lin 123
Line 62
link 10
link grammar 123
link type—*see* relation type
linking rule 172–3, 234–6
Liu 126
localist network 21
localist semantics 234
logic—*see* predicate logic, default
    inheritance
logical form 236
logical operator 33–6
    see also operator, 'not' operator, or
    operator
long-term memory 5, 7–8
long-term working memory 42, 44
lowering 141, 144, 189

Macdonald, 42
Macwhinney 129
Macwhinney 38
making 216

Malouf 167, 183, 184, 186, 188–90, 197, 200, 204, 207
Mandarin 241
Manning 123
markedness 29, 69, 159, 160
Marrantz 74
Marslen-Wilson 41, 42
McCawley xi
McClelland 42
McRae 42
meaning 18, 211–48
meaning-text theory 122
Meidner 213
Mel'cuk 122
member 29–30, 229
metalinguistic knowledge 240
metaphor 225
metonymy 225
Michaelis 152
Miller 7, 40
Milroy 247
mind-reading 223
minimalism, minimalist
    program 121
mismatch 75, 77, 172
mixed category 88, 167–71
Moder 76
module, modularity 6–7, 9, 42
Mollá 123
monotonic reasoning 25
morph 63, 67, 73
morpheme 73
morpho-syntactic feature 70
morphological process 68
morphological structure 94–6
morphology 60, 63–117
morphomic form 67
morphomic function 81
movement 119, 121, 160
multiple inheritance 21, 27–8, 72, 167, 183, 198–9
multiple membership 12, 49
mutation 126

name, naming 175, 236–7
nativism 3–4
negation 36, 227
neighbour 37
network morphology 63
network postulate 1, 9, 119, 121
network strength 247–8
network typology 8–9, 10–11
network viii–ix, 1, 2–3, 53, 232–3
neuro-psychology 6–7
Ninio 128
Nivre 123
Nixon diamond 27
node creation 43–4
nominalization 202, 208
non-canonical phrase 166, 186
non-human cognition 18
non-monotonic reasoning 25
non-selected complement 164
Norwegian 241
'not' operator—*see* logical operator
no-tangling principle 140
notation 11, 17, 19–20, 44, 64, 65, 119, 131, 225
noun, noun phrase 183, 186–7, 192–9
number 29, 69–71, 159

O'Connor 151
object 235
obligatory adjunct 164
obliqueness 122
Old English 202, 206–10
ontology 13, 214–19
operator—*see* logical operator
optimality theory 147
or operator—*see* logical operator
order 75, 111, 118, 126; *see also* word order,
    full ordering, partial ordering
order concord 140
overriding 24, 26–7
Owens 117

Pake 57, 128, 129
Panini 117

parameter 2, 3, 151
parent 118, 132, 179–80
parents are landmarks rule 146
parsing 7–8, 46, 52, 123, 131–2
part1, part2 64, 68, 110, 112–13
partial ordering 133
partial VP fronting 143–4
participle 170, 199, 207
part-whole structure 96, 118
PEN treebank 128
perception 42–5, 237
Percival 117
performance vii–ix
person type 243
phonetic form 236
phonetics 64
phonological loop vii, 8
phonology 64, 73, 79, 102, 105, 115,
    160, 220–1
phrase 118, 130
phrase structure 118–31, 151, 154, 156, 183,
    190, 210, 228
Pickering 41, 125
Pinker 3, 63, 217
pivot 167
place 214
plural 228–32
pluralia tantum 174
politeness 239
Pollard xi, 66, 74, 119, 120, 122, 190, 212
Ponapean 99
popular etymology—*see* etymology
Portuguese 100
position 113, 132
POSS-ING 185
Postal 192
post-dependent, post-modifier 160–1,
    165, 195
Poutsma 184
power 174, 236–9
Powesland 241
pragmatics—*see* enrichment, processing,
    inference, situation

pre-adjunct 206
precedence concord 140
pre-dependent, pre-modifier 133, 160–1, 165, 195
predicate 33
predicate logic 21, 31–6
predicative, predicative adjective 175–7
prefrontal cortext 222–3
prejudice 241–2
preposition meaning 234
prepositional pied-piping 146–50
primate, non-human primate 219, 237
priming 37–9
primitive relation 12, 16–17, 20, 47
principle 2, 144
PRO, *pro* 172–82
probability 245–8
pocedural analysis—*see* declarative analysis
processing 8, 20, 39–40, 63, 84–5, 124–6, 138, 180, 214, 222–3, 245–6
processing domain 126
production 42, 45
productivity 91
projection 146
projectivity 130–1, 135–40
pronoun 190–6, 227
pronunciation 79
proper noun 190, 192
property 232
property types 39
proposition 31
proto-agent, proto-patient 234
prototype effects, prototype semantics 24, 61, 216
proxy 146–8
psycholinguistics 7, 36, 244
psychological reality 60
psychology i, 8, 36, 61
Pullum 189
purpose 215–9

quantification, quantifier 31–4, 228–32
quantifier 19

quantitative dialectology 246–8
quantity 12, 19–20, 36, 178–9, 229
Quillian 42, 50
Quirk 75, 185, 186, 193

raising principle 141
raising rule 144–6
raising verb 130, 140–1
Rambow 122
Rappaport Hovav 165
rationalism 232
realization 65, 79–81, 98, 178–81, 218–19
recency viii, 53
recursion 131, 219
recycling 233–6
redescription 79, 217–18
redundancy 22, 25, 50–1
reduplication 99
reference assignment 46
referent 89, 211–13, 224–8, 236–7
referential meaning 212–13, 236
reflexive pronoun 194, 227
relation 12–18, 39–40
relation noun 234
relation type 42, 59, 68, 119, 224, 234–6
relational 200–1
relational grammar 120
relative clause 110–11, 152–3, 193–5
relevance theory 46
representational redescription—*see* redescription
result, resultative verb 215–19, 235
Richards 141
Robins 67
Robinson 120, 129
Roelofs 42
Roland 42
Role and Reference Grammar 120
root 74
Rosch 56
Rosta 102, 121, 122, 137, 146, 173, 204
rule 2–3, 144
rule of referral 84–5

Rumbaugh 219
Rumelhart 42
Rushton 42
Rusteberg 184

Sadock xi, 67, 74, 75, 109
Sag xi, 66, 74, 119, 120, 122, 190, 212
Sangal 117
Sapir 1
Saussure 1
Savage-Rumbaugh 219
scale-free network 8, 123
Schmidt 22
second-order network 15, 224
second-position clitic 113–14
selection 156–7, 162, 187, 198, 206
semantic network 5, 10
semantic phrasing 122, 162
semantic relation 232–6
semantic role 162
semantics 60, 122, 173, 211–37
semitic-type morphology 92
sense 89, 224–8
sentence-root 118, 131
Serbo-Croatian 63, 105, 113–14
set 30, 34, 159, 228–32, 244
Seyfarth 223, 237
Sgall 122
sharing 128, 172
Shieber 25
short-term memory i, 7–8
Siewierska 120
sign 74
signal, signalling 217–19
simple clitic 104
sister transitivity 136–7, 139
sister-ordering 135–6
situation 212, 214, 215, 242–3
situation-language 243
size 229
Slobin xi
Slovene 86–7
small-world network 128

Smith 132
SOAR 42
social fact 1–2
social meaning, social restriction 213, 237
social psychology 241
social relation, social structure 223, 237, 246–8
social semiotic 1
social type 241–2
sociolinguistics 60, 75, 174, 211–13, 236–48
Solé 8, 123, 128
solidarity 174, 236–9
Somers 164
source 96
Spanish 100
speaker 212–15, 236–9
special clitic 105, 107
specifier 119
speech community 2
speech error 37–8, 48, 77
spelling 79, 95
Sperber 46
spreading activation vii, 27, 36–41, 43–4, 46–50, 138, 217–18, 225, 233, 245
Sproat 104
starling 219
statistics 124–5
Steedman 122
stem—*see* base
stemma 130
stereotype 241–8
stipulation 188
stochastic process 245, 247
Stratificational Grammar 2, 41
structural priming viii
structuralism vii, 1, 214
structure dependence 132
structure-sharing 119, 140
Stump 84
Sturt 41
subclassification 29, 132–3, 190
subject 59, 133, 165, 234–5

subject form 202
subject-predicate analysis 122
subject-verb agreement 71, 174
sub-lexeme 94, 156
subordinate 141, 227
subordinate parents are not landmarks
    rule 146
subordinate transitivity 136–7, 139
subset 29
Sun 21
supercategory 11
superior 238
superordinate 141
suppletion 86, 97
surrogate 146
Sutcliffe 123
Swahili 63
Swan 209
Swedish 241
syllable structure 80
symbol 18, 217–19, 220–4
symbolic network 9, 42, 63
syncretism 82, 84–7
syntactic dependency—*see* dependency
syntax 38–9, 51–2, 57, 60, 76, 78, 195–7, 219
synthetic knowledge 232
system network 29
systemic functional grammar xi, 2, 29,
    120, 212

t/d deletion 58
Tajima 184
Tallerman 126–7
Talmy 215, 234
tense 228
terminology 14
Tesnière 117, 130
thought 217–18
time 132, 214–15, 228
tip-of-the-tongue state 79
token x, 3, 20, 25, 30, 42–4, 54–5,
    134, 214
Tomasello xi, 7, 53, 129, 152, 223

topic 167
topological distance 36, 67; *see also*
    dependency distance
Touretzky 27, 61
trace 119, 172
trajector 132
transformation, transformational
    grammar viii, 172, 189
transitive pronoun 192
transitive verb 156
transitive-isa 23, 30
tree-adjoining grammar 122
tree-bank 123
truth 212
truth value 225
type x, 3, 43, 54–5
typed variable 21w
typology 126, 161
Tzanidaki 134

unary branching 121
under-specification 84
universal categories, universal
    grammar 116, 151, 160, 233–4
universal quantification 31–4, 230
unrealized word 127, 178–81, 192
usage, usage-based learning, usage
    statistics 3, 22, 53, 57–8, 124–5,
    211–12, 214
utterance—*see* token

valency 89, 192, 202
valent 165–6
value 12, 16–17, 71
Van Langendonck 129
Van Valin 120
variable (logical) 20–1, 31
variable (sociolinguistic) 246–8
variant 81–7, 96, 246–8
verb 199–202
visitor 160
vocabulary 219–20, 224
vocabulary spurt 220–2

Vosse 42
vowel 79, 98
vowel-alternation 97–8
VP 122, 151

wanna 63
Warneken 223
Wells 118
Welsh 101, 126–7
Wescoat 189
WG—*see* word grammar
wh question 142
Wierzbicka 232, 233
Wik 184
Williams 219, 234
Wilson 46
Winograd xi, 48
word 64, 68–81, 93–6, 117, 150, 214–19,
    236, 244–5

word class—*see* lexeme class
word grammar xi, 5
word order 131–52
word string 139
word-and-paradigm morphology 67, 78
word-form 104
working memory 8, 40–1, 124–5
writing 79, 213
Wurff 184, 188, 207–9
WXDY 156–7, 166

X-bar phrase structure 117
Yoon 189

Zapotec 147–50
Zwicky 76, 104